A

CONCISE HISTORY

OF THE

KEHUKEE BAPTIST ASSOCIATION

FROM ITS

ORIGINAL RISE DOWN TO 1803

LEMUEL BURKITT AND JESSE READ

REVISED AND IMPROVED
BY HENRY L. BURKITT

ARNO PRESS

A New York Times Company
New York • 1980

Editorial Supervision: Steven Bedney

———————

Reprint Edition 1980 by Arno Press Inc.

Reprinted from a copy in the Southwestern Baptist
Theological Seminary Library

THE BAPTIST TRADITION

ISBN for complete set: 0-405-12437-6
See last pages of this volume for titles.

Manufactured in the United States of America

———————

Library of Congress Cataloging in Publication Data

Burkitt, Lemuel, 1750-1806.
  A concise history of the Kehukee Baptist Association,
from its original rise down to 1803.

  (The Baptist tradition)
  Reprint of the 1850 ed. published by Lippincott,
Grambo, Philadelphia.
  1. Primitive Baptists. North Carolina. Kehukee
Primitive Baptist Association. I. Read, Jesse, joint
author. II. Burkitt, Henry Lemuel, b. 1818.
III. Title. IV. Series: Baptist tradition.
BX6384.N84B87 1980   286'.4   79-52591
ISBN 0-405-12458-9

A
CONCISE HISTORY

OF THE

KEHUKEE BAPTIST ASSOCIATION,

FROM ITS

ORIGINAL RISE DOWN TO 1803.

WHEREIN ARE SHOWN ITS FIRST CONSTITUTION, INCREASE, NUMBERS,
PRINCIPLES, FORM OF GOVERNMENT, DECORUM, REVOLUTION, RE-
VIVALS, MINISTERS, CHURCHES, CONFESSION OF FAITH, TIMES
AND PLACES WHEN AND WHERE ASSOCIATIONS HAVE BEEN
HOLDEN, QUERIES AND THEIR ANSWERS, AND ALL
OTHER USEFUL ARTICLES RELATIVE TO
CHURCH HISTORY.

BY

ELDERS LEMUEL BURKITT AND JESSE READ,

MINISTERS OF THE GOSPEL IN NORTHAMPTON AND HALIFAX COUNTIES,
NORTH CAROLINA.

When the Lord shall build up Zion, he shall appear in his glory. This
shall be written for the generations to come; and the people which shall
be created shall praise the Lord.—PSALM cii. 16-18.

REVISED AND IMPROVED
BY HENRY L. BURKITT.

PHILADELPHIA:
LIPPINCOTT, GRAMBO AND CO.,

SUCCESSORS TO

GRIGG, ELLIOT AND CO.,

14 NORTH FOURTH STREET.

1850.

CIRCUIT COURT.

DISTRICT COURT OF THE UNITED STATES
For Middle Tennessee District:

Be it remembered that, in conformity to an Act of Congress of the United States of America, entitled "An Act to amend the several acts respecting copyrights," on this 13th day of March, A. D. 1850, and in the seventy-fourth year of the Independence of the United States, Henry L. Burkitt, of said district, hath deposited in this office the title of a book, the right whereof he claims as proprietor, and which is as follows, viz: A Concise History of the Kehukee ·Baptist Association, from its original rise down to 1803: wherein are shown its first constitution, increase, &c. By Elders Lemuel Burkitt and Jesse Read, Ministers of the Gospel in Northampton and Halifax Counties, North Carolina. Revised and improved by Henry L. Burkitt.

[L. S.] In testimony whereof, I, Jacob M Gavock, clerk of said court, have hereto set my hand and affixed the seal of said court at office in Nashville, this 13th day of March, A. D. 1850.

JACOB M'GAVOCK.

PHILADELPHIA:
PRINTED BY T. K. & P. G. COLLINS.

TO ALL THE

ELDERS AND BRETHREN

BELONGING TO THE

Kehukee, Virginia Portsmouth, and Neuse

ASSOCIATIONS;

AND TO ALL THE

MINISTERS AND MEMBERS

OF THE SEVERAL

Baptist Churches throughout the United States, with
all those who wish well to Zion,

ARE THE

FOLLOWING SHEETS

HUMBLY DEDICATED

BY THEIR AFFECTIONATE AND HUMBLE SERVANTS,

L. BURKITT,
JESSE READ.

THE EDITOR'S PREFACE.

" THE Baptists have, under every form
of government, been the advocates of liberty; and, for this reason, they have never
flourished much except in those govern-
ments where some degree of freedom has
been maintained. Arbitrary states have
always oppressed them, and driven them
for refuge to milder regions. They cannot
live in tyrannical states, and free countries
are the only places to seek for them, for
their whole public religion is impracticable
without freedom. In political changes,
they have always been friendly to the
cause of liberty, and their passion for it
has, at different times, led some into acts
of indiscretion and scenes of danger. But,
with a few exceptions, we may say, in
truth, that the Baptists have always adhered to their leading maxim, to be *subject
to the powers that be;* and all the favor they,

as Christians, have asked of civil govern-
ments has been, *to give them their Bibles,
and let them alone.*"*

The favorable reception which this work
met with from those for whom it was written, in its first edition, published during
the life of its authors, has induced the sub-
scriber to prepare a second edition. Considerable amendments and alterations have
been made ; no fact or statement of the authors, however, has been changed ; their
accuracy having been such, that none of
the numerous friends with whom the present editor has corresponded, has suggested
any material changes of this kind.

A distinguished gentleman of Elizabeth
City, N. C., in a recent letter, says : "The
churches in that region, *planted by Elder
Burkitt*, are, in most cases, very large and
flourishing. Generally, they have built
large and handsome meeting-houses, &c.
Similar information has been received from
other points, and it is hoped and believed
that all those churches will be pleased to
read the unpretending narrative of their

* Benedict.

early trials, by authors who lived and labored with them in the perilous days of
their beginnings.

It has been suggested to the editor that
the narrative ought to be brought down to
the present time. From this opinion, however, he begs leave to differ. The Baptists
in the United States, and, perhaps, throughout the whole world, at the time of the original publication of this history, stood upon
one general platform, and there was no division among them. But now, it is widely
different. There are divisions, and subdi-
visions in the Baptist church ; and the
editor, being desirous to see a return to
former principles, thinks the work most
acceptable in its original form.

The work has been revised and corrected
with care as it passed through the press.
In this, and other respects, the editor has
had the kind assistance of several friends,
to whom he tenders his sincere thanks. It
is not doubted that the present edition will,
in style and accuracy, favorably compare
with any similar publication of the day. It
is, therefore, respectfully submitted to the

members of the church to which its authors belonged, and in which they labored so long.

My warm and sincere attachment to the author (who is my ancestor), and the unusual popularity of the first edition of this work, are my only apologies for offering to the public a second edition. I need add nothing in relation to its merits. The great demand for it throughout the United States, and especially in the States of North Carolina, Virginia, Tennessee, and Kentucky, is a higher recommendation than I could give. I therefore submit the work to a generous public without any further remarks, and only ask a continuance of that liberal patronage which it has heretofore received.

HENRY L. BURKITT.

LAWRENCEBURG, TENNESSEE.
  January, 1850.

PREFACE.

HISTORY is so genuine and familiar to men of all estates, ages, qualities, sects and conditions, that among the many eulogies it hath received from the learned pieces of ancient and modern writers, it may be justly accounted rather the recreation than the application of a *studious man*.

It is, indeed, that *telescope* by which we see into distant ages, and take up the actions of our forefathers, with as much evidence as the news of the latest Gazette; it is the mirror that represents the various transactions of times past, and shows us the dress of *antiquity*, according to which we may rectify or adjust our present fashions. In a word, it is the last will and testament of our deceased progenitors; which, though it does not expressly leave every one of us a particular legacy, yet it shows us how we may be possessed of their inheritance; and accordingly as we follow their example, live in reputation or ignominy.

Insomuch that the ruder ages of the

world, who were unacquainted with letters, and consequently ignorant of refined sciences, thought *history*, next to their *religion*, the only useful and proper study of mankind; and judging the forming of the manners, and regulating the actions of man, to be the duty and care of societies, they thought documents, precepts, and laws too weak a means to work so great effect, without they were confirmed and strengthened by the *examples* of their predecessors; to which prone nature, even among the most barbarous, does willingly render an implicit veneration: and, therefore, seeing their libraries were their memories, and words their characters, so songs and rude rhymes were their only books, whereby their *Bards* and *Druids* instructed their children in the histories of former ages, making the famous actions of their ancestors so much the more the pattern of their conduct and manners, as it was the subject of their innocent melody and mirth: and this custom is at this day in practice among the uncultivated heathens of Africa and America.

But when the kind heavens were pleased to gratify the industry of man with the invention of letters, no subject seemed to the ancients so worthy of the prerogative of being transmitted to posterity as that of *history:* and, indeed, the most ancient of

their writings that can be found is of this
kind. Whether it was that they knew no
immortality but that of *fame*, or found no
better way to provide with security for their
offspring, in whom they were to live to posterity, than by handing down to them the
methods and honest courses, by which
some attained to honor, wealth and command, whilst others, by the contrary ways,
lived and died in obscurity, poverty, and
contempt.

But what satisfaction soever dying men
may have in the prospect of a lasting name,
it is certain the living reap great benefit
from the register of their actions; for, would
a *Prince* have measures to govern, a *Subject*
how to obey, a *Statesman* how to give
counsel, a *Judge* and *Magistrate* how to
execute justice, a *Husband* and *Father* how
to command and cherish, a *Wife* or *Child*
how to love, honor, and obey, all conditions
of men how to perform mutual good offices
in every kind of society, history, and especially the truest and most ancient of all, the
Holy Scriptures is that repository from
whence they may draw the truest *maxims*
for all *duties*, exemplified with the good or
bad successes of those who have followed or
transgressed the same. And thus much, in
short, of *history* in general.

It has been, of late, the wish of some of

the leading characters in the churches belonging to the Kehukee Association, for a brief history of that Association to be published, from its origin to the present time, hoping it may prove a blessing to the churches in general, and their *posterity* in particular; that they may be fully acquainted with the faith and practice of the churches to which their forefathers belonged. It was, therefore, the request of some of the churches and ministers that we should engage in this work.

It was a subject which had not engaged our attention before; but, upon a serious reflection that, whereas, we had been members of this Association as long perhaps as any now living, and one of us had been *Clerk* of the Association for *thirty* years, and acquired a considerable degree of information relative to the Association and churches in general, and being persuaded of the general utility of such an history, we were encouraged to undertake the publication thereof.

As to the history now about to be published, it is an history of a *Baptist Association;* it might, therefore, be thought necessary by some that something should be said respecting the origin of that society. The name might probably have originated from the word Anabaptist, which was a

stigma prefixed on us by the Pedobaptists,
who suppose that, because we baptize persons on the profession of their faith, who
were sprinkled in infancy, that we *re-baptize*
them. But it is the general opinion of the
Baptists that, where any person has a *valid*
baptism, agreeable to the Scriptures, that
on such, baptism ought not to be *repeated;*
and, as infant sprinkling is not *scriptural,*
and baptizing such persons on profession of
their faith in Christ, who were sprinkled in
infancy, cannot be re-baptism, therefore we
disown the name of *Anabaptists.* The
word *Baptist* may be considered as a *society,* or as a *baptizer.* If by it we are to understand a particular *society* of people, we
may claim the the *highest* original, since
we read in the very front of the New Testament, " In those days came *John the Baptist,* preaching in the wilderness, &c." It
does not say, in those days came John the
Churchman, nor John the Presbyterian,
nor John the Methodist, nor John the
Quaker, but John the *Baptist.* And we
know that where a Baptist preacher comes
into any place and baptizes a number of
believers, they are immediately called Baptists. But it may be that he was so called
because he was a *baptizer;* and *we* may
be called Baptists because we hold with
his baptism, in the manner it was by him

and the apostles administered : if so, we think it no *disgrace* to be called by that name. It is most certain that the Baptists do administer the ordinance of baptism agreeable to the word of God, in the practice of *John* and the *apostles.*

In the first place, we find from the Scriptures that baptism is a *duty.* Mat. iii. 15. " Jesus answering, said, suffer it to be so now : for thus it becometh us to fulfil all righteousness." Mat. xxviii. . 19. " Go teach all nations, baptizing them in the name of the Father, and of the Son, and of the Holy Ghost." Acts x. 47, 48. " Can any man forbid water that these should not be baptized, which have received the Holy Ghost as well as we ? and he *commanded* them to be baptized."

2. We have reason to believe that *John* the *Baptist* and the *apostles* baptized none, only such as, within the judgment of charity, they believed to be possessed of *Faith* and *Repentance.* This appears from the following scriptures. Mat. iii. 5, 6. " Then went out unto him Jerusalem and all Judea, and all the region round about Jordan, and were baptized of him in Jordan, confessing their sins." Verse 7. " But when he saw many of the Pharisees and Sadducees come to his baptism, he said unto them, " O generation of vipers ! who hath

warned you to flee from the wrath to come?
Bring forth, therefore, *fruits* meet for repentance," &c. Mark xvi. 16. " He that
believeth and is baptized, shall be saved."
Acts ii. 38. "*Repent*, and be baptized every
one of you in the name of the Lord Jesus."
Verse 41. " They that *gladly received the
word* were baptized," &c. Acts viii. 37.
"If thou *believest* with all thy heart thou
mayest."

3. We also have reason to believe that,
in the primitive times, baptism was administered by *dipping*, or plunging the party
baptized all under water. This seems to
appear from the practice of John and the
apostles—from the practice of John who
baptized our Lord, and many others in Jordan; and was baptizing in Enon near Sa-
lim, because there was much water there.
John iii. 23. Also from the practice of
the apostles. Acts viii. 38, 39. " And
they went *down into* the water, both Philip
and the Eunuch; and he baptized him.
And when they were *come up out* of the
water, the spirit of the Lord caught away
Philip, that the Eunuch saw him no more."
But perhaps some may say, can we trace
the practice of *adult* baptism by *immersion*
from us to the apostles' times? If this was
required of the *Pedobaptists* to trace the
practice of *baptizing infants* from the pre-

sent time to the days of the apostles, we
should find the Episcopalians, Presbyte-
rians, and Methodists at a very great loss.
For, after they had dragged it through
Rome, and had the sanction of Popes,
Councils, Churches, and some of the ancient fathers, so far from tracing it to the
apostles' days, it cannot be carried farther
back, by *positive proof*, than the *third* century, in which mention is made of it by
Tertullian, *Origen*, and *Cyprian*. And the
first of these *dissuades* from it, and advises
to defer baptism to riper years. Origen,
with all his corruptions, mentions it; but
his translations are so imperfect that it
is observed by some that "Origen is not
to be found in Origen." And, although it
is allowed that infant baptism began to be
practiced in Cyprian's day, yet it was esteemed an upstart notion, since it was not
till then determined at what time it should
be administered. But it is evident that
believer's baptism by immersion was the
primitive practice, and that there have been
some, no doubt, ever since the apostles, in
some parts of the world, who practiced it;
as is evident there were in Bohemia, Ger-
many, Piedmont, and other places, notwithstanding the general apostacy which took
place since the apostles' times throughout
the whole world. And as we think we are

sufficiently authorized to baptize believers by immersion, so we think that gathering, and organizing particular churches, and their union in an *association* way, is agreeable to the standard of truth, the unerring word of God. And for the satisfaction of the reader, we will give a proper definition of the *church*, and the utility of an *association of churches*, which we think is agreeable to the Holy Scriptures. On the Church.—The word *church*, in the New Testament, must necessarily mean an *assembly*, and not the *house* in which they assemble. Mat. xviii. 15, 16, 17. " Moreover, if thy brother shall trespass against thee, go and tell him his fault between thee and him alone : if he shall hear thee, thou hast gained thy brother. But if he will not hear thee, then take with thee one or two more, that in the mouth of two or three witnesses every word may be established. And if he shall neglect to hear them, tell it to the *church*." It cannot be supposed our Lord meant that we should tell it to the house. Again. Acts ii. 47. " The Lord added to the *church* daily such as should be saved." 1 Cor. xiv. 23. " If therefore the church be come together into one place." These places in the sacred writings must undoubtedly allude to the people, and not to the building. The New

2

Testament writers always apply the word
church to a *religious assembly*, selected and
called out of the world by the doctrine of
the Gospel, to worship the true God according to his word. And is emphatically represented in the nineteenth article of the
Episcopal church, which saith, " The visi-
" ble church of Christ is a congregation of
" faithful men, in the which the pure word
" of God is preached, and the sacrament be
" duly administered, according to Christ's
" ordinance, in all those things that of ne-
" cessity are requisite to the same."

When we consult the sacred writings,
we have sufficient reason to believe that
the word *church* is intended to signify the
church catholic, triumphant, invisible, and
particular.

The church *catholic* means all that have
been, or ever will be *saved*. Eph. i. 22,
23. " And gave him to be head over all
things to the church which is his body, the
fulness of him that filleth all in all." Col-
los. i. 18, 24. The church *triumphant*
means all the saints who are now already
in Heaven. Heb. xii. 23. " The general
assembly and *church* of the first-born, which
are written in Heaven—and to the spirits
of just men made perfect." The church
militant means all the saints on earth.
There are about nine passages in Scripture

which refer to this church. Acts viii. 3.
1 Cor. x. 32; xii. 28; xv. 9. Gal. i. 13.
Phil. iii. 16. 1 Tim. iii. 15. The *invisible* church means all the elect not yet
called. " Other sheep I have, which are
not of this fold : them also must I bring,
and they shall hear my voice ; and there
shall be one fold and one shepherd." John
x. 16.

A *particular* church is a little distinct
and separate society, called out of the
world, and professing faith in Christ Jesus,
have given themselves up to the Lord and
to one another, to be governed and guided
by a proper discipline agreeable to the
word of God. Of this sort of church, frequent mention is made in the word of the
Lord. Some of the passages relative thereto, are, " The church in their house."
Rom. xvi. 5 1 Cor. xvi 9. " The church
in thine house." Phil. 2. " The church
in Jerusalem." Acts viii. 1. At Antioch,
at Rome, Corinth, Philadelphia, Ephesus,
Smyrna, &c. &c.

The churches which compose the Kehukee Baptist Association, profess to be of
this description ; and churches *baptized
upon profession of their faith* in Christ Jesus, and well organized, we think it is
agreeable to those particular Congrega-

tional churches mentioned in the Holy Scriptures.

An *Association* is a *combination* of churches uniting together in one body, governed by certain rules when met together, and whose business it is to hear from, and inquire into the state of the churches in the union, and give advice, in order to reconcile differences, detect errors, and remove difficulties ; so as not to lord it over God's heritage, but sit and act only as an advisory council.

The divine authority of this ancient custom seems manifest in the example of our Lord and his holy apostles. Our blessed Lord when entering on his divine mission, and laying a plan for the establishment of his kingdom, as soon as he entered on his public ministry, made choice of *twelve,* with whom he associated, not, indeed, to assist him by their counsel, but to train them up to assist one another. And we find the apostles themselves assembled on certain occasions to confer about the affairs of the churches. See Acts xv. If Paul, Barnabas, and others, therefore, were delegated by their brethren of the churches at Antioch, to assemble, or associate with the apostles and elders at Jerusalem, how much more will the propriety and necessity of such meetings or assemblies appear to us, who do not enjoy their *abilities*, nor possess their *powers*. And, as the Scriptures support its divine authority and expediency, so from the experience we have had of its well known benefits, we are the more easily persuaded that the churches will always find it of general *utility*, in maintaining and supporting—1. A general *union*. 2. The *communion* of the churches. 3. The increase of brotherly love. 4. To gain information of the state of the churches. 5. Remove difficulties. 6. Grant supplies to destitute churches. 7. The extirpation of false doctrines; and, 8. The benefit arising to the church and neighborhood where the association is holden.

1. The association is of general utility in supporting and maintaining a general union. Now, the more firmly any civil or religious society is knit together by *love*, and coalesce in *unity*, by so much the better they are secured against their common enemies and dangers, and become still the more prosperous and flourishing. United force, we all know, is more than single; and hence it is, we are so frequently in the sacred Scriptures exhorted to a general unanimity. Rom. xii. 16. 1 Cor. i. 10. Phil. ii. 2. Psal. cxxxiii. 1.

2. The general utility of an association also consists in the *communion* of the

churches. It is through this sameness of
love, mind, and rule, that a chain of communion is, or can be kept up with the
churches. Christ's church is a *family*.
Anything that is lawful and right, that
will maintain an union among the children,
so they, with love and fellowship, can from
time to time eat bread together in the spirit
of meekness, must be of use. Christ's
church is a body. All proper means that
have a tendency to keep the members in
place, should be used for that purpose; for
the beauty and strength of a *body* depend
on its not being maimed or disordered.
We therefore think that it is impossible
that so endearing a privilege, and particular duty as the communion of the churches,
can be preserved sacred and inviolable
without some such mode of associating together; where we can hear from the different churches, know each other's principles,
and be acquainted with the proper discipline
of each church; we therefore think that an
association is useful.

3. We not only think that it tends to
preserve a communion of churches, but we
also believe it has a tendency to *increase
brotherly love*. It is through this medium
that an acquaintance is cultivated amongst
the brethren, and brotherly love increased
and continued. Heb. xiii. 1.

4. *To gain proper information of the state of the churches.* It is by the means of an association that we obtain this information, and, from the accounts given, be able to ascertain whether they be in prosperous or declining circumstances; and can propose measures accordingly, so as to mourn with them that mourn, and rejoice with them that do rejoice.

5. By means of an association, *brethren under difficulties of mind* may be relieved, by presenting their queries to the association, and having them properly discussed; which often tends to the satisfaction of the aggrieved party; and as, in the multitude of counsellors there is safety, we believe an association is useful.

6. It is through this mode of assembling together that information is communicated to the association of the *state of destitute churches,* and on their request, and by the consent of the brethren in the ministry, supplies can be granted. Ministers receive the intelligence, make their appointments, and the destitute churches get furnished at proper seasons, and the ordinances administered to them.

7. It is useful for the extirpation of *heterodoxy.* "Do not err, my beloved brethren," was the exhortation of the apostles to primitive Christians; and another

apostle warrantably informs us that some should bring in damnable heresies. Now, if this was the case in ancient times, we may reasonably expect it in this corrupt age of the world. And where are we so likely to gain the information of these heretical principles amongst the church, if there be any, as at the association? and where so proper a place to nip them in the bud as at this time? Thus, we see the primitive churches, and that under the immediate inspection of the apostles themselves, were likely to err in this point, had they not had recourse to the assembly of the apostles and others met at Jerusalem. Witness the great disputation of Paul, with all his experience, his learning, his oratory, and his inspiration (for we may suppose he used all his efforts) to refute an error then getting birth in the church; and all would not do—it must be carried up to the association of the apostles and elders delegated at Jerusalem.

8. The good effects which have attended the church and neighborhood where these numerous assemblies have attended, bespeak the utility of the association of churches.

Thus, dear reader, we have given sufficient reasons to believe that the mode of gathering churches, by baptizing believers, and their union in an association way, is purely scriptural and apostolical.

Before we entirely close the subject of gathering churches after this mode, it might not be amiss to say something with respect to the *particular communion* of the Baptist churches. We have been, by some, judged as a singular, narrow-hearted set of Christians, because we would not commune with *other societies*. But we apprehend ourselves justifiable in so doing, and without this we could not be consistent with our own principles. For we believe that *Christian baptism is the first ordinance* a believer ought to comply with; and persons cannot become regular church members without first being baptized according to the word of God. This appears from the conduct of the apostles in the first gathering of the churches of Jesus Christ. Acts ii. 41, 42. "They that gladly received the word were baptized; and the same day there were added unto them about three thousand souls. And *they* (*i. e.* those *baptized*) continued steadfastly in the apostles' doctrine and fellowship, and in *breaking of bread*, and in prayers." Also it is said, "By one spirit we are all baptized into one body." 1 Cor. xii. 13. That is, by the leading and teaching of the Holy Spirit we are all baptized into one body,

i. e. the church.   And we cannot find from
the Holy Scriptures, and we think no man
can, that since the ascension of our Lord
and Saviour Jesus Christ, that any were
received members of the visible church before they submitted to the ordinance of
baptism.   And we also believe that it is
out of the power of any person to prove
that any one was ever admitted to the ordinance of the *Lord's Supper* before he was
first baptized.   Were any of *John's* prose-
lytes?   No.   The ordinance of the supper
had never then been administered.   Were
any of the members of the church at Rome,
Corinth, Galatia, Philippi, Ephesus, &c. ?
We have no reason to believe they were.
The apostle's exhortation to the people was,
"*Repent,* and be *baptized* every one of you
in the name of Jesus Christ, for the remis-
sion of your sins."   Acts ii. 38.   And it is
evident, from sundry examples, that *baptism* was the first ordinance to be complied
with, before they were admitted to other
ordinances, or to church privileges.   What
was the first ordinance the three thousand
who gladly received the word were admitted to ?   It was *baptism,* the same day.
What was the first the Eunuch complied
with, after he believed with all his heart?
It was *baptism.*   What was the first the
Jailer and his house were admitted to, after

he believed in God, with all his house? It
was *baptism*, the same hour of the night.
Acts xvi. 33. What was the first Lydia
complied with, after the Lord opened her
heart? It was *baptism*. Acts xvi. 15.
What was the first the Apostle Paul submitted to after Ananias laid his hands on
him, and said, "Brother Saul, receive thy
sight?" It was *baptism*. He does not say,
and now why tarriest thou? arise, and go
preach the gospel; nor does he say, now,
why tarriest thou? arise, and come to the
Lord's table; but arise, and be *baptized*.
Acts ix. 18; xxii. 16.

We, therefore, do believe that it is a
duty for every real Christian to comply
with baptism in the first place, agreeable to
the word of God, and then be entitled to
the privileges of the church, and to the ordinances in general. And, except they do
comply with their *duty* in this respect, they
are disorderly; and we are commanded to
withdraw from every brother that walks
disorderly. 2 Thes. iii. 6. We, therefore,
think we are justifiable, from God's word,
to raise a bar of communion against all
churches and persons who have not a baptism that is valid, agreeable to the word of
the Lord.

These are a few of our reasons for *particular communion*, which we hope may be

duly considered, and weighed in the balance of the sanctuary with an *even* hand.

As to the ensuing history we are about to publish, we can assure thee, reader, that we have endeavored to collect all the materials we could come at; and obtain all the information we could, in order to render the work complete. Notwithstanding all, it may be imperfect in many things, as it is well known that writings of this kind are subject to errors. But we hope to obtain a pardon from the public, when we assure them that *we have done the best we could.*

The greatest part of the history, our readers may depend on the reality of those facts recorded, as we were both eye and ear witnesses to them.

To conclude, we may add that this little compendium will present you with the glorious increase of Christ's kingdom, in calling poor sinners to the happy privileges of the Gospel, and the increase of his churches. When our association was first established, there were only ten churches, and now near about ninety, which have become three associations in thirty years. Blessed be God, we hope the happy day is fast approaching when the kingdoms of this world shall become the kingdoms of our Lord and his Christ. May we all pray, "*thy kingdom come.*"

We are, dear reader, your soul's well wishers, and affectionate servants in the gospel of our dear Lord Jesus

LEMUEL BURKITT,
JESSE READ.

NORTHAMPTON COUNTY, NORTH CAROLINA,
October, 1803.

|

A CONCISE HISTORY

OF THE

KEHUKEE BAPTIST ASSOCIATION.

CHAPTER I.

1. The State of the Churches at first, before they were
United in an Association at all.—2. The Revolution
those Churches passed through before they became an
established Association.—3. The Form of a Church
Covenant, and the Plan on which they were Established. — 4. Biographical Sketches of some of those
Ministers who died before the Establishment of the Association on its present Order.

SOME of the churches which at first
composed the Kehukee Association, were,
the church at Tosniot, in Edgecomb county; the church at Kehukee, in Halifax
county; the church at the Falls of Tar
River, in Edgecomb county; the church
on Fishing Creek, in Halifax county; the
church on Reedy Creek, in Warren county; the church at Sandy Run, in Bertie
county; and the church in Camden county, North Carolina. The most of these

churches, before they were ever united in an
association, were *General Baptist*, and held
with the Arminian tenets. We believe
they were the descendants of the *English
General Baptists*, because we find, from
some original papers, that their Confession
of Faith was subscribed by certain elders
and deacons, and brethren, in behalf of
themselves and others, to whom they belonged, both in *London*, and several counties in *England*, and was presented to King
Charles the Second.

They preached, and adhered to the Arminian, or Free-will doctrines, and their
churches were first established upon this
system. They gathered churches without
requiring an experience of grace previous
to their baptism; but baptized all who believed in the doctrine of baptism by *immersion*, and requested baptism of them. The
churches of this order were first gathered
here by Elders *Paul Palmer* and *Joseph
Parker*, and were succeeded by a number
of ministers, whom they had baptized; and
some of whom, we have no reason to believe, were converted when they were baptized, or first began to preach. We cannot
learn that it was customary with them to
hold an association at all; but met at *yearly meetings*, where matters of consequence
were determined.

This was the state of these churches until divine Providence disposed the Philadelphia Baptist Association to send Messrs. *Vanhorn* and *Miller*, two of the ministers belonging to that Association, who lived in New Jersey, to travel into the southern Colonies, and visit the churches and preach the Gospel. And it appears that it was attended with an happy effect. When they came into North Carolina, some of the members belonging to these churches seemed to be afraid of them, as they were styled by the most of people *New Lights*; but by the greatest part of the churches they were cordially received.

Their preaching and conversation seemed to be with power, the hearts of the people seemed to be open, and a very great blessing seemed to attend their labors.

Through their instrumentality, many people were awakened; many of the members of these churches were convinced of their error, and were instructed in the doctrines of the Gospel; and some churches were organized anew, and established upon the principles of the doctrine of *grace*. These churches, thus newly constituted, adopted the Baptist confession of faith, published in London in 1689, containing thirty-two articles, and upon which the *Philadelphia* and *Charleston* Associations

3

are founded. And, as it is customary for churches thus formed, at their first constitution, to have a church covenant, in which they solemnly agree to endeavor to keep up the discipline of the church; the following specimen will show the reader something of the nature of that covenant compact. It is to this effect :—

FORASMUCH as Almighty God, by his grace, has been pleased to call us (whose names are underneath subscribed) out of darkness into his marvellous light, and all of us have been regularly baptized upon a profession of our faith in Christ Jesus, and have given up ourselves to the Lord, and to one another, in a Gospel church way, to be governed and guided by a proper discipline agreeable to the word of God: We do, therefore, in the name of our Lord Jesus, and by his assistance, covenant and agree to keep up the discipline of the church we are members of, in the most brotherly affection towards each other, while we endeavor punctually to observe the following rules, viz :—

1. In brotherly love to pray for each other, to watch over one another, and, if need be, in the most tender and affectionate manner to reprove one another. That is, if we discover anything amiss in a bro-

ther, to go and tell him his fault according to the direction given by our Lord in the 18th of Saint Matthew's Gospel; and not to be whispering and backbiting. We also agree, with God's assistance, to pray in our families, attend our church meetings, observe the Lord's day and keep it holy, and not absent ourselves from the communion of the Lord's Supper without a lawful excuse; to be ready to communicate to the defraying of the church's expenses, and for the support of the ministry; not irregularly to depart from the fellowship of the church, nor remove to distant churches without a regular dismission.

These things we do covenant and agree to observe and keep sacred, in the name of, and by the assistance of the Holy Trinity. *Amen.* Signed by the mutual consent of the members whose names are underneath subscribed.

THUS, by means of those ministers who visited the churches, several were reformed, and the work of reformation progressed, until the greater part of what few churches were gathered in North Carolina, both ministers and members, came into the *Regular Baptist* order. Elder *Palmer*, we believe, died before the reformation took place; and Elder *Joseph Parker*, we cannot learn, was ever convinced of his errors, or receded from them ; but continued in his way as before. And we cannot understand he was very successful, because all the ministers of that party were brought over to embrace the Calvinistic scheme, except himself, Elder *Winfield*, and Elder *William Parker ;* and we presume, but a few others, either ministers or members, except the members of *their* churches.

The churches thus reformed, although but few in number, entered into an association compact about the year of 1765, and first convened at Kehukee, from whence the Association took the name of the " Kehukee Association." Thus, being formed in a body, they corresponded with the Charleston Association ; and in this situation they continued some years, until the year 1774, when an alteration took place, which our readers will be favored with in the next chapter.

The principal ministers which belonged to the Association on its first establishment, were, Elders Jonathan Thomas, John Thomas, John Moore, John Burges, William Burges, Charles Daniel, William Walker, John Meglamre, James Abington, Thomas Pope, and Henry Abbot. All of whom, except Elders John Meglamre and James

Abington, we believe, were baptized by ministers of the Free-will order.

As some of these ministers died before those remarkable events took place, mentioned in the succeeding chapter, it would be necessary to give a few sketches of their biography in the close of this.

ELDER JAMES ABINGTON.

ELDER JAMES ABINGTON was a resident of Bertie county, North Carolina. Before he became religious, he was a man much addicted to sporting and gaming, and very vicious in his life and conversation. But it pleased God by his great goodness to convince him of his dreadful state by nature, and to reveal his dear Son Jesus Christ to his soul; and, after he was converted, he was baptized, and began to preach the Gospel. He became a member of the church at Sandy Run, and after preaching some time, he was ordained pastor of that church, and was instrumental in gathering a considerable number of members. He was a man of a bright genius, a ready mind, a good voice; and was a *Boanerges* in preaching the Word. He was remarkably gifted in distinguishing between the *Law* and the *Gospel*. The *insufficiency* of the one to justify a sinner in the sight of

God, and the *suitableness* of the other to
recommend us into the favor of God. He
continued but a few years in the work of
the ministry—how long we are not able to
say—but at last, being taken very ill, he was
taken away from the evil to come. He departed this life, February, 1772 His funeral sermon was preached by Elder *Jonathan Thomas*, from 2 Tim. iv. 7, 8. " I
" have fought a good fight, I have finished
" my course, I have kept the faith : hence-
" forth there is laid up for me a crown of
" righteousness, which the Lord, the right-
" eous judge, shall give me at that day."

ELDER JONATHAN THOMAS.

JONATHAN THOMAS was the son of John
Thomas, of Edgecomb county, North Carolina. He had a brother by the name of
John. Both his father and brother were
preachers of the Baptist denomination.
Jonathan, at first, was received into a
church and baptized by a minister of the
Free-will order. But, in process of time,
embraced the Calvinian plan, and became
an eminent preacher of the *regular* Baptist
Society. He was ordained in December,
1758. He was a man of talents, very affable in his address, and a great orator. He
had the general esteem of the churches,

and was revered by all men of character
with whom he was acquainted. He was
exceeding orthodox in his principles, and
had a peculiar faculty in reconciling seem-
ing contradictions in the Scriptures; and
on intricate passages of Scripture, his judgment was thought exceeding good. In a
word, he appeared as a pious, good Christian, a sensible, zealous minister of the Gospel, and one who aimed at the peace and harmony of the churches in general : insomuch,
that where discord or division was likely to
take place in a church, he was very careful
to endeavor to reconcile them again ; and
he very often proved successful in his
attempts. Towards the latter end of his
life, he appeared to be more zealous, and
more constantly employed in traveling and
preaching. His last sermon was preached
at Sandy Run meeting house, in Bertie
county, from Luke xiv. 23. "Compel
"them to come in, that my house may be
"filled." He said, "his master had sent
"him to compel them to come in, and they
"need not begin to make excuse, for no ex-
"cuse could be received, nor denial taken."
There was a large assembly, and but few
in the congregation but what were in floods
of tears; and many cried out loudly. This
was in December, 1774 ; and from Sandy
Run he went home, being under complaint

of a bad cold, and the last of January, or
first of February following, he died.

CHAPTER II.

1. The Revolution the Association passed through before
established on the present plan.—2. Her Organization
at the Falls of Tar River, and the Principles on which
she is founded, adopted at Sappony, in Sussex county,
Virginia; and afterwards published by order of the
Association, held at Whitfield's Meeting House, Pitt
county, North Carolina, October, 1789.—3. Biographical Sketches of Elder James Bell.—4. Persecution of
Elder John Tanner.

SOME years after the Association was established on its original plan, in Virginia,
and some parts of North Carolina, the *Separate Baptists* (as they were then called) increased very fast. The *Separates* first arose
in New England, where some pious ministers and members left the Presbyterian, or
the Standing Order, on the account of their
formality and superfluity, viz. 1. Because
they were too extravagant in their apparel. 2. Because they did not believe
their form of church government to be
right. But chiefly because they would admit none to the ministry only men of class-

ical education, and many of their ministers, apparently, seemed to be unconverted. They were then called *Separate Newlights.* Some of these were baptized and moved into the southern provinces, particularly Elders *Shubal Sterns* and *Daniel Marshall,* whose labors were wonderfully blessed in Virginia, North and South Carolina, and Georgia. Many souls were converted, and, as the work of the Lord progressed, many churches were established in Virginia, and some in North Carolina. Their preachers were exceeding pious and zealous men, and their labors wonderfully blessed : and such a work appeared to be amongst the people, that "some were amazed, and stood in "doubt, saying, what means this?" The distinction between us and them was, that they were called *Separates,* and the Philadelphia, the Charleston, and the Kehukee Association, were called Regular Baptists.

The Kehukee Association, desirous of fellowship and a general communion between these two parties, sent Elders *Jonathan Thomas* and *John Meglamre* to the Separate Baptist Association, which was holden in one of the northern counties in Virginia, to endeavor to effect an union. Accordingly their Association delegated Elders *Elijah Craig* and *David Thompson* to the Kehukee Association, which was holden at Ke-

hukee meeting house, in Halifax county,
North Carolina, August, 1772, and rendered
their reasons why they could not commune
with the Regulars. Their reasons were as
follows, viz. 1. They complained of the
Regulars not being *strict enough in receiving experiences*, when persons made application to their churches for baptism, in order to become church members. 2. They
refused communion with Regular Baptist
churches, because they believed that faith
in Christ Jesus was essential to qualify a
person for baptism, yet many of the Regular churches had members in them who
acknowledged they were *baptized before
they believed*. 3. The Separates found fault
with the Regulars for their *manner of dress*,
supposing they indulged their members in
superfluity of apparel. These, with a few
other non-essentials, were the reasons they
refused communion with us: but the most
weighty reason was, " the Regulars hold-
" ing persons in fellowship in their churches,
" who were baptized in unbelief;" which
was a matter of some consequence, and
operated strongly on the minds of many
belonging to the Kehukee Association.
Accordingly, in 1774, the church in *Bertie*,
under the care of Elder *Lemuel Burkitt*,
held a conference, and declared they would
commune with none who confessed they

were baptized before they believed in
Christ. And the reasons why they did so
were, because they believed that from the
practice of John the Baptist, from the commission given by our Lord to his apostles,
and the conduct of the apostles in executing that commission, that *repentance* towards God, and *faith* in our Lord Jesus
Christ, were required as a pre-requisite to
baptism of all they baptized. If so, it appears reasonable that even *adult* persons
themselves, if baptized in a state of *impeni-
tency* and *unbelief*, are no more the proper
subjects of the ordinance than *infants*, as
the age of the person does not qualify him
for baptism, but his faith in Christ. These
things had such weight on the minds of the
members of that church, that they declared
in open conference, non-fellowship with all
churches and persons who held and maintained the contrary doctrine. And some of
the members of that church, who we baptized in unbelief, came forward and petitioned for baptism, and were baptized upon
confession of their faith in Christ.

The church at Sandy Run had no sooner
set up a bar of communion against such
churches and members, than they received
information that the church in Sussex, in
Virginia, under the pastoral care of Elder
John Meglamre; the church in Brunswick,

under the care of Zachary Thompson; the
church in the Isle of Wight, under the care
of David Barrow, had done the same. All
these churches belonged to the Kehukee
Association.

In October, 1775, the Kehukee Regular
Baptist Association, according to their annual appointment, by their delegates, met
at the Falls of Tar River, John Moore's
meeting house, and on Saturday, being assembled in the meeting house, information
was received by the other churches belonging to the Association, what the churches
in Bertie, Sussex, Brunswick, and the Isle
of Wight had done. And a great dissen-
sion arose amongst the churches respecting
the propriety of their proceedings; and the
other party claimed the prerogative of being
the Kehukee Association, and *we* who had
engaged in the reformation, insisted on being *the true*, genuine Association, as we believed we had never departed from the original plan on which that Association was
first founded. We argued that, it was well
known, that we all held *faith* in Christ essential to qualify a person for baptism, and,
if so, they who were baptized before they
believed, were not baptized agreeable to
God's word; and, as their baptism is not
valid, they remain unbaptized members;
and not to commune with unbaptized per-

sons was a principle of the Association on which we were at first established. We, therefore, argued that *we* were the true Association who had not departed from their original principles. After some desultory conversation, the Association divided, and those churches which had begun the reformation sat and held an Association in the meeting house; and the other party went into the woods, the first day, and held an Association, and the second day, removed to a private house in the neighborhood.

This division, our readers may be well assured, afforded great grief to many truly pious and godly souls; but, that God, who *works* all things by his divine providence, according to the counsel of his own will, was pleased to bring order out of confusion, and good out of evil, for by these means he was pleased to effect a reformation in the churches, and bring about a glorious revival of religion throughout the churches in general. It was not many years before all the churches were united again, and the names *Regular* and *Separate* buried in oblivion, and we were known to the world by the name of the "United Baptists." And, blessed be God, the distinction, at this time, has become obsolete, and the different names lost throughout the United States,* and we hope throughout the world.

One particular reason why those churches were at first dissatisfied with others, and were so forward in setting up a bar of communion against churches and individuals, who held members in fellowship who were baptized in unbelief, was, because several of those churches, that at first belonged to the Kehukee Association, were gathered by the *Free-will Baptists*, and as their custom was to baptize any persons who were *willing*, whether they had an experience of grace or not, so, in consequence of this practice, they had many members, who were baptized before they were converted ; and after they were brought to the knowledge of the truth, and joined the Regulars, openly confessed they were baptized before they believed : and some of them said they did it in hope of getting to Heaven by it.

* Until about twelve months before the writing of this history, the distinction was kept up in the State of Kentucky. There were a few churches in that State which still retained the name of *Separates*, and the ministers and members seemed rather inclined to believe in *General Redemption*. These churches chiefly lay in the counties of that State, south of the river Kentucky, and were formed into an Association, called the Separate Association, and they did not commune with the other Associations. But by a letter from Elder David Barrow to Elder Burkitt, we learn there is a happy union taken place amongst all the Associations, and these names lost.

Some of their *ministers* confessed they had endeavored to preach, and administer the ordinance of baptism to others, after they were baptized, before they were converted themselves; and so zealous were they for baptism (as some of them expected *salvation* by it), that one of their preachers confessed, if he could get any willing to be baptized, and it was in the night, that he would baptize them by *fire-light*, for fear they should get out of the notion of it before the next morning.

We, therefore, in conscience thought, and that from God's word, that we ought to withdraw from every brother that walked disorderly, and we were under very great impressions to begin a reformation in the churches.

The principal churches which stood in opposition to our measures, at the time when the division took place at the Falls of Tar River, were the church at Tosniot, the church on Fishing Creek, formerly under the care of *Charles Daniel;* the church at Kehukee, under the care of *William Burges;* the church in Warren county, on Reedy Creek, formerly under the care of *William Walker;* and part of the church at the Falls of Tar River—for it appears that church was divided—Col. Horn, who was a member of that church, was a chief speaker in the time of the contention, and had a very warm debate with Thomas Daniel, a minister of the other party; and Col. Horn insisted on the propriety of our procedure, and justified our raising a bar of communion against them. The chief ministers belonging to those churches who opposed the reformation, were, Elders *John Moore*, *William Burges*, *John Thomas*, and *Thomas Daniel*. The churches on the other side of the question were, the church at Sandy Run, the church in Sussex, the church in Brunswick, and the church in Isle of Wight, Virginia. Their chief ministers present were, Elders *John Meglamre*, *David Barrow*, and *Lemuel Burkitt*.

Very little business of consequence was done at this Association, except their engagements to keep up the order and rules of an Association; and accordingly agreed to meet the next time at Elder *James Bell's* meeting house, on Sappony Creek, in *Sussex* county, Virginia.

On the Saturday before the second Sunday in August, 1777, delegates from ten churches (some of which were what was then called *Separates*, and others which formerly belonged to the Kehukee Association, and had raised a bar against unbaptized members, of which mention was made before) met in an annual Association at Elder James Bell's meeting house, on Sappony, in Sussex county, Virginia, and by their delegates, presented a confession of their faith to the Association; which was unanimously acceded to. At which time and place, the Association to which we now belong was settled and established on its present order.

It was necessary at this time, for the churches to present in *their* letters to the Association, a confession of their faith; because, 1. Some of them were churches that claimed the prerogative of being the Kehukee Association, that never had departed from their original principles; therefore, in order to convince the other churches, and the world at large, that they still held the same faith and order they were at first established on, it was necessary to present to this Association, and make public, their confession of faith.

2. As some of those churches which at this time were about to unite in the Association with us, had never before been members, and were what was then called *Separates*, it was necessary they should present a confession of their faith, that it might be known whether we all agreed in *principles* or not.

The churches, by their delegates, then
4

convened, and the number of members they contained, and their present order, whether *Regulars* or *Separates*, are as follows, viz :—

	No.
1. The church in Bertie county, N. Carolina, under the care of Elder Lemuel Burkitt,	217
2. The church in Sussex, Virginia, under the care of Elder John Meglamre,	209
3. The church in Brunswick, Virginia, under the care of Elder Zachary Thompson,	320
4. The church in the Isle of Wight, under the care of Elder David Barrow,	142
5. A newly constituted church in Chowan county, North Carolina,	84
6. The church in Granville county, North Carolina, under the care of Elder Henry Ledbetter,	70
7. The church in Bute, North Carolina, under the care of Elder Joshua Kelly,	109
8. The church in Sussex, Virginia, under the care of Elder James Bell,	200
9. The church at Rocky Swamp, North Carolina, under the care of Elder Jesse Read,	139

10. The church in Edgecombe county, under the care of Elder John Tanner, } 100

—————

1590

Of which churches, the first six were *Regulars*, and the last mentioned four were *Sepdrates*.

An abstract of the principles then agreed to, and the substance of which afterwards was published in print, by order of the Association at Whitfield's meeting house, Pitt county, North Carolina, 1799, is as follows, viz:—

1. WE believe in the being of God, as almighty, eternal, unchangeable, of infinite wisdom, power, justice, holiness, goodness, mercy, and truth : and that this God has revealed himself in his word, under the characters of Father, Son, and Holy Ghost.

2. We believe that Almighty God has made known his mind and will to the children of men in his word ; which word we believe to be of divine authority, and contains all things necessary to be known for the salvation of men and women. The same is comprehended or contained in the books of the Old and New Testament, as are commonly received.

3. We believe that God, before the foundation of the world, for a purpose of his

own glory, did elect a certain number of men and angels to eternal life; and that this election is particular, eternal, and unconditional on the creature's part.

4. We believe that when God made man at first, he was perfect, holy, and upright, able to keep the law, but liable to fall, and that he stood as a federal head, or representative of all his natural offspring, and that they were to be partakers of the benefits of his obedience, or exposed to the misery which sprang from his disobedience.

5. We believe that Adam fell from this state of moral rectitude, and that he involved himself and all his natural offspring in a state of death; and for that original transgression, we all are both filthy and guilty in the sight of an holy God.

6. We also believe that it is utterly out of the power of men, as fallen creatures, to keep the law of God perfectly, repent of their sins truly, or believe in Christ, except they be drawn by the holy spirit.

7. We believe that in God's own appointed time and way (by means which he has ordained) the elect shall be called, justified, pardoned, and sanctified; and that it is impossible they can utterly refuse the call; but shall be made willing, by divine grace, to receive the offers of mercy.

8. We believe that justification in the

sight of God is only by the imputed righteousness of Jesus Christ, received and applied by faith alone.

9. We believe in like manner, that God's
elect shall not only be called, and justified,
but that they shall be converted, born again,
and changed by the effectual working of
God's holy spirit.

10. We believe that such as are converted, justified, and called by his grace, shall
persevere in holiness, and never fall finally
away.

11. We believe it to be a duty incum-
bent on all God's people, to walk religiously in good works; not in the old covenant
way of seeking life, and the favor of the
Lord by it; but only as a *duty* from a principle of love.

12. We believe baptism and the Lord's
Supper are Gospel ordinances, both belonging to the converted, or true believers; and
that persons who were sprinkled, or dipped,
whilst in unbelief, were not regularly baptized according to God's word, and that
such ought to be baptized after they are
savingly converted into the faith of Christ.

13. We believe that every church is independent in matters of discipline; and that
associations, councils, and conferences of
several ministers or churches, are not to
impose on the churches the keeping, hold-

ing, or maintaining any principle or practice contrary to the church's judgment.

14. We believe in the resurrection of the dead, both of the just and the unjust, and a general judgment.

15. We believe the punishment of the wicked is everlasting, and the joys of the righteous are eternal.

16. We believe that no minister has a right to the administration of the ordinances, only such as are regularly called, and come under imposition of hands by the Presbytery.

17. Lastly, we do believe that, for the mutual comfort, union, and satisfaction of the several churches of the aforesaid faith and order, we ought to meet in an association way; wherein each church ought to represent their case by their delegates, and attend as often as is necessary to advise with the several churches in conference; and that the decision of matters in such associations, not to be imposed, or in any wise binding on the churches without their consent, but only to sit and act as an advisory council.

These principles were adopted by the Association at Elder James Bell's meeting house, on *Sappony*, Sussex county, Virginia; and afterwards re-examined and recommended by the Association at *Pottacasy* meeting house, in Northampton county, North Carolina, 1778.

At this Association on *Sappony*, Sussex county, being the first after the division took place at the Falls of Tar River, the following business was done :—

The Association was opened by prayer, Elder John Meglamre chosen Moderator, Elder Lemuel Burkitt, Clerk. Letters from the several churches were read—all agreed in judgment about principles, and an answer given to the following queries:—

Query 1. From the church in Chowan— *Suppose a man to be a member of the* Presbyterian *church, and therein ordained a minister of the Gospel, and administrator of the ordinances thereof with approbation of them in their way, afterwards submits to believer's baptism—is his ordination valid to the Baptists?* Answer. *No.*

2. From the church in the Isle of Wight — *What shall a church do with a minister who labors to make them believe that, difference in judgment about water baptism ought to be no bar to communion?*

Ans. Such a practice is disorderly, and he who propagates the tenet ought to be dealt with as an offender.

3. From brother Thompson's church— *What shall a church do with a member, who*

*is suspected to be guilty of a fault, and de-
nies it, and no plain proof can be had, and
yet circumstances appear very plainly that
he is guilty?*

Ans. That if the church shall think that
the circumstances are good, that they ought
to act accordingly, and deal with him.

The Association further agreed to hold
two Associations yearly, viz. one in the
spring, the other in the fall. It was also
ordered that Elder Burkitt should procure
a book, and keep the records of the Associations. The next Association appointed at
Elder Burkitt's meeting house, in Northampton county, on Pottacasy Creek, the
Saturday before the third Sunday in May,
1778.

Extracts from the Minutes of the Association held at Pottacasy, May,
1778.

Saturday, the 16th of May, the delegates
from the several churches being assembled,
Elder John Meglamre was chosen Moderator, and Elder L. Burkitt, Clerk. The
letters from the churches being read, we
proceeded to business.

A church at Cashie, in Bertie county,
N. C., under the pastoral care of Elder Jeremiah Dargan, presented a letter by their

delegates, desiring admission into the Association ; and some difficulties appearing in the way, they were received on condition of having a hearing of those difficulties afterwards, in the Association.

A church in Brunswick county, Virginia, under the care of Elder Moses Foster, on petition, was received.

Then adjourned till Monday morning.

On Monday, the 18th of May, the Association being convened, those difficulties respecting the church under the care of Elder Dargan, were taken into consideration ; and the Association resolved that, Elders *James Bell, Jesse Read,* and *William Andrews* be appointed to attend his meeting, and give advice, and further inquire into the state of the church, and returns be made to our next Association.

Query 1. From Elder Burkitt's church —*By what rule shall a church approve or disapprove of a minister's gifts, who thinks he is called to the work of the ministry ?*

Ans. We give it as our opinion, that if the following things attend the ministry of a brother, that the church may approve of his gifts, and encourage him to go on in the work : 1. If he preach the truth. 2. If his preaching tends to the conviction and conversion of sinners. 3. If it be instructive and consolatory to the people of God. 4.

And, if need be, to call other ministers to the examination of his call to that work.

2. *Is the marriage of servants lawful before God, which is not complied with according to the laws of the land?* Ans. *Yes.*

3. *Is it duty to hold a member in fellowship who breaks the marriage of servants?* Ans. *No.*

Elders James Bell, John Meglamre and Zachary Thompson were appointed to visit the Regular Baptist Association, viz. the churches we were formerly *connected* with, who had formed themselves into an Association, and, in the most friendly manner, endeavor to effect a reconciliation between us.

Before we conclude this chapter, we think it our duty to give our readers a brief account of the persecution that was against Elder John Tanner; and a few biographical sketches of Elder James Bell, who departed this life before the sitting of the next Association.

ELDER JOHN TANNER.

A CERTAIN woman by the name of Dawson, in the town of Windsor, N. C., had reason to hope her soul was converted, saw baptism to be a duty for a believer to comply with, and expressed a great desire to join the church at Cashie, under the care of Elder Dargan. Her husband, who was violently opposed to it, and a great persecutor, had threatened that, if any man baptized his wife, he would shoot him; accordingly, baptism was deferred for some considerable time. At length, Elder Tanner was present at Elder Dargan's meeting, and Mrs. Dawson applied to the church for baptism, expressing her desire to comply with her duty. She related her experience, and was received; and, as Elder Dargan was an infirm man, he generally, when other ministers were present, would apply to them to administer the ordinance in his stead. He therefore requested Elder Tanner to perform the duty of baptism at this time. Whether Elder Tanner was apprised of Dawson's threatening or not; or whether he thought it was his duty to obey God rather than man, we are not able to say; but so it was, he baptized sister Dawson And, in June following, which was in the year 1777, Elder Tanner was expected to preach at Sandy Run meeting house, and Dawson, hearing of the appointment, came up from Windsor to Norfleet's Ferry, on Roanoke, and lay in wait near the banks of the river, and when Elder Tanner (who was in company with Elder Dargan) ascended the bank from the ferry

landing, Dawson, being a few yards from
him, shot him with a large horseman's pis-
tol, and seventeen shot went into his thigh,
one of which was a large buckshot, that
went through his thigh, and lodged between his breeches and thigh on the other
side.   Elder Burkitt was present when the
doctor (who was immediately sent for) took
part of the shot out of his thigh.   In this
wounded condition Elder Tanner was carried to the house of Mr. Elisha Williams, in
Scotland Neck, where he lay some weeks,
and his life was despaired of; but, through
the goodness of God, he recovered again.
Dawson seemed somewhat frightened, fear-
ing he would die, and sent a doctor up to
attend him.   And, after Elder Tanner recovered, he never attempted to seek for any
recompense, but submitted to it patiently as
persecution for Christ's sake.

ELDER JAMES BELL.

Elder James Bell was born in Sussex
county, Virginia, of parents who professed
the Episcopal religion, but there was no
great reason to believe they were acquainted with an experience of grace.   He, as his
parents before him had done, frequently attended the church of England, and complied with the forms of the church.   He

was a man of bright intellectuals, and at a very early period became popular in the county where he lived. He first received a commission in the military department; he was appointed captain of a militia company; then a justice of the peace; and, some time after, became sheriff of the county. His popularity increasing, he gained the general esteem of every respectable character in Sussex, and the adjacent counties. He was at length solicited to offer himself a candidate for the General Assembly, and accordingly did, and was elected by a large majority, and continued to represent that county for some time. All the time he was anxiously pursuing popularity he had no concern about religion, nor anxiety for the salvation of his soul, until his brother, Benjamin Bell, who had for some time been removed to the south, came in to see him. His brother Benjamin was converted, and had joined the Baptists in the south State, and when he came into Virginia and saw his brother James Bell, he told him what the Lord had done for his soul, and what a miserable state he apprehended his brother to be in; insomuch that it took a very powerful effect on his brother, so that he never was truly satisfied until he had reason to hope the Lord had converted his soul. And he

was then willing to part with all his worldly honor and preferments for that honor
that comes from God only. He was baptized in Sussex county, by Elder John
Meglamre, in the year of 1770, and soon
after became a zealous preacher of the Gospel of our Lord Jesus Christ; and it is well
known he always continued a remarkable
pious and zealous Christian until his death.
He became a member, and took the care of
the church on Sappony, in Sussex county,
Virginia, which was formerly under the
care of Elder *John Rivers*, and continued
preaching and baptizing until September,
1778, when he died. In his last sickness
he said he was apprehensive he should not
be in his senses when he died. He therefore wished to have his children called together, that he might talk to them while he
had the exercise of his reason. Which was
accordingly done, and all his children who
were present, stood around him, and he
very affectionately exhorted them all before
he bid the world adieu! He requested
Elder Burkitt (who was then present) to
preach his funeral sermon from 1 Tim. i.
15. "This is a faithful saying, and worthy
" of all acceptation, that Christ Jesus came
" into the world to save sinners, of whom I
" am chief." It is this, said he, upon
which my soul depends for life and salva-

tion. He departed this life, September, 1778, aged about 43 years.

CHAPTER III.

1. Some of the proceedings of the Association, and remarkable Events that took place from the year 1778
until 1785.—2. The Decorum or Rules by which the
Association is Governed, when made and adopted, and
the Rules at large.—3. The Nature of a Minister's Call
to the Office of the Ministry, and the Manner of his Ordination.—4. Biographical Sketches of Elder Jeremiah
Dargan, who departed this life the 25th of December,
1786.

In the year 1778, September 28th, the Association met at Elder Meglamre's meeting house, in Sussex county, Virginia. Elder Meglamre, Moderator; Elder Burkitt, Clerk. From the great respect we still had for our sister churches, which were former-ly in union with us, it was resolved that Elders John Meglamre, Z. Thompson, and Elder Burkitt (instead of Elder Bell, deceased, who was appointed by last Associa-tion) were at this Association appointed to visit those churches, and endeavor to effect a reconciliation with them if possible, and returns be made to our next Association.

A query proposed at this Association from Elder Burkitt's church—*Suppose a member is accused of a fault and denies it, and a person who is not a member, and is not interested in the matter, has made oath before a justice of the peace that he is guilty —what shall a church do in that case?*

Ans. That the church shall judge of the veracity of the person who swore, and the circumstances attending it, and act accordingly thereto.

At this time the churches began earnestly to desire a revival of religion, and sat apart two days of fasting and prayer, to solicit the throne of grace for a revival.

The next Association was appointed at Fishing Creek, at the new meeting house, on the Saturday before the third Sunday in May next

The Association met at the time and place before mentioned, and on account of the present distress of our country, but few delegates met, and but little business was done. It was at this time we received information that the *British* were at Suffolk, in Virginia, and had burned the town; and the people were fearful they were on the way to North Carolina; but the Association sat, and we continued a short space of time —the following business was done, viz :—

A church in Camden county, N. C., by

their delegates, presented a letter to the Association desiring admission. On examination they were found to' be an orderly church, and they were received. This church was one of those which was formerly in union with us before the reformation took place, and was a very ancient, respectable church. It appears that this church had for some time believed the principles on which the reformation was grounded at first. But they did not so readily accede to the measures which were fallen on at the Falls of Tar River, because their pastor, Elder *Henry Abbot*, was baptized in unbelief, and had not seen it his duty to comply with baptism since he was converted; but before this Association, which was holden at Fishing Creek, he complied with his duty, and a reformation in that church, in this respect, took place, and they have again united with us. Blessed be God for the union of saints.

It was at this time that the church under the care of Elder Dargan was received. All those difficulties before mentioned, which were for some time a bar to their being admitted, were all removed.

By reason of the distress in our country, and the molestation of our enemies, being the time of the war, we were prevented from holding any regular Association, of

5

which we have the minutes, until the Saturday before the fourth Sunday in May, 1782, which was holden at Mr. *Arthur Cotten's*, in Hertford county, North Carolina.

Saturday, 25th May, 1782. The Association being open, Elder Meglamre was chosen Moderator, Elder Burkitt Clerk. A church in Pitt county, under the care of Elder John Page, presented a letter by their delegates, desiring admission into the Association, and were received. Also the church at the Falls of Tar River was received. And also the church in Edgecomb, under the care of Elder Joshua Barns; and one in the county of Currituck, North Carolina, under the care of Elder James Gamewell, were received.

Elders Silas Mercer, Abraham Marshall, and David Barrow were appointed to preach on Sunday.

The clerk was requested to prepare a *Decorum* for the Association, and present it on Monday morning.

Monday morning, 27th May, 1782, the decorum, or rules of the Association, which the clerk had prepared, was read and approved of. A copy of which is as follows, viz :—

1. The Association shall be opened and closed by prayer.

2. A Moderator and Clerk shall be chosen by the suffrage of the members.

3. Only one person shall speak at once, who shall rise from his seat, and address the Moderator when he makes his speech.

4. The person thus speaking shall not be interrupted in his speech by any, except the Moderator, till he be done speaking.

5. He shall strictly adhere to the subject, and in no wise reflect on the person who spoke before, so as to make remarks on his slips, failings, or imperfections; but shall fairly state the case and matter as nearly as he can, so as to convey his light or ideas.

6. No person shall abruptly break off, or absent himself from the business of the Association, without liberty obtained from it.

7. No person shall rise and speak more than three times to one subject, without liberty from the Association.

8. No member of the Association shall have liberty to be whispering or laughing in time of a public speech.

9. No member of this Association shall address another, in any other terms or appellations but the title of *Brother*.

10. The Moderator shall not interrupt any member in, nor prohibit him from speaking, till he give his light on the subject, except he break the rules of this decorum.

11. The names of the several members of the Association shall be enrolled by the Clerk, and called over as of ten as the Association requires.

12. The Moderator shall be the last person who may speak to the subject; and may give his light on it, if he please, before he puts the matter to a vote.

13. Any member who shall willingly and knowingly break any of these rules, shall be reproved by the Association as they shall see proper.

These rules being confirmed and established, we then proceeded to business; wherein there was much disputing about the power of Associations, their business and foundation. But at last there was a unanimity among the whole upon the following plan, viz: The Association did agree that we should answer queries when approved, when presented by a member of the Association, and not as coming from the church; and the proceedings of the Association to be returned in writing to the respective churches. Here a motion was made for a division in the Association, but the Association did not agree to it. But for conveniency, the Association advised that four general Conferences should be holden at different places, and that the churches convenient might represent themselves in those Conferences, and their proceedings be transmitted to the annual Association. Accordingly, the four following were appointed, viz: At Elder Meglamre's meeting house, the Saturday before the second Sunday in August; at Yoppim, the Saturday before the fourth Sunday in August; at Camden, the Saturday before the first Sunday in September; at Elder Page's, the Saturday before the second Sunday in September.

The next annual Association to be at Davis's meeting house, on Roanoke, in Halifax county, North Carolina, the Saturday before the last Sunday in May, 1783.

According to the appointment, the Association met at Davis's meeting house; at which time and place the following business was done. 1. They thought proper to set aside the practice of general Conferences, and appointed four occasional Associations in their stead; and for each church convenient to represent their case by letters and delegates, and consult the affairs of the churches; and the minutes of these Associations to be transmitted to an annual Association, where all the churches which possibly could, should attend. 2. The following queries were answered at this Association, viz:—

Query 1. By Elder Mercer—*Is washing feet an ordinance of Christ's church which ought to be continued in the church?*

Ans. We look upon it a duty to be continued in the church.

2. By brother Peter Mercer—*Has a church of Christ any right to try causes of a civil nature?*

Ans. We look upon it that the church has a right from God's word, to try all causes which may arise amongst themselves.

3. The proceedings of the general Conferences appointed by the last annual Association, and which were held last year, were read in this Association, and the minutes ordered to be recorded in the Asso-

ciation book.   Queries of consequence answered at these Conferences were as follows, viz:—

Query 1. By brother Lancaster, in the
Conference at Elder Meglamre's meeting
house—*Has a church any right to suspend
a member from communion, who has been
guilty of a crime, and still hold him as a
member of the church?*

Ans. As our Lord in the 18th of St.
Matthew's Gospel, has given a sufficient
rule to deal with offending members, we
generally think there is no degree of church
censure to be inflicted on an impenitent
member, after a public hearing in the
church, besides excommunication; which
we believe consists in putting him out of
communion and membership.

2. *Has a church any authority from
God's word, to lay it upon their minister to
get up in a congregation, and publish the excommunication of a disorderly member?*

Ans. We think that the offending member being dealt with in a public conference,
is sufficient without any more publication.

3. By brother Shelly—*What way is
thought best for a church to act in supporting their minister?*

Ans. That each member ought to contribute voluntarily, according to his or her

ability; and in no wise by taxation or any other compulsion.

4. *What method shall be taken with a member, who shall rend himself off from his own church and join another?*

Ans. We think it is disorderly for a member to rend himself off from his own church, and disorderly for a church to receive him.

5. *Is the baptism of a believer a legal baptism, if performed by an unauthorized minister?*

Ans. It is our opinion, that the person who administered the ordinance was very much out of his duty, and displeasure ought to be shown to such a practice; but as for the person's baptism, as it was done in faith, we esteem it legal.

6. By Elder Abbot, in the Conference at Yoppim—*Is a person who is called to the work of the ministry, in his duty to travel out into different parts of the world to preach, without a letter from his church signifying their approbation of his personal conduct, and call to the ministry?*

Ans. We do not think they are in their duty.

7. By Elder Burkitt, in the Conference at Camden—*What shall a church do with a member who shall absent himself from the communion of the Lord's Supper?*

Ans. That it is the duty of the church to inquire into the reason of his thus absenting himself from the communion, and if he does not render a satisfactory reason the church shall deal with him.

8. By brother Forbes—*What number of members can be thought sufficient, in an arm, branch, or wing of a church, in order for their constitution?*

Ans. We give it as our opinion, that a number of members who are capable to carry on a proper discipline in the church, are sufficient for a constitution.

9. *Has an itinerant minister, who has not the care of a church, a right to baptize on any occasion?*

Ans. We suppose he has not a right on all occasions, but only on some. The occasions which we conceive he has a right to baptize on, are as follows, viz : 1. When he visits a church destitute of a pastor, and is called by the church to baptize. 2. When he travels into dark places, destitute of ministerial helps, and persons get converted and desire baptism of him, and they are not capable to make application to any church by reason of their distance from them.

After the Association had heard and approved of the procedure of these general Conferences, they then appointed their next annual Association, which was to be holden at Sandy Run, in Bertie county, N. C., the Saturday before the third Sunday in May, 1784.

By a resolve of this Association there were four occasional Associations to be holden in 1783, viz : At Ballard's Bridge in August, at Camden in September, at South Quay in October, and at the new meeting on Fishing Creek, the Saturday before the third Sunday in September, and the minutes to be transmitted to the annual Association.

EXTRACTS FROM THE MINUTES OF THESE OCCASIONAL ASSOCIATIONS.

At the Association at Ballard's Bridge, the following queries were answered, viz:—

Query 1. By Elder Burkitt—*Is it agreeable to God's word, for Christians to marry unconverted persons ?*

Ans. We do not know that God's word does actually forbid such marriages, but we would advise the members of our churches to comply with Christian marriages, as nearly as they can judge, for their own comfort and satisfaction.

2. *What shall the master of a family do with his slaves, who refuse to attend at the time of public prayers in the family ?*

Ans. We think it is the duty of every master of a family to give his slaves liberty to attend the worship of God in his family; and, likewise, it is his duty to exhort them to it, and endeavor to convince them of their duty; and then leave them to their own choice.

3. By Elder Welsh—*Is it thought regular for a church to restore a deacon upon repentance, from suspension to office, as well as to membership?*

Ans. It is our opinion, that if the church be fully satisfied with his conduct in executing his office before, that they may restore him to office again, as well as to membership.

4. By Elder Burkitt—*What way is thought best for a church to put members upon a trial of their gifts, who think they are called to the work of the ministry?*

Ans. We judge it necessary that all ministers should be called of God to preach the Gospel, and when any member thinks he has a call to preach, he ought to inform his church of it; and then we would advise the church to deal very tenderly with him, and give him all the encouragement necessary: and we would advise that brother to follow the direction of the church with respect to the manner of beginning to preach.

At the occasional Association held on Fishing Creek the same year, a church on Black Creek, in Wayne county, N. C., petitioned for admission into the Association, and was received. And at this Association the following queries were answered:—

Query 1. By Elder Meglamre—*What shall a church require of a person for satisfaction, who had been excommunicated from another church at a great distance, and now being removed convenient to them and desires fellowship with them?*

Ans. That such a person ought (if possible) by a letter of recommendation from the church where he lives, apply to the church from which he was excommunicated, and regain fellowship with them, and then take a letter of dismission from them, and join the church amongst whom he lives.

2. *What are the essentials of church communion?*

Ans. That a person shall, before being admitted to commune, give a satisfactory account of his being savingly converted to the Lord Jesus Christ, and publicly declare the same by being regularly *baptized* by *immersion.*

At the occasional Association at South Quay, very little was done, except a motion for a division in the Association; which was rejected.

THE ANNUAL ASSOCIATION AT SANDY RUN.

The 15th of May, 1784, the annual Association commenced at Sandy Run meeting house, Bertie county, North Carolina. The Association was opened by prayer— Elder Meglamre was chosen Moderator, and Elder Burkitt Clerk. Then proceeded to business. A church in Pitt county, under the care of Elder Abram Baker, on petition, was received into the Association. Elders Jesse Read, John Meglamre, Philip Hughes, and David Barrow were appointed to preach on Sunday.

This Association agreed to correspond with the Salisbury Association, in Maryland, by letter and delegate. Elder Edward Mintz was appointed our delegate. Elder Burkitt was requested to prepare letters to the Salisbury Association, and to the general committee at Dover, in Virginia. An answer to the following queries were given, viz:—

Query 1. *Is a pastor or bishop of a church bound by the word of God, to the congregation he agrees to take the oversight of, for life; or is he, in this case, at liberty to be governed by his inclination, interest, or what he may suppose to be a call from God. Yea or nay?*

After debating the query some time, and it appearing ambiguous, by the consent of the Association the query was altered to read thus—

Is it thought that a bishop, or pastor of a church, stands upon the same footing in the church as any other member, with respect to his having a right to a dismission on his request?

Ans. It is our opinion that, as a member, he is accountable to the church, and as a minister he is accountable to God.

2. *Is it agreeable to Gospel rule and order, to call a minister to take the pastoral care of a church, without the unanimous consent of the members of said church?*

Ans. We think they ought to be unanimous.

The Association agreed to hold only one occasional Association this year, which was appointed at Fishing Creek, Daniel's meeting house, the Saturday before the second Sunday in October. The annual Association was appointed next at Shoulder's Hill, in Virginia.

At the occasional Association on Fishing Creek, a church in Craven county, N. C., under the care of Elder James Brinson, joined the Association. Also another in

said county on Swift Creek, was received.
Another in Franklin county, formerly under the care of Elder William Walker,
presented a letter, setting forth their desire
to be in union with us, and wished to know
what were those bars which heretofore subsisted between the churches. Accordingly
information was given. This church was
one of the Regular Baptist Association
which was formerly in union with us.

EXTRACTS FROM THE ANNUAL ASSOCIATION HOLDEN AT SHOULDER'S HILL.

Saturday, the 14th of May, 1785, the
Association met at Shoulder's Hill, in Nansemond county, in Virginia, and after it
was opened by prayer, Elder Meglamre
was chosen Moderator, and Elder Burkitt
Clerk.

Letters from twenty-one churches were
read.

A church at the North-west River bridge,
in Norfolk county, Virginia, a church at
Shoulder's Hill, a church on Scuppernong,
in Tyrrel county, N. C., a church at Pungo, Princess Anne county, Virginia, and
a church on Blackwater, Princess Anne,
were all received in this Association.

Elders John Leland, Lemuel Burkitt,

David Barrow, and Jonathan Barns, were appointed to preach on Sunday.

On motion of Elder Barrow, the *engrossed bill*, respecting a general assessment, was taken into consideration; and on motion of Elder Leland, a petition of the inhabitants of Charles City county, Virginia, was read; and the Association advised that this petition, or one similar thereto, should be adopted by the delegates of this Association who reside in Virginia, and be presented to the inhabitants of their respective counties, and when they have gotten a sufficient number of subscribers, be presented to the General Assembly of Virginia.

Here at this Association, the churches were still sensible of the declining state of religion; accordingly a day of fasting and prayer was appointed, to solicit the throne of grace for a revival.

The next Association was appointed at Kehukee, the Saturday before the second Sunday in October, 1785.

At this Association the most of the churches complained of coldness in religion; a few informed us of a great stir amongst them.

A church at South Quay, in Virginia, a church at Bear Creek, in Dobbs county, N. C., a church in the upper end of Tyrrel county, on Morattuck, were received into membership in this Association.

On motion of Elder Read, Elders John Meglamre and Jesse Read, and brothers Charles Champion and Thomas Gardner were appointed a committee to meet the Regular Baptist brethren in conference to endeavor to effect a reconciliation with them.

Elders David Barrow, Lemuel Burkitt, John Meglamre, and Jonathan Barns were appointed to preach on Sunday.

Query 1. *Has a woman any right to speak in the church in matters of discipline, unless called upon?*

Ans. We think they have no right unless called upon, or where it respects their own communion.

In consequence of a motion made by Elder J. M'Cabe, the Association thought proper to advise the several churches (in order to remove the general complaint of coldness in religion) to set apart some time every day, between sunset and dark, to be engaged in private prayer to the Lord for a revival of religion.

The next Association is to be holden at the house of brother Joshua Freeman, in Bertie county, May, 1786.

We shall conclude this chapter, by showing the nature of a minister's call to the

KEHUKEE BAPTIST ASSOCIATION.

office of the ministry, and the manner of his
ordination; and a few sketches of the biography of Elder Dargan, who departed this
life the 25th of December, 1786.

A MINISTER'S CALL AND ORDINATION.

It is by many thought absolutely necessary, that the first qualification of a minister
of the Gospel, should be a classical education; and such persons think that a minister
cannot be. qualified to preach the Gospel,
except he be a man of *erudition*. But is it
not evident, that many who have spent
years in the schools to acquire a liberal education, and yet notwithstanding all their
acquirements, are ignorant of the *true knowledge* of God, and are unacquainted with the
spiritual meaning of his word. "The natural man receiveth not the things of the spirit of God, neither can he know them, for
they are spiritually discerned." 1 Cor. ii.
14. "And the wisdom of this world is
foolishness with God." Chap. iii. 19.—
Learning is a very good handmaid, but we
are far from supposing that it is essentially
necessary for a man to be acquainted with
the *oriental* languages, before he is qualified
to preach the Gospel. Many may be acquainted with these languages, and yet be,
as a poor African told a young gentleman:
6

"I perceive (said he) that there are many *learned* fools." Upon the whole, we suppose that it is necessary every minister of Christ should, in the first place, be truly converted, and regenerated by the grace of God; that he have a general acquaintance with the Word of God, and that he should be called of God to preach the Gospel. "No man taketh this honor to himself, but he that is called of God, as was Aaron." Heb. v. 4. An evidence of his call, for his own satisfaction, is, first, if his views in preaching the Gospel be not for the sake of lucre, nor for honor, nor applause; but, secondly, if he aim at the glory of God and the good of souls. An evidence of his call, to the satisfaction of others, is, first, his spiritual understanding in the Word of God; second, his ability in explaining the meaning of the Word; third, the success of his ministry in the conviction and conversion of sinners, and comfort of the saints. It is necessary that a person thus called to the ministry, should preach on trial for some time, and when the church is satisfied with his call and usefulness, he shall then be set apart by fasting and prayer, by the hands of the Presbytery, in manner and form something like the following example:—

1. It is necessary that a fast should be observed. Acts xiii. 3. 2. That a Presby-

tery of two ministers, at least, should be present.

The day appointed for ordination being come, and the church being assembled, a sermon shall be delivered by one of the ministers suitable to the occasion. The sermon being over, the solemnity may begin with singing a suitable hymn, and prayer to Almighty God. Then one of the ministers standing up, ought to address the *candidate* and church after this manner: "When the church at Jerusalem, the mo ther of us all, had chosen men to office, it is recorded that they set them before the Apostles to be ordained, by laying on of hands and prayers; we desire, therefore, that this church will set before us the man whom they have chosen to the ministry."

Then let some of the church conduct the candidate to the ministers, and one of them may address him in this manner :—

"The regard we pay to that sacred charge, *lay hands suddenly on no man*, obliges us to use caution—Sir, we would be certified of your call to preach."

The candidate may relate his call, or present a copy of his call, and it may be read.

"We would also see your license, which may be to us a testimony of your good morals, and the approbation which your ministerial abilities have obtained."

Let the license be read, or let the church testify.

Then add, "Hitherto your advances towards the ministry appear to have been regular and fair, but we are obliged to seek for further satisfaction, which you alone are capable of giving: permit me therefore to ask you—Do you, Sir, willingly, and not by constraint, out of a ready mind, and not for filthy lucre, devote yourself to the sacred office?"

The candidate shall answer, that the ministry to him is of free choice, and that his view is not lucrative.

"Do you believe that you are moved hereto by the spirit of God, so that a necessity is laid on you to preach the Gospel, and that a wo will be to you if you preach it not?"

The candidate shall answer the question in the affirmative.

"Do you take the *Bible* to be the word of God, in such a sense as to hold yourself bound to believe all it declares; to do all it requires of you as a Christian; to abstain from all it forbids? Do you consider that book as the only *rule* of *faith* and *practice* in matters of religion; and a sufficient rule, so that there is no occasion for any other judge of controversies; or for creeds, confessions of faith, traditions, or acts of councils of any denominations, to supply its supposed defects? Do you hold that book as your *creed* or *confession of faith*; and will you make it your directory, whether in preaching, administering ordinances, exercising government and discipline, or in performing any other branch of your function?"

The candidate shall confess that he owns it as the word of God, and that his resolution is to be directed by it as a Christian, and as a minister.

After this the candidate shall be desired to kneel, and the ministers lay their hands on him, and pray, each of them. Then the ministers to withdraw their hands, and when the ordained person rises, to salute him in the following manner:—

"We honor you, dear brother, in the presence of all the people, and give you the right hand of fellowship as a token of brotherhood and congratulation; and wish you success in your office, and an answer to those prayers which two or three have heartily agreed on earth to put up for you."

Then the solemnity is to be concluded by a charge given to the ordained minister, and a certificate of his ordination as follows:—

State of N. Carolina,
   Bertie County.

   This may certify that A. B. (a minister of the Baptist society, and a member of the church in the county and state aforesaid, being before proved and recommended by said church), was set apart by fasting and prayers, on the 3d day of October, 1803, by the imposition of hands of C. D., E. F. and G. H., ministers of the Gospel, who were called as a Presbytery for that purpose, whereby the said A. B. is ordained a minister of the Gospel, and entitled to the administration of all the ordinances thereof. Witness our hands the day and date above written.   C. D.
                                     E. F.
                                     G. H.

ELDER JEREMIAH DARGAN.

ELDER JEREMIAH DARGAN was converted and baptized in the south state, but divine Providence so ordered that he should move in, and become a resident of Bertie county, N. C. The manner and means by which it was effected through the divine agency of Him, *who worketh all things according to the counsel of his own will,* was sister Dargan, whose name before married was *Anne Moore,* who resided at Cashie, in Bertie county, got converted, and as there was no administrator near to administer baptism, she travelled out into the state of South Carolina, under a sense of duty and a desire to comply with it. Here she met with Elder Dargan, whom she soon after married, and he moved into Bertie county. He was a remarkable pious Christian, and a

KEHUKEE BAPTIST ASSOCIATION.   87

very zealous minister of the Gospel. He was so tender-hearted, that it was hardly ever known that he preached a sermon without plentifully shedding tears; so that he could say with the Apostle Paul, *For the space of three years I have warned every one, night and day, with tears.* Acts xx. 31. Elder Dargan was an instrument of first planting the Gospel at Cashie, and of first gathering that church. He did not continue a great many years among them, but his labors were wonderfully blessed among that people, and in that part of the country near Wiccacon. He was a means, in the hands of God, of planting that church, called *Wiccacon church,* now under the care of Elder Hendry. Being greatly afflicted, he did not travel much; and towards the latter end of his days he was grievously afflicted with the gravel, of which he at last died. He was very patient in his affliction, submissive to the will of Divine Providence, and expressed a desire to depart and to be with Christ, which was far better. He departed this life on the 25th of December, 1786. He requested that Elder Burkitt should preach his funeral sermon, and that a copy of the sermon should be written (as nearly as could) for the benefit of his friends. Accordingly Elder Burkitt attended at his funeral solemnity, and preached to a crowded

audience, from Luke ii. 29, 30. "Lord,
now lettest thou thy servant depart in peace,
according to thy word: For mine eyes have
seen thy salvation." The sermon afterwards was printed.

CHAPTER IV.

On the 20th of May, 1786, the Association met at brother Joshua Freeman's, in
Bertie county, N. C. The Association was
opened by prayer, Elder John Meglamre
was chosen Moderator, Elder Burkitt Clerk.
Letters from twenty-one churches were
read. They mostly complained of coldness;
but there were added to the churches since
last Association, nearly seventy members.

Here, a church at Knobscrook, in Pasquotank county, N. C., and one in Brunswick county, Virginia, on Fountain's Creek, were received into the Association.

Elder Read, who was appointed (with some others) to attend a committee of the Regular Baptist Society, informed the Association that he attended the committee, and made to them the following proposals :—

1. We think that none but believers in Christ have a right to the ordinance of baptism ; therefore we will not hold communion with those who plead for the validity of baptism in unbelief.

2. We leave every church member to judge for himself whether he was baptized in unbelief or not.

3 We leave every minister at liberty to baptize, or not, such persons as desire to be baptized, being scrupulous about their former baptism.

The Association concurred with the report; and recommended those propositions to the several churches in our union, and desired their opinion thereon.

Query 1. *Is it legal to administer the Lord's Supper to a single person, in case of inability to attend public worship?*

Ans. We believe it may be lawful in some cases.

2. *Is it orderly for a church to hold com-*

munion with a member who frequents the Free-Mason Lodge?

Ans. We think it disorderly.

The next Association to be holden at South Quay, in Virginia, the first Sunday in October, 1786.

On the 30th day of September, being the Saturday before the first Sunday in October, 1786, the Association met at South Quay. The following business done:—

A church at Black Creek, Southampton county, Virginia, was received.

On motion of Elder Barrow, a committee of six, viz: Elders Meglamre, Barrow, Mintz, Stansil, Etheridge and Read, were appointed to devise ways and means for the encouragement of itinerant preaching. On Monday the 2d of October, the committee reported that they were divided in their sentiments, and had concluded on nothing decisive. Whereupon it was ordered that Elder Meglamre, the chairman of said committee, report the difficulties which occasioned the division as aforesaid; and after hearing those difficulties and considering them, the Association ordered that the proceedings of said committee be entered on the Minutes of the Association, and be transmitted to the different churches for their consideration and approbation; and they were requested to signify their minds to the next Association. The proceedings were as follow, viz:—

1. From the frequent requests, in the church letters to the Association, we think it necessary that four ministers be appointed to visit the churches in our connection, each one to go through the churches twice in one year.

2. For the support of those ministers, we think necessary for the Association to advise the congregations thus visited, to contribute as they may think to be duty; and favor the next Association with an account of what they shall do for that purpose.

3. That the said Itinerants equally partake of the bounty of the people.

4. That this work be begun the 1st day of November, at South Quay.

Query 1. *Has a church a right to excommunicate a member on the single testimony of a worlding, in any case?*

Ans. No: unless corroborating circumstances be sufficient to induce the church to believe the testimony to be true.

At this Association the churches agreed to divide, in a measure—that is, they agreed to hold one Association in Virginia in the spring, and the Carolina Association in the fall; and that each Association shall send five ministers, and each of the ministers to take with him one of the members of his church, as a delegate; and that either of the Associations may dismiss or receive any church in the connection for the sake of conveniency.

The next Association in Virginia to be at Fountain's Creek, in May; and the Carolina Association to be at Daniel's meeting house, on Fishing Creek, in October next.

On the 19th of May, 1787, the Association met at Fountain's Creek.

A church at Otterdam's, Sussex county, Virginia, was received.

This Association agreed to reconsider the business of *itinerant* preaching. A committee was appointed for that purpose, and after deliberation thereon, reported as follows :—

1. It is thought expedient that every quarterly meeting should be attended by some neighboring itinerant preacher.

2. That not only ordained preachers, but young gifts also be advised and called upon by the church to which they belong, to engage in the work, not only amongst the churches, but in other places where it may appear necessary.

3. That as many appointments as can be conveniently attended, be by the present Association made, in order to begin the work.

An amendment to these rules was proposed by Elder Barrow, and concurred with by the Association, viz:—

That this Association would recommend it to the several churches to search among themselves for such members as have useful gifts, and pressingly lay it upon them to exercise them without delay.

Query 1. *What number of ministers are sufficient to compose a Presbytery?*

Ans. Two or more.

The next Virginia Association appointed at Elder Meglamre's meeting house, in Sussex county, on the Saturday before the third Sunday in May next.

On the Saturday before the second Sunday in October, 1787, the Carolina Association met at Daniel's meeting house, on Fishing Creek. Elder Meglamre, Moderator; Elder Burkitt, Clerk.

At this Association, a church in Martin county, under the care of Elder Martin Ross, was received into the Association.

Query 1. *What measures shall a deacon take, who sees the necessity of the minister's support, and his conscience binds him to do his duty, in consequence of which he frequently excites the brethren to their duty; yet after all, to his daily grief, he finds they neglect their duty?*

Ans. It is our opinion that it is the mem-

bers' duty voluntarily to contribute to the
minister's support, and if the deacon dis-
covers any member remiss in his duty, that
he shall cite him to the church ; and, if the
church finds him negligent in his duty, we
give it as our advice, that the church should
deal with him for covetousness.

The churches were requested, both in
Carolina and Virginia, to send in their letters to our next Association, whether they
approve of a division of the Association,
according to the proceedings at South
Quay, in 1786.

On the Saturday before the third Sunday in May, 1788, the Association convened
at Elder Meglamre's meeting house, in Sussex, Virginia.   Elder Meglamre chosen
Moderator; Elder Burkitt, Clerk.

A church at Seacock, in Sussex county ;
a church near the Cut Banks, on Nottoway, Dinwiddie county; a church in the
same county, on Rowanty, and a church
on Great Creek, in Brunswick county, Virginia, were received into the Association.

On motion of Elder Barrow, a committee was appointed to examine the minds of
the delegates from South Quay church, respecting a certain sentence in their letter to
this Association.   On examination of the
delegates, the committee reported as follows, viz :—

That this church had adopted a certain plan for discharging their duty towards traveling preachers by a public fund; which plan the church recommended to the approbation or disapprobation of this Association.

The plan was as follows, viz:—

" By raising a fund, in the first place, " by their own contribution. 2. By public " collections from the inhabitants, twice in " the year at least. Which money so col-" lected and deposited in the hands of some " person, and subject to the orders of the " church, to be appropriated to the aid of " any and every traveling preacher, whom " they shall judge to be sent of God to " preach. And they conceive that such a " plan, with them alone (beautiful as it ap-" pears) will not answer the desired pur-" pose; therefore have thought it necessary " to present it to this Association for their " approbation."

Upon a further investigation of the matter, the Association determined that the plan proposed be inserted in the minutes of the Association, and the following answer be prefixed:—

The Association, after a mature deliberation upon the matter, do think that, according to Scripture, there ought to be some provision made in the churches for the ministry; and, therefore, thought it improper to decide on the proposed plan; but, do recommend it to the consideration of the different churches for their approbation or disapprobation.

On the mature consideration of the division of the Association, it was thought expedient for the two bodies to be again united in one, as formerly: And it was also resolved that there should be two Associations in the year; one in Virginia, the other in Carolina; one in the spring, the other in the fall. And that they should be appointed by the respective brethren in each State, when and where they please; i. e. the brethren belonging to Virginia to appoint the Association in their State, and the brethren in Carolina to have the privilege of appointing the Association in that State; and that every church in each State be under an obligation to attend each Association, in each State, according to their former compact, before the division took place.

The next Association, in Virginia, is appointed the Saturday before the third Sunday in May, 1789.

The Association in Carolina met, the Saturday before the second Sunday in October, 1788, at the Falls of Tar River.

Elder Meglamre was chosen Moderator, and Elder Burkitt, Clerk.

A church on Newport River, in Cartaret county; and one on New River, in Onslow county, under the care of Elder Robert Nixon, were received.

On motion, the Association was requested to give their opinion what they believe the real work of a Deacon is.

Ans. That we think that there ought to be such officers in the church as Deacons, and that their work is to serve tables. That is, the table of the Lord; the table of the minister; and the table of the poor. And to see that the church makes proper provision for them.

Query 1. *How far can a church that has no pastor, or ordained minister (though they have some other ordained officers), proceed in discipline to receive or turn out members, and be orderly in their proceedings?*

Ans. We think that such an organized church has full power to receive persons to baptism, and call upon an authorized minister to baptize them; and that such a church has full power to excommunicate disorderly members.

2. *Suppose a man should be married to a woman who was under twelve years old, he knowing her age when he married her; and should afterwards forsake her, and marry*

7

another: Can such a man be justifiable in so doing; or ought that man to be held in the fellowship of a Gospel church? Ans. No.

Whereas, the church at Kehukee are fallen into disorder, and stand in great need of our assistance, to advise them to such suitable measures as they may think proper to effect their union again—

It is ordered that Elders Burkitt, Read and White be a committee to attend said church, and propose suitable measures for that purpose.

It was the opinion of this Association that those *bars* which heretofore subsisted between the baptists amongst us, formerly called *Regulars* and *Separates*, be taken down; and a general union and communion take place according to the terms proposed at brother Joshua Freeman's, in Bertie county, May, 1786; and that the names *Regular* and *Separate* be buried in oblivion, and that we should be henceforth known to the world by the name of the *United Baptist*.

The next Association in Carolina is appointed to be at Whitfield's meeting-house, in Pitt county, the second Saturday in October, 1789.

May, 1789, the Association met at the Isle of Wight meeting-house, in Virginia. A church on Meherrin, Southampton county, under the care of Elder Murrell, was received into the Association.

Elder Isaac Backus, of New England, and Elders John Pollard, Thomas Read, and Thomas Armistead, being present, were invited to a seat in the Association.

Query 1. *Is it the duty of a minister to take little children in his arms (at the request of their parents or others), and name them, and pray to the Lord to bless them?*

Ans. We think it duty for ministers to pray for infants as well as others, but not to take them in their arms and name them at that time.

2. *Is it orderly for a minister to withdraw from a church he is pastor of, and refuse to preach or administer the ordinances amongst them, because they do not pay him?*

Ans. By the law of Christ, ministers are required to watch for souls as they that must give an account, and their hearers are required to communicate unto them in all good things. Heb. xiii. 7. Gal. vi. 6. We believe that no minister can justly refuse to feed the flock he had taken the charge of, without either having their consent therefor, or else referring the case to the judgment of impartial brethren.

Whereas, our sister church at Pungo, Princess Anne county, Virginia, has not associated with us for a considerable time—

It is advised that the minutes of this Association, together with a letter of admonition (which Elder Barrow is requested to prepare), be sent to that church.

The next Association in Virginia, to be holden at Reedy Creek, in Brunswick county, the Saturday before the third Sunday in May, 1790.

On the 10th of October, 1789, the Association convened at Whitfield's meetinghouse, in Pitt county, North Carolina, brother Elisha Battle was chosen Moderator, and Elder Burkitt, Clerk.

A church at Lockwood's Folly, in Brunswick county, and a church in Robeson county, North Carolina, under the care of Elder Jacob Tarver, joined the Association.

On motion, Elders Burkitt, Barrow, Read, Ross, and Moore, were appointed a committee to prepare a plan or constitution for the future government of the Association.

Elder Burkitt, from the committee appointed by a resolution of the last October Association, to propose measures for a reconciliation in the church at Kehukee, reported, that the committee attended according to appointment, and thought it best to advise that church to relate their experiences to each other, and come under re-examination, in order to regain a general fellowship; which was unanimously agreed to by the church, and accordingly put in practice. The Association concurred with the report.

Elders Burkitt, Barrow, and Read were appointed to preach on Sunday.

A church in Bladen and New Hanover counties, under the care of Elder William Cooper, were received into union with us.

THE JUNCTION OF THE ASSOCIATION.

Whereas, a division heretofore subsisted between the churches in the Association, called the Kehukee Association, those bars being taken down by the churches themselves, and approved by the Association; and as it is the desire of the churches and this Association that we again become one body as formerly, it was agreed that the following churches should be considered as part of our body, viz :—

1. The church in Warren county, under the care of Elder Lewis Moore.

2. The church in Franklin county, under the care of Elder William Lancaster.

3. The church on Tosniot, under the care of Reuben Hayes.

4. The church in Johnston and Wake counties, under the care of John Moore.

5. The church in Duplin, Wayne, and Johnston, under the care of Charles Hines.

6. The church in Sampson, Wake, and Cumberland, under the care of W. Taylor.

7. The church in Sampson county, under the care of Fleet Cooper.

Elder Burkitt, from the committee appointed to prepare a Plan or Constitution for the future Government of the Association, reported, that they had prepared a plan, which to them was thought the most advisable; which was read, and debated article by article, and amendments being made thereto, the Association resolved to adopt the following Plan or Constitution for the future Government of the Association, viz :—

THE PLAN OR CONSTITUTION OF THE UNITED BAPTIST ASSOCIA-
TION, FORMERLY CALLED THE KEHUKEE ASSOCIATION.

Preamble.

From a long series of experience, we, the churches of Jesus Christ, being regularly baptized upon the profession of our faith in Christ, are convinced of the necessity of a combination of churches, in order to perpetuate an union and communion amongst us, and preserve and maintain a correspondence with each other in our union: We therefore propose to maintain and keep the orders and rules of an Association, according to the following plan or form of government.

Article I. The Association shall be composed of members chosen by different churches in our union, and duly sent to represent them in the Association; who shall be members whom they judge best qualified for that purpose, and, producing letters from their respective churches, certifying their appointment, shall be entitled to a seat.

II. In the letters from the different churches, shall be expressed their number in full fellowship, those baptized, received by letter, dismissed, excommunicated, and dead since the last Association.

III. The members thus chosen and convened shall be

denominated the *United Baptist Association, formerly called the Kehukee Association;* being composed of sundry churches lying and being in North Carolina and the lower parts of Virginia: Who shall have no power to *lord it* over God's heritage; nor shall they have any classical power over the churches; nor shall they infringe any of the internal rights of any church in the union.

IV. The Association, when convened, shall be governed and ruled by a regular and proper decorum.

V. The Association shall have a Moderator and Clerk, who shall be chosen by the suffrage of the members present.

VI. New churches may be admitted into this union, who shall petition by letter and delegates, and upon examination (if found orthodox and orderly), shall be received by the Association, and manifested by the Moderator, giving the delegates the right hand of fellowship.

VII. Every church in the union shall be entitled to representation in the Association; but shall have only two members from each church.

VIII. Every query presented by any member in the Association shall be once read; and before it be debated, the Moderator shall put it to vote; and if there be a majority for its being debated, it shall be taken into consideration, and be deliberated; but if there be a majority against it, it shall be withdrawn.

IX. Every motion made and seconded shall come under the consideration of the Association, except it be withdrawn by the member who made it.

X. The Association shall endeavor to furnish the churches with the minutes of the Associations. The best method for effecting that purpose shall be at the discretion of the future Associations.

XI. We think it absolutely necessary that we should have an Association Fund for defraying the expenses of the same: For the raising and supporting of which, we think it the duty of each church in the union to contribute voluntarily such sums as they shall think proper, and send by the hands of their delegates to the Association; and those moneys thus contributed by the churches, and received by the Association, shall be deposited in the hands of a Treasurer, by the Association appointed, who shall be accountable to the Association for all moneys by him received and paid out, according to the direction of the Association.

XII. There shall be an Association book kept, wherein the proceedings of every Association shall be regularly recorded, by a Secretary appointed by the Association, who shall receive a compensation yearly for his trouble.

XIII. The minutes of the Association shall be read (and corrected if need be), and assigned by the Moderator and Clerk before the Association rises.

XIV. Amendments to this plan or form of government may be made at any time by a majority of the union, when they may deem it necessary.

XV. The Association shall have power—

1. To provide for the general union of the churches.

2. To preserve inviolably a chain of communion amongst the churches.

3. To give the churches all necessary advice in matters of difficulty.

4. To inquire into the cause why the churches fail to represent themselves at any time in the Association.

5. To appropriate those moneys by the churches contributed for an Association Fund, to any purpose they may think proper.

6. To appoint any member or members, by and with his or their consent, to transact any business which they may see necessary.

7. The Association shall have power to withdraw from any church in this union, which shall violate the rules of this Association, or deviate from the orthodox principles of religion.

8. To admit any of the distant brethren in the ministry, as assistants, who may be present at the time of their sitting, whom they shall judge necessary.

9. The Association shall have power to adjourn themselves to any future time or place they may think most convenient to the churches; provided it be holden once in the year in the State of *Virginia*, and once in the year in *North Carolina;* and the Association in North Carolina interchangeably, one year on the *north* side of *Tar River*, and the next year on the *south* side of *Tar River:* and the members living within each district to fix the time and place for holding the Asssociation within said district.

The minutes of the Association had never before this time been printed. It was at this Association ordered that two hundred and fifty copies of the minutes of this Association should be printed; and that the Constitution or Form of Government and an abstract of our principles be inserted in the same; which was done accordingly. There were now fifty-one churches and three thousand nine hundred and forty-four members in the Association. So that, through the goodness of God, we had increased forty-one churches and one thousand three hundred and fifty-four members in twelve years, and we have great reason to be thankful to Almighty God that an happy union had taken place between all the churches of *Regulars* and *Separates*.

The next Association was holden at Reedy Creek meeting-house, in Brunswick county, Virginia, May, 1790. Elder Meglamre, Moderator; Elder Burkitt, Clerk.

At this Association, a church in Portsmouth, and one in Mecklenberg, Virginia, under the care of Elder John King, were received into the Association.

At this Association, the business of dividing the Association was under consideration, but it was judged not expedient to divide at this time.

Elder Burkitt was appointed to write a

Circular Letter for the next Association, on the doctrine of sanctification.

It was also resolved, that it be recommended to the churches in our connection to give their unordained preachers, who travel amongst the churches, a suitable recommendation.

The next Association was appointed at Davis's meeting-house, in Halifax county, North Carolina, on the Saturday before the second Sunday in October, 1790.

October, 1790, the Association met at Davis's meeting-house, according to appointment. Elder Barrow preached the introductory sermon from Luke xii. 15. *Take heed, and beware of covetousness.* Brother Elisha Battle, Moderator; Elder Burkitt, Clerk. Letters from fifty-four churches were read.

A church on Flatty Creek, Pasquotank county; a church near Wiccacon, in Bertie county; a church on Sawyer's Creek, Camden county; a church on Trent, Jones county; a church on Hadnott's Creek, Carteret county, and a church in Dobbs county, North Carolina, were received into membership in this Association.

A committee of five, viz: Elders Barrow, Burkitt, and Brethren Battle, Lemmon, and Col. Bryan, were appointed to devise ways and means for the encouragement of

itinerant preaching ; who reported that,
Whereas, it does appear to us, from a varie-
ty of circumstances, that itinerant preaching
is necessary, and we hope would be a blessing, we therefore advise the Association to
recommend to the several churches in the
union, to signify in their letters to the next
Association whether they approve of the
following plan, viz. 1. That the Association be divided into certain districts. 2.
That a certain number of ministers be appointed by the Association to travel, attend
at, and preach to each church once at least
in six months, or more often. 3. That
such ministers as are nominated, shall have
no power or superiority over the churches
by virtue of their delegation, or otherwise,
more than to advise. 4. We would advise
every church when visited, to call those
ministers to their assistance in conference
about any matter of difficulty, whether it
be in principle or practice. 5. That the
Association do recommend the respective
churches of their connection to consider
what the apostle says concerning this matter,
"That they who preach the Gospel should
" live of the Gospel ;" and accordingly advise the churches to consider the expenses
of those ministers, and use proper means in
each church (which they themselves may
prescribe) to answer that purpose, and vo-

luntarily contribute to them for the defraying of such expenses.

Elders Burkitt, Ross, and Barns were appointed to attend the church at Flat Swamp, who were under difficulties respecting the doctrine of Universal Restoration, strenuously propagated amongst them by a certain John Stansill, and propose measures for their relief.

At this Association, it was again solicited for a division of the Association; and after a long deliberation on the subject, it was resolved, that the Association be divided into two distinct Associations, and that the state line between Virginia and North Carolina be the dividing line between the two Associations, and that they should constantly visit each other by two delegates and a letter of correspondence.

REMARKS ON THE DIVISION.

The division of the Association was not occasioned by any discordant principles, nor any difference of judgment with respect to church government, nor want of love; but purely for convenience. The Association had become very numerous, and the churches lay at a great distance from each other. The Association now consisted of sixty-one churches, which contained five thousand and seventeen members, and

many of the churches being at a great distance from the centre of the Association, it
was thought best to divide into two bodies.
For the convenience of the churches, 1.
There were appointed four general Conferences in different parts of the Association,
which were empowered to transact business similar to the Association, and their
proceedings transmitted to the annual Association: then it was thought best to have
only two occasional Associations, and their
minutes returned to the annual Association.
Some of the churches repeatedly requesting
a division, and as many of the churches lay
in Virginia, the Association agreed to hold
two Associations annually; one in Virginia, the other in Carolina; the Association
in Virginia in the spring, the Association
in Carolina in the fall. This continued until the Association at Davis's meeting-house,
in 1790, when, according to a resolution of
the last Association, the subject of a division was again taken up, and they agreed
to divide, and the state line between Virginia and North Carolina was to be the dividing line between the two Associations.
The Association in North Carolina then
consisted of forty-two churches, and still retained the name of the *Kehukee Association*.
The Association in Virginia first assembled
at Portsmouth, and called themselves by

the name of the *Virginia Portsmouth Association.* They consisted of nineteen churches at their first meeting.

Biographical sketches of Elders Samuel Harrell and Henry Abbot.

ELDER SAMUEL HARRELL.

ELDER SAMUEL HARRELL was born the 25th of December, 1756, in Hertford county, N. C. He embraced religion in his youth, and joined the church near Wiccacon, now under the care of Elder Hendry. He began to preach in a few years after he became a member, and was much approved of by all who heard him. He was a man of a bright genius, masculine voice, a ready mind, and a good orator. He appeared to be a man of eminent piety, and a zealous preacher of the Gospel, notwithstanding his worldly embarrassments. He was Major of the militia in Hertford county, Clerk of the court of said county, and employed in the mercantile line, in the time he exercised his public ministry; yet we never found he neglected the worship of God in his family, or omitted attending at his own church, Conferences, or public worship when convenient. He was elected a member of the Convention, in 1788, for the deliberation of the Federal Constitution. He continued

preaching a few years, but was never ordained. He departed this life in January,
1791, aged 35 years.

ELDER HENRY ABBOT.

ELDER HENRY ABBOT was the son of the
Rev. John Abbot, Canon of St. Paul's, London. He left England while young, without the consent or knowledge of his parents,
and came over to America. He had a
tolerable education, and was chiefly employed in keeping school until converted
and called to the ministry. He was baptized by a minister of the *free-will* order before he was converted, as he afterwards
acknowledged. But it pleased God to
reveal his dear Son to his soul, the hope of
glory, and also to convince him of the doctrines of free and sovereign grace, and he
joined the Regular Baptists, and became a
preacher of that society. He acted as an
itinerant preacher for a few years, and
about the year of 1764 or 1765, he took the
care of the church in Camden county, N. C.,
which was formerly under the care of Elder
John Burges, a worthy character. He continued preaching and baptizing here until
the revolution took place at the Falls of Tar
River, mentioned in page 44. After this,
being dissatisfied with his former baptism

in unbelief, he was baptized upon a confession of his faith in Christ Jesus, and still continued his pastoral functions in that church, and his labors were blest. He was a man of a strong mind, very orthodox, well acquainted with church discipline, and of a distinguished character. He was much esteemed by men of character in the county where he resided, and very useful as a statesman. He was chosen several times a member of the State Conventions. He was a member of the Provincial Congress when the State Constitution was formed and adopted; and to him we owe our thanks, in a measure, for the security of some of our *religious rights.* He was also a member of the Convention for the deliberation of the Federal Constitution, and at the time of his election had a greater number of votes than any man in the county. After he had for many years been useful, it was the will of his Lord and master to call him away to receive the crown of righteousness he had laid up for him. Towards the latter end of his life, he said he did not delight much in reading controversies, but experimental divinity met his approbation. He was frequently reading, and seemed much delighted in a book, titled " *Pious Memorials,*" which contained the life and death of many eminent saints. At last, after a violent affliction of a few days, he cheerfully resigned his immortal soul into the hands of a dear and ever blessed Saviour. He departed this life, May, 1791. He requested, a long time before he died, that if Elder Burkitt survived him, that he should preach his funeral sermon; which he did, to a crowded and much affected audience, from ii. Tim. iv. 7, 8. *I have fought a good fight, I have finished my course, I have kept the faith,* &c.

CHAPTER V.

1. Proceedings of the Association until the Division took place between the Kehukee and Neuse Associations, concluded on at the Association, holden at Skewarkey, in October, 1793.—Proceedings continued until 1796.—2. Biographical Sketches of Elder John Page, Jonathan Barnes, and Brother Joshua Freeman.—3. A few remarks on Itinerant Preaching.—4. The Association Fund.

OCTOBER, 1791, the Association convened at Flat Swamp meeting-house, in Pitt county, North Carolina. This was the first Association after the division. Delegates from thirty-seven churches were present.

8

The introductory sermon was preached
by Elder Burkitt, from Rev. xii. 3, 4.
Col. Nathan Mayo was chosen Moderator,
and Elder Burkitt, Clerk.   Elders Barrow
and Browne were messengers from the Virginia Portsmouth Association.

A church on Morattuck Creek, in Tyrrel county, a church at Mattamuskeet, a
church on Little Contentney, and a church
on Bear March, in Duplin county, North
Carolina, on petition, were received into
the Association.

As there was a plan proposed by the last
Association for the encouragement of *itinerant preaching*, and recommended to the
churches for their approbation or disapprobation; it appeared by the letters to this Association that there are a great majority of
churches against the adoption of the proposed plan.   This Association thought proper to certify to the churches that they still
thought itinerant preaching useful, therefore advised the churches to fall on some
measures to encourage it.

It was also, at this time, resolved to recommend it to the churches, to signify in
their letters to the next Association whether they would approve of an alteration of
the last section of the last article of the
Constitution, or not.: the words are, " The
" Association shall have power to adjourn

" themselves to any time or place they may
" think most convenient to the churches,
" provided it be interchangeably holden
" one year on the *north* side of Tar River,
" and the next year on the *south* side of
" Tar River."

Elder Ross and Elder Baker were appointed our delegates to the next *Virginia Portsmouth Association*. Elder Read was appointed to write a circular letter for our next, on the doctrine of *original sin*.

The next Association was appointed at Elder Baker's meeting-house, on Bear Creek, then Dobbs, but now Lenoir county, the Saturday before the second Sunday in October, 1792.

October, 1792, the Association convened at Bear Creek. The introductory sermon was preached by Elder Ross. The circular letter prepared by Elder Read was received, and ordered to be printed. The Association, after some time sitting, adjourned to their next annual appointment; which was appointed at Skewarkey meeting-house, in Martin county, the Saturday before the second Sunday in October, 1793.

At which time and place the Association met, and an introductory sermon was delivered by Elder Thomas Etheridge, from John iii. 16. Col. Nathan Bryan was

chosen Moderator, and Elder Burkitt,
Clerk. Letters from forty-three churches
were read in this Association. Elder Murrell was a delegate from the Portsmouth
Association. A letter from Georgia Association was received and read. A church
in Franklin county, at the Poplar Spring;
a church at the Maple Spring, in said
county; and a church on Durham's Creek,
in Beaufort county, on petition, were received into this Association.

The Association had now increased, and
some of the churches were very desirous
for another division to take place. The
Kehukee Association now consisted of forty-
nine churches, which contained three thousand four hundred and forty members,
according to the returns made to this Association. It was therefore thought necessary to divide a second time; accordingly
it was resolved, that Tar River be the dividing line between the Associations; and
the Association between Tar River and
Virginia line still retained the name of the
Kehukee Association; and the other, south
of Tar River, was called the *Neuse Association*.

It was also agreed that each Association should annually visit the other with
two delegates, and a letter of correspondence.

Our delegates to the Association south of Tar River, were Elders Jesse Read and Lewis Moore.

Our next Association was appointed at Sandy Run, in Bertie, North Carolina— Elder M'Cabe to preach the introductory sermon, Elder Lancaster to write the circular letter, *On the saints' final perseverance in grace.*

On the 27th of September, 1794, the Association, according to her respective appointment, met at Sandy Run. The introductory sermon was delivered by Elder M'Cabe, according to appointment, from John xv. 14. *Ye are my friends, if ye do whatsoever I command you.* After prayer by Elder Burkitt, Colonel Mayo was chosen Moderator, and Elder Burkitt, Clerk.

This was the first meeting after the second division took place, and we were reduced to only twenty-six churches. Letters from only twenty-two were received and read in this Association. Brethren Wall, Murrell, and Barnes, ministers from our sister Associations, being present, were invited to seats with us. Elders Lancaster, Ross, and Murrell were appointed to preach on Sunday. A church on Meherrin, formerly under the care of Elder William Parker (a General Baptist) petitioned by letter and delegate for admission into this

Association. On examination, it appears
there has been a revolution in this church,
and believing them now to be of our *faith*
and *order*, they were received.

Our next Association is appointed at
Yoppim meeting-house, in Chowan county,
the Saturday before the fourth Sunday in
September, 1795. Elder Read was appointed to preach the introductory sermon,
and Elder Burkitt was appointed to write
the circular letter, *On effectual calling.*

At this Association, it was resolved that
the Saturday before the fourth Sunday in
every month should be appointed a day for
prayer meetings throughout the churches;
whereon all the members of the respective
churches are requested to meet at their
meeting-houses, or places of worship, and
there, for *each of them,* as far as time will
admit, to make earnest prayer to God for a
revival of religion amongst us.

September, 1795, the Association met
at Yoppim. The introductory sermon was
preached by Elder Read, from 1 Pet. v. 2,
3. *Feed the flock of God, which is among
you, taking the oversight thereof, not by
constraint, but willingly; not for filthy lucre,
but of a ready mind: Neither as being lords
over God's heritage, but being ensamples to
the flock.*

Col. Nathan Mayo, Moderator; Elder

Burkitt, Clerk.   Elder Barrow was messenger from the Virginia Portsmouth Association.   A letter of correspondence from
the Neuse Association was received, but
the delegates failed attending.   A letter of
correspondence from the Georgia Association was received and read.

Elders Barrow, Burkitt, and Spivy were
appointed a committee to devise ways and
means to encourage the brethren in the
ministry to visit the churches.   Who, after
mature deliberation on the subject, reported, that it was their opinion that this Association should appoint four ministers who
are ordained, to travel and preach at every
meeting-house or meeting place in this
whole connection, that can be made convenient this year, viz: The first in the nomination (if to him convenient, if not, to sub-
stitute one of the other three in his stead),
to begin at Kehukee, on Sunday, the 15th
of November, and to continue till he has
gone through all the churches ; and that
the appointments be sent forward from this
place.   And that day three months, the
second in nomination to follow him, beginning at the same place ; the first notifying
the people of the second coming on, the
second the third, &c.

The committee also added, that they did
not intend by the plan they proposed to

discourage any other brethren in the ministry who are not in the nomination, from traveling and preaching to the churches as much as they think the Lord calls them to.

The Association concurred with the report; and by ballot of the Association, Elders Burkitt, Etheridge, John M'Cabe, and Spivy were chosen.

The next Association to be holden at Parker's meeting-house, in Hertford county, September, the fourth Sunday, 1796. Elder Lancaster appointed to preach the introductory sermon, Elder M'Cabe to write the circular letter.

Saturday, 24th September, 1796, the Association met pursuant to the appointment, at Parker's meeting-house, on Meherrin. Elder Lancaster preached the introductory sermon from Songs iv. 12. *A garden inclosed, is my sister, my spouse; a spring shut up, a fountain sealed.*

Elder M'Cabe chosen Moderator, Elder Burkitt, Clerk. Letters from twenty-two churches were received and read. Elders Browne and Morris were Corresponding Delegates from the Virginia Portsmouth Association. Elders Totewine and Tison were Delegates from the Neuse Association. Elders Murrell, Barnes, Wall and M'Clenny, from our sister Associations, being present, were invited to seats with us.

A church on Great Swamp, in Pitt county, under the pastoral care of Elder Noah Tison, was received into membership with this Association.

This Association did not think proper to continue the mode adopted by the last for the encouragement of itinerant preaching.

Query. *Is it agreeable to the word of God to hold a man in fellowship that has married a woman who has another husband living in the same county, or hold her in communion?*

We humbly conceive that such a practice is diametrically opposite to the word of God, and therefore give it as our opinion that such members ought not to be held in communion.

The next Association appointed at Flatty Creek, in Pasquotank county, N. C., on the Thursday before the fourth Sunday in September, 1797. Elder Spivey to preach the introductory sermon, and Elder Gilbert to write the circular letter, *on regeneration.*

BIOGRAPHICAL SKETCHES.

BROTHER JOSHUA FREEMAN was the son of William Freeman, of Chowan county, N. C. His parents were both strict Episcopalians. He was converted under the ministry of Elder Dargan, about the year of 1777, and was received and baptized a

member of his church near Wiccacon, now
under the care of Elder Hendry. He was
one of the Deacons of that church. He was
so remarkably zealous and tender under
preaching, that he hardly ever heard a sermon zealously delivered but what he would
break out in raptures, praising and glorifying God. He very frequently attended our
Associations, and he was so loving that he
gained the general esteem of all the brethren
with whom he was acquainted; and we felt
happy when he was present, and when he
was absent something seemed wanting.
He was a man of considerable fortune, and
some years past was captain of a company
of militia in Bertie; but had long since resigned that office, for it was evident that he
sought not the honor that comes from man,
but that which comes from God only.
Although he had many slaves, his lenity
towards them was very remarkable. If any
of them transgressed, his general method to
chastise them was to expose their faults before the rest of his servants and the whole
family, when they came in to family worship in the morning; who, when assembled
at morning prayer, would talk to them, exhort and rebuke them so sharply for their
faults, that made others fear. Elder Burkitt
had often been at his house the time of
public prayer, and he was so very much

affected for the spiritual welfare of his family
that often he seemed almost convulsed.
And this extraordinary zeal was not the
impulse of a moment, but his constant practice for seventeen years, and continued to
his dying moment, and instead of declining
rather increased. On Saturday night before he died he went to prayer with his
family, and was immediately afterwards
seized with a paralytic fit (for he had been
under that complaint for about twelve
months), the operation of which continued
till Monday evening, the 10th of November,
1794, when he died. And we hope he is
now where his longing soul is satisfied with
beholding his Saviour's face without a glass
between. His death was sincerely lamented
by all his friends and acquaintance; and
every person who was acquainted with his
merit, on hearing the melancholy news of
his death, can but drop a tear. His funeral
sermon was preached by Elder Burkitt,
from Phil. i. 21. *For to me to live is Christ,
and to die is gain.*

ELDER JOHN PAGE.

Elder John Page embraced religion
under the preaching of Elder Jonathan
Thomas, and became a member of a branch
of his church at Connetoe. At what time

he was called to the ministry we are not
able to say; but exercising his gift for a
while, he was at length ordained Pastor of
the church at Flat Swamp, which was dismissed from Tosniot, and became a constituted body. He continued preaching for
several years, and his labors were blessed.
And although his church at times was
greatly distressed on account of a division
amongst them, by reason of *Armenianism*
and *Universalism*, yet Elder Page appeared
always steadfast in the Calvinistic doctrines.
After finishing the work which his Heavenly Father designed for him to do, he
departed this life October, 1796.

ELDER JONATHAN BARNES.

ELDER JONATHAN BARNES was a resident
of Currituck county, North Carolina; and
was a member of the church at Cowenjock,
in said county. *He was born blind;* and
it is very certain that he never saw anything with his natural eyes. He was converted in his youth, and was baptized; and
began to preach while young. His mother
and others were frequently reading to him,
and he was remarkable for a retentive
memory. There were not many passages
of scripture, but what he would tell the
book, chapter, and verse where they were, if

applied to. And in preaching he would prove his doctrine by citing texts of scripture, and telling the place where they were, far exceeding any other minister we ever heard. It was said he could repeat about two hundred of Watts' hymns, and there were none in the book but he knew some verses of them. He had such a faculty in knowing the voices of people, that if he heard a person of his acquaintance talk in conversation with him half an hour, and was not to hear him speak again in five years, he would know him again on hearing him talk. He married a wife in Currituck, but we do not know whether he had any children. He traveled considerably, but always had a guide when he did so. He was much approved by the people, and many were amazed at his gifts and memory. He moved out to Whitfield's meeting-house, on Little Contentney, where he lived awhile, then removed back to Currituck, where he died; which was in the year 1796.

ITINERANT PREACHING.

For a great many years, it was thought that itinerant preaching was calculated to prove a blessing to the churches; therefore sundry attempts were made by the Association to bring about the desirable effect. A plan was first laid in the church at South

Quay, in 1786. A committee was appointed
to investigate it, but did not agree on it.
The next Association another plan was
adopted, but did not prove successful.
Some of the churches and ministers still
kept soliciting for ways and means to be
devised for its encouragement, until the
Association at Davis's meeting-house, where
a certain plan was devised by three laymen
and two preachers, in committee, and appro-
bated by that Association, was sent to the
churches, to know whether they would
approve or disapprove of said plan. Accordingly, a majority of the churches in
their letters to the next Association dis-
approved of it, and all the attempts for the
encouragement of *itinerant preaching* proved
ineffectual, until the Association at Yoppim,
in 1796. Then a new plan was laid and
put into execution at the time appointed.
But we believe only two of the four ministers who were appointed, traveled through
all the churches, viz. Elder Burkitt and
Elder M'Cabe. We still believe, that if
ministers were to travel and preach more,
that it would prove a blessing to the
churches.

ASSOCIATION FUND.

It became necessary that there should be
an Association fund, to defray the expenses

thereof; but no regular plan was laid to bring it to pass, until the Association at Whitfield's meeting-house, in 1789. When the minutes were first printed, and the Constitution formed, it was an article in the Constitution, and Elder Burkitt appointed Treasurer. The fund was chiefly intended to defray the expenses of printing the minutes, and other charges arising therefrom, and may lawfully be applied to any other use the Association may deem necessary. The mode of contributing is for every church to send what they please, and the sum by them contributed to be inserted in the minutes; and a regular statement of the money contributed from *all* the churches, and the expenses of the Association, to be printed yearly, so that all may know the state of the fund.

CHAPTER VI.

1. Proceedings of the Association until 1802.—2. Biographical Sketches of Elder John Meglamre and Brother Elisha Battle, who departed this life in 1799.

THE Association met at Flatty Creek, Pasquotank county, N. C., on Thursday,

21st September, 1797.   Elder Spivey preached the introductory sermon, from Psal. cxxxiii. 1.   *Behold, how good and how pleasant it is for brethren to dwell together in unity.*   Elder M'Cabe, Moderator, Elder Spivey, Clerk.   Letters from nineteen churches were read   Elder Morris, Corresponding Delegate from the Virginia Portsmouth Association, took his seat, and presented to the Association a letter of correspondence and twenty-seven copies of their minutes.   Elders William Soary and James M'Clenny, ministering brethren from our sister Portsmouth Association, being present, were invited to seats in this Association.   Elder M'Cabe was appointed a Delegate to next Neuse Association : Elder Ross to the Virginia Portsmouth.   The next Association to be at Cashie, in Bertie county, N. C., September, 1798.

September 20th, 1798, the Association convened according to appointment at Cashie, in Bertie county.   The introductory sermon by Elder Davis Biggs, from 1 Pet. iii. 12.   *For the eyes of the Lord are over the righteous, and his ears are open to their prayers : But the face of the Lord is against them that do evil.*   Prayer by Elder Ross.   Col. Mayo was chosen Moderator; Elder Burkitt, Clerk.   Letters from twenty-three churches were read.   Received letters from the following corresponding Associations, viz: Virginia Portsmouth, with her minutes; Elder Brown and Jacob Gregg, Messengers. Neuse, with their minutes; Joshua Barnes, Messenger: and Georgia, with minutes. We also received minutes from Philadelphia, New York, Charleston, Danbury, Middle District, Stonington, Delaware, Woodstock, Ketockton, Warren, Roanoke, Goshen, Dover, Shaftsbury, and Hepzibah Associations.

A church· in Franklin county (Haywood's meeting-house) was received into this Association

Query. *What shall a church do, when one member brings an accusation against another member, and he denies the charge—shall the testimony of the accuser, unsupported by any other evidence, be received by the church or not?* Ans. No.

At this Association it was resolved to have as many copies of the minutes printed as would amount to £18, and to sell the minutes to defray the expenses. But, on experience, it was found ineffectual. It was the first time that an attempt of this kind was made, and it has been the last. This Association also thought proper to discontinue the practice of paying the cor-

9

responding delegates from us to our sister Associations.

The next Association appointed at the new meeting-house on Fishing Creek. Elder Amariah Biggs to preach the introductory sermon, and Elder Spivey to write the circular letter.

Saturday, the 5th of October, 1799, the Association met at Fishing Creek. Brother Amariah Biggs preached the introductory sermon, from Heb. xiii. 1. *Let brotherly love continue.* Prayer by Brother Davis Biggs. Col. Mayo, Moderator; Elder Burkitt, Clerk. Letters from twenty-two churches were read. Elders Jesse Mercer, from Georgia, Elder Barnes, from the Neuse Association, and Elder Brame, from Virginia, were invited to sit with us. A newly constituted church at Quankey, in Halifax county, was received into this Association. Letters of correspondence from Virginia Portsmouth, Georgia, and Hepzibah Associations were received and read.

As several of the churches in their letters to this Association, complain of their destitute state with respect to ministerial helps, and some others have earnestly requested the ministers to visit them, on motion by Elder Burkitt, it was resolved that Elders Mercer, Lancaster, Read, Gilbert, and

Burkitt be a committee to devise ways and means for the encouragement of itinerant preaching. The committee sitting, and taking the matter into consideration, reported that—Whereas sundry of the churches in our Association are deprived of ministerial helps to administer the ordinances to them, and several others have requested the brethren in the ministry to visit them, we, your committee, do advise this Association to make out their appointments, and grant supplies to those destitute churches, and visit them, at least at each of their quarterly meetings; and to visit as often as convenience will admit, all other churches who have so particularly in their letters requested the ministers to visit them. The Association concurred with the report. The church who convene at Parker's meeting house, representing their destitute case with respect to ministerial helps to administer the ordinances to them, the following brethren in the ministry did agree to attend them at their quarterly meetings the ensuing year, viz: Elder Harrell, the Saturday before the first Sunday in November; Elder Burkitt, on the Saturday before the first Sunday in February; Elder Lancaster, on the Saturday before the first Sunday in May; and Elder Read, the Saturday before the first Sunday in August next.

Query. *Should a minister who has been regularly ordained as an itinerant preacher be called upon to take the pastoral care of a particular church; is there anything necessary to be done, more than the consent of each party?*

Ans. Nothing more is necessary.

Minutes from the following Associations were received, viz: Shaftsbury, New Hampshire, Leyden, Woodstock, Danbury, Warren, Delaware, Culpepper, Ketockton, Philadelphia, and New York Associations.

The next Association was appointed at the Falls of Tar River, the Saturday before the first Sunday in October, 1800. Elder Gilbert appointed to write the circular letter; Elder Hendry appointed to preach the introductory sermon, and, in case of failure, Elder Joseph Biggs.

Thursday, 21st of November, was appointed a day of general thanksgiving to Almighty God, throughout the churches, for His temporal blessings on our fields and farms, and that our country seems happily delivered from the fearful apprehensions of want and scarcity.

The Association next convened at the Falls of Tar River, Nash county, pursuant to appointment, on the Saturday before the first Sunday in October, 1800.

Sermon by Elder Joseph Biggs, from 1

Kings, vi. 8. *The door for the middle chamber was in the right side of the house: and they went up with winding stairs into the middle chamber, and out of the middle into the third.* Col. Mayo, Moderator; Elder Burkitt, Clerk. Letters from twenty-one churches were read. Elder Lewis Moore from Tennessee being present, was invited to a seat. Letters of correspondence from Virginia Portsmouth and Neuse Associations were read; and their Messengers, Elders Murrell, Barnes, and Oliver took their seats. Elders James M'Cabe and Gilbert were appointed Messengers to the Neuse Association; Elders Lancaster and Read to the Virginia Portsmouth. Elders Murrell, Moore, and Burkitt were appointed to preach on Sunday.

Query. *Is it not wrong for a man who is a member of a church, and the head of a family, wholly to neglect family worship on account of the smallness of his gifts in prayer?* Ans. It is wrong.

Received seven copies of the minutes of the Charleston Association, as a token of their respect. One was read in the Association.

Query 2. *Ought not deacons to be regularly ordained before they use the office of a deacon in any respect?*

Ans. Yes.

The next Association was appointed atthe Great Swamp meeting-house, in Pitt county, October, 1801. Elder Martin Ross to preach the introductory sermon, Elder Etheridge to write the circular letter.

October the 3d, 1801, the Association met according to appointment, at Great Swamp, Pitt county, North Carolina. Introductory sermon by Elder Ross, from Rev. xvi. 15. *Behold, I come as a thief. Blessed is he that watcheth and keepeth his garments, lest he walk naked, and they see his shame.* Col. Mayo, Moderator ; Elder Burkitt, Clerk. Letters from twenty churches were read. Elder Brame being present, was invited to a seat. A letter from the Virginia Portsmouth Association was received from their messengers, Elders Browne and Grigg. A letter of correspondence from the Neuse Association was received. Elder Barnes was their delegate. Elder Burkitt appointed to write to the Portsmouth, Elder M'Cabe to the Neuse, and Elder Ross to the Georgia Association. The circular letter which Elder Etheridge was appointed to write for this year, was presented to the Association in an unfinished, imperfect state ; it was therefore resolved that Elder Burkitt write such an one as he may think proper, which shall contain as accurate an account of the revivals of religion in the different States, as have come within his knowledge, and insert it in these minutes; which said letter shall be deemed the circular letter from this Association to the respective churches. Elders Brown, Burkitt, and Grigg were appointed to preach on Sunday. The circular letter in the minutes of the Dover Association was read, which informed us of a happy revival among them. Elders James M'Cabe and Tison were appointed delegates to the Neuse Association. Elders Burkitt and Ross to the Portsmouth Association.

Minutes from Flat River, Dover, Ketockton, Roanoke, Middle District, and Goshen Associations were received. The next Association appointed at Elder Hendry's church near Wiccacon, October, 1802. Elder Moses Bennett appointed to preach the introductory sermon, and, in case of failure, Elder Lancaster. Elder Read appointed to write the circular letter.

By the letters to this Association there were one hundred and thirty-eight baptized last year; and it appeared by the success of the word preached at this time, and the general engagement of the ministers, and the great desire of the brethren, that a glorious revival was not far distant; which shortly appeared, and the particulars of which our readers will be furnished with in the subsequent chapters.

October 2, 1802, the Association met at Elder Hendry's meeting-house, in Bertie, North Carolina. The ministers appointed by the last Association to deliver an introductory sermon to this, not being present, a sermon was preached by Elder Davis Biggs, from 2 Cor. v. 10. *For we must all appear before the judgment seat of Christ, that every one may receive the things done in his body, according to what he hath done, whether it be good or bad.* Col. Mayo, Moderator; Elder Spivey, Clerk. Elder Jeremiah Ritter, from Virginia, being present, was invited to a seat. Letters from twenty churches were read.

Letters from Portsmouth and Neuse Associations were received and read; and their messengers, Elders Browne, Biggs, Whitfield, and Cooper took their seats. Elder Gilbert appointed to write to the Portsmouth, Elder Spivey to the Neuse Association. It was agreed at this Association to reprint a sermon published by Elder Leland, of Massachusetts, titled, a " Blow at the Root." Elders Browne, Whitfield, and Ross were appointed to preach on Sunday. Elders James Ross and Holloway Morris Messengers to the

Neuse, Elders Read and Martin Ross
Messengers to the Portsmouth Association.
The next Association to be held at the
Log Chapel, in Martin county, on Connoho Creek, on the Friday before the first
Sunday in October, 1803, and continue
four days. Elder Wall to preach the introductory sermon, Elder Ross to write the
circular letter. As Elder Burkitt was absent from this Association by reason of
sickness, it was resolved by the Association
that the following minute should be made
in the proceedings of the Association, viz :
" Our very respectable and highly esteem-
" ed Brother Lemuel Burkitt, whose labors
" in the Gospel have been much blessed in
" the churches belonging to this Associa-
" tion, especially in the late revival of reli-
" gion, has manifested his sincere desire to
" be with us at this Association by coming
" to this place through many difficulties ;
" but sickness soon obliged him to leave
" us, which has grieved our hearts, and he
" has been greatly missed. But we must
" submit to the hand of the Lord." A glorious revival took place the past year according to expectation : and the letters
from the churches say that eight hundred
and seventy-two were added to the churches by baptism since the last ; and blessed
be God the work was going on. The par-

ticulars of the revival we mean to speak of in time and place.

BIOGRAPHICAL SKETCHES.

ELDER JOHN MEGLAMRE was born and raised in one of the northern states, and being somewhat religiously inclined in his youth, at length moved into North Carolina. He joined the Baptist Society about the year 1764 or 1765. After preaching some time, he was ordained and took the pastoral care of the church at Kehukee. But having some invitations, he traveled into Sussex county, Virginia, where he preached, and his labors were attended with a blessing. And, through his instrumentality, and Elder John Rivers, and some others, a church was gathered in that county, and through their solicitations he removed to that place, and gave up his pastoral charge at Kehukee to Elder William Burges. After continuing in Sussex for a few years, a large and very respectable church was gathered, and Elder Meglamre continued to be their pastor as long as he was capable of preaching. He very frequently attended the Association, and almost every Association acted as Moderator for upwards of twenty years, until the division took place at Davis's meeting house, and then he became a member of the Portsmouth Association, and generally served that Association in the same capacity until his death. He was a very useful member, seemed well acquainted with church discipline; but by reason of the asthmatic complaint, he was prevented from preaching some time before he died. He departed this life December 13th, 1799, about three o'clock in the afternoon, aged sixty-nine years, six months, six days.

BROTHER ELISHA BATTLE.

BROTHER ELISHA BATTLE was born in Nansemond county, Virginia, on the 9th day of January, 1723-4. In the year of 1748 he moved to Tar River, Edgecomb county, North Carolina. About the year 1764, he joined the Baptist church at the Falls of Tar River, and continued in full fellowship until his death. He was chosen a deacon of the church, and served the church in that office about twenty-eight years, until he resigned by reason of old age. He usually attended Associations, at which he sometimes acted as Moderator; and was very suitable for that office. It is well known he was a remarkable pious, zealous member of society. He also was very useful as a statesman. About the

year 1756 he was appointed a justice of the
peace, and continued in that office until the
year 1795, when he resigned on account of
his infirmities. He was chosen a member
of the General Assembly in the year 1771,
and continued to represent the county, and
was never left out for about twenty years,
until he declined offering himself a candidate by reason of his advanced state in life.
He served in that capacity throughout the
war, and was in almost all the State Conventions. He was a member of the State
Convention at the formation of the State
Constitution ; and was also a member of
the Convention for the deliberation of the
Federal Constitution, and when the Convention formed itself into a Committee of
the whole House, Brother Battle was appointed *Chairman.* In 1799, he requested
his youngest son to come and take posses-
sion of the land and plantation whereon he
lived (which he had before made him a
deed for), that he might give up the care of
a family and live with him. About this
time he desired his children to meet him,
that he might have some private discourse
with them, and concluded to have his will
written and execute it, although he had for
many years kept a written one by him, al-
tering it when he found it necessary. He
divided his property amongst his children,

only reserving a sum of money and notes, as security for himself in his decent maintenance. Soon after he was taken more unwell than usual, and weakened till he became so helpless that he could not turn in his bed. In his sickness he seemed to have no desire to recover; he said he was willing to go, but must wait the Lord's time. After being about eight weeks in this helpless condition, without the least apparent doubt of future felicity, he departed this life the 6th of March, 1799, being the 76th year of his age. His funeral sermon was preached by Elders Gilbert and Burkitt, from Psal. xxxvii. 37. Elder Gilbert preached from the former part of the text, viz: *Mark the perfect man, and behold the upright.* And Elder Burkitt preached from the latter part of the same text, viz: *For the end of that man is peace.*

CHAPTER VII.

1. The happy Revival which took place in the Churches belonging to the Kehukee Association in 1802 and 1803.—2. Means which the Lord blessed in the Revival.—3. Constitution of an Union Meeting.

AFTER a long and tedious night of spirit-

ual darkness and coldness in religion, blessed be God, the sable curtains are withdrawn, the day has dawned, and the Sun
of righteousness has risen with healing on
his wings. The churches appeared to be
on a general decline. Many of the old
members were removed from the church
militant to the church triumphant. Some
had moved to the western countries, and
some had gone out from us, "that it might
be made manifest that they were not all of
us." These things reduced the number of
members in the churches greatly. So that
in some churches there were hardly members enough to hold conference, and in
some other churches the Lord's Supper
was seldom administered. *Iniquity abounded, and the love of many waxed cold.* The
Association, nevertheless, met annually,
and in every church there were a *few*
names still left, who seemed anxiously con-
cerned for a revival. There were but few
added by baptism for several years. In
1789, only fifteen members were added in
all the churches. In 1790, there were four
hundred and forty-six baptized. In 1791,
ninety-nine. In 1792, one hundred and
ninety-two. In 1794, fifty-seven. In 1795,
only nineteen. In 1796, only thirty-three.
In 1797, thirteen. In 1798, forty-three.
In 1799, seventy-two. In 1800, one hun-

dred and twenty-nine.   At the Association
in 1801, one hundred and thirty-eight were
returned in the letters from the churches to
the Association. Thus the work progressed
but slowly, but there always appeared some
worthy characters in every church sensible
of the coldness of religion, and at almost
every Association would be devising some
ways and means to bring on a revival.   As
early as the year 1778, a revival was greatly desired, and a fast was proclaimed, to
humble ourselves before the Lord, and to
solicit the throne of grace for a revival.   In
1785, at Shoulder's Hill, another fast was
proclaimed.   The same year, at an Association at Kehukee, it was agreed to set apart
some time between sun-set and dark every
day, for all the churches to unite together
in prayer, and earnestly pray for a revival.
And in 1794, the Association agreed to appoint the Saturday before the fourth Sunday in every month, a day for *prayer meetings* throughout the churches; whereon all
the members of the respective churches
were requested to meet at their meeting-
houses, or places of worship, and there for
each of them, as far as time would admit,
to make earnest prayer and supplication to
Almighty God for a revival of religion.
Thus the means were used, and the request
was so laudable that there was no doubt

but the Lord would grant the *desires* of the righteous. For the Lord has promised, *Ask and ye shall receive, seek and ye shall find, knock and it shall be opened to you. The eyes of the Lord are over the righteous, and his ears are open to their prayers.* And where the Lord puts it into the hearts of his people so earnestly to desire the increase of Christ's kingdom, and the revival of his work amongst his churches, the request is so laudable, that Christians need not doubt but the Lord will hear them in his own time and way. So when the set time to favor Zion was come, he heard the prayers of the Kehukee Association. There was a small appearance of the beginning of the work in Camden, and the Flat Swamp, and Connoho church, in 1800—thirty-two this year were baptized in Camden, twenty-two in the Flat Swamp church, and twenty-four at Connoho. But at the Association at Great Swamp, in 1801, Elder Burkitt just returning from Tennessee and Kentucky, brought the news to this Association, and proclaimed it from the stage, that in about eight months six thousand had given a rational account of a work of grace on their souls, and had been baptized in the State of Kentucky, and that a general stir had taken place amongst all ranks and societies of people, and that the work was

still going on. The desirable news seemed
to take such an uncommon effect on the
people, that numbers were crying out for
mercy, and many praising and glorifying
God. Such a Kehukee Association we
had never before seen. The ministers all
seemed alive in the work of the Lord, and
every Christian present in rapturous desire,
was ready to cry, *Thy kingdom come.* The
ministers and delegates carried the sacred
flame home to their churches, and the fire
began to kindle in the greatest part of the
churches, and the work increased. The
first appearance that was discovered was,
great numbers of people attended the ministry of the word, and the congregations
kept increasing. It was observed in some
places, that as many people would now
meet at a meeting on a common day, as
used to meet on a Sunday, and as many
would come on Sundays as used to attend
at great meetings. And it was also observed that the audience was more *solemn*
and *serious* than usual. This was the first
beginning. Thus the work began to revive in many places within the bounds of
the Association. The word preached was
attended with such a divine power, that at
some meetings two or three hundred would
be in floods of tears, and many crying out
loudly, *What shall we do to be saved?* An-
10

other thing was observed, *old Christians*
were so revived they were all on fire to see
their neighbors, their neighbors' children
and their own families so much engaged.
Their souls seemed melted down in love,
and their *strength renewed like the eagle's.*
Many *backsliders* who had been runaway
for many years, returned weeping home.
The ministers seemed all united in love,
and no strife nor contention amongst them,
and all appeared to be engaged to carry on
the work, and did not seem to care whose
labors were most blessed so the work went
on ; and none of them seemed desirous to
take the glory of it to themselves, which
ought carefully to be observed. God is a
jealous God, and will not suffer any of his
creatures to take the glory of *his* work to
themselves. We hope that no person will
ascribe the glory of the work to any person
or persons whatever, but to the Lord alone ;
for true religion is a *work of God.* The
work increasing, many were converted,
and they began to join the churches. In
some churches where they had not received
a member by baptism for a year or two,
would now frequently receive, at almost
every conference meeting, several members. Sometimes twelve, fourteen, eighteen, twenty, and twenty-four at several
times in one day. Twenty-two and twenty-

four were baptized several times at Flat
Swamp, Cashie, Parker's meeting-house,
Fishing Creek, Falls of Tar River, &c.
Some of the churches in the revival received nearly two hundred members each.
In four churches lying between Roanoke
and Meherrin Rivers, in Bertie, Northampton, and Hertford counties, were baptized
in two years about six hundred members:
and blessed be God the work seems yet progressing. The work has engaged the attention of all sorts of people—rich and poor, and
all ranks. Many very respectable persons in
character and office have been called in in
this revival. There are a few churches
within the bounds of the Association that
have not as yet experienced a revival, but
we hope for them. According to the accounts returned to the two last Associations
fifteen hundred have been added to the
churches by baptism in the Kehukee Association.

It has been objected by some that we
ought not to number the Lord's people,
and bring, for example, the bad consequences which attended David's number-
ing the people of Israel. But we think
ourselves justifiable in mentioning our
numbers, when we are actuated by good
principles. David might number them to
boast of the number, and to put *confidence*

in a *multitude*, not considering *the race was
not to the swift, nor the battle to the strong*.
But we number them to exult in the riches
of God's free grace, in magnifying his
mercy in the conversion of thousands. We
find that the Scripture makes mention of
the great addition at the day of Pentecost
—*The same day were added about three
thousand souls.* Acts ii. 41.

The Lord was pleased to make use of
weak and simple means to effect great purposes, that it might be manifest that the
work was *his* and not *man's*. *Singing* was
attended with a great blessing : Elder Burkitt published two or three different pam-
phlets, which contained a small collection
of spiritual songs, some of which he had
brought from the western countries. They
were in very great demand. As many as
about six thousand books were disposed of
in two years. We might truly say, *the
time of singing of birds had come, and the
voice of the turtle was heard in the land.*
At every meeting, before the minister began to preach, the congregation was me-
lodiously entertained with numbers singing delightfully, while all the congregation seemed in lively exercises. Nothing
seemed to engage the attention of the people more ; and the children and servants at
every house were singing these melodious

songs.   From experience, we think, we can assure our readers, that we have reason to hope that this, with other means, proved a blessing in this revival. *Shaking hands* while singing, was a means (though simple in itself) to further the work. The ministers used frequently, at the close of worship, to sing a spiritual song suited to the occasion, and go through the congregation, and shake hands with the people while singing ; and several, when relating their experience, at the time of their admission into church fellowship, declared that this was the first means of their conviction. The act seemed so friendly, the ministers appeared so loving, that the party with whom the minister shook hands, would often be melted in tears.   The hymn

> " I long to see the happy time,
>   When sinners all come flocking home,
>   To taste the riches of his love,
>   And to enjoy the realms above :"

And especially that part of it,

> " Take your companion by the hand ;
>   And all your children in the band,"

—many times had a powerful effect. *Giving the people an invitation to come up to be prayed for*, was also blessed.

The ministers usually, at the close of preaching, would tell the congregation, that if there were any persons who felt

themselves lost and condemned, under the
guilt and burden of their sins, that if they
would come near the stage, and kneel
down, they would pray for them. Shame
at first kept many back, but as the work
increased, numbers, apparently under strong
conviction, would come and fall down before the Lord at the feet of the ministers,
and crave an interest in their prayers.
Sometimes twenty or thirty at a time.
And at some Union Meetings, two or three
hundred would come, and try to come as
near as they could. This very much engaged the ministers; and many confessed
that the Lord heard the prayers of his ministers, and they had reason to hope their
souls were relieved from the burden of their
sins, through the blood of Christ. It had a
powerful effect on the spectators to see
their wives, their husbands, children,
neighbors, &c., so solicitous for the salvation of their souls; and was sometimes a
means of their conviction. Many ladies
of quality, at times were so powerfully
wrought on, as to come and kneel down
in the dust in their silks to be prayed for.
The act of *coming to be prayed for* in this
manner had a good effect on the persons
who came, in that they knew the eyes of
the congregation were on them, and if they
did fall off afterwards it would be a dis-

grace to them, and cause others to deride them ; this, therefore, was a spur to push them forward.

Relating experiences, and the administration of the ordinance of baptism were greatly blessed in this revival. When the churches held conference to receive members (which they always did in a public assembly) the congregation would draw up in such crowds, as they would tread one on another, anxious to hear the experiences of their neighbors and families. And while the candidates were relating their experience, the audience would be in floods of tears, and some almost convulsed, while their children, companions, and friends were relating their conversion. And several declared this was the means of their conviction.

And when the ordinance of baptism was administered, nothing had a more solemn effect. Sometimes *fifteen* or *twenty* would be received at one time ; and at the time appointed for baptism, great numbers would attend; from two hundred to one thousand and more would assemble at such times. And then to see fifteen or twenty persons suitably attired to go into the water, who usually stood in a row, a small distance from the water, hand in hand, and the minister joining the rank at the head, would march down into the water regularly, like *soldiers of Jesus*, singing as they went,

"Come, all ye mourning souls, who seek rest in Jesus'
　　love,
Who set your whole affections on things that are above;
Come, let us join together, and hand in hand go on,
Until we come to Canaan, where we no more shall
　　mourn,"

—would take a solemn effect on the numerous assembly. Numbers would be in floods of tears, and so greatly affected could scarcely stand, while they would express their sincere wishes that they were prepared to go in with their children and companions.

Sometimes they had the pleasure to see the father and the son, the mother and her daughter, the wife and the husband, go into the water together hand in hand. This proved conviction to many. Thus the Lord carried on his work.

Evening meetings were greatly blessed. Some years past it was customary to hold night meetings; but for some time they were disused When the revival commenced they began to revive. In some neighborhoods they met once a week on an evening; and numbers would attend. At some times, and in some places, nearly two hundred people would meet, and some would come ten miles to a night meeting. And when they had the opportunity for a

minister to attend them, they usually had
a sermon preached, and the rest of the time
they were together, would be spent in exhortation, singing and prayer.   And we
are fully satisfied the Lord blessed these
meetings.

Where they had not the privilege of a
minister to attend and preach, the time
would be spent in singing, exhortation,
prayer, religious conversation, &c.   Sometimes they would tell each other their experiences, and examine others whether
they had any experience to relate.   Thus
the work went on.

Union meetings have also been attended
with a blessing.   An union meeting consists of several churches, being convenient
to one another, of the same faith and order,
who meet at stated times to confer in love,
about matters relating to peace, brotherly
union, and general fellowship.   The time
the meeting holds is generally three days.
On the first day when they meet, one of
the ministers delivers a suitable sermon introductory to business; then all the brethren present from every church, who are
in fellowship, sit in conference, and any
brother is at liberty to propose such cases
of conscience, as he wants advice on : or
any difficult passage of Scripture on which
he wants light; or anything else which

tends to the harmony of the churches, or to love and peace amongst brethren. And when the conference adjourns, the rest of the time is employed in preaching, praying, singing, &c.

There are four Union meetings within the bounds of the Kehukee Association, viz: *On the east side of Chowan River*, which is composed of the churches at Cowenjock, Camden, Sawyer's Creek, Knobscrook, Flatty Creek, Yoppim, and Ballard's bridge. The *Bertie Union meeting* is composed of the Bertie, Cashie, Wiccacon, Meherrin, and Connaritsey churches. *Flat Swamp Union meeting* comprehends the Flat Swamp, the Great Swamp, Connoho, Skewarkey, and Morattuck churches. The *Swift Creek Union meeting* contains the churches at the Falls of Tar River, Kehukee, Fishing Creek, Rocky Swamp, and Quankey. There are a few churches that have not joined in any of these Union meetings. We do not know what is the reason, unless it be on account of the inconveniency of their local situation.

To give our readers a more general idea of the nature of an Union meeting, we will insert the Constitution of one of them, and we presume that, in substance, they are all nearly similar.

CONSTITUTION OF THE BERTIE UNION MEETING.

Article I. This meeting shall in future consist of the members who may attend the same, from Bertie, Cashie. Wiccacon, Meherrin, and Connaritsey churches, and members who may attend the same at their respective appointments from all sister churches and Associations.

II. This meeting shall be known by the name of the " Bertie Union Meeting."

III. Each meeting shall have power to adjourn themselves to any time or place they may see proper; so that the different churches in the union be equally benefited by their several appointments.

IV. When assembled they shall make choice of a Moderator and Clerk; and the Clerk of said meeting shall enter the minutes of the conference, and transmit them to the next meeting.

V. A book shall be procured, in which all the minutes of the different conferences shall be inserted from time to time, and a person appointed to record the same.

VI. In time of conference, each member shall be entitled to the liberty of speech, and shall first arise and address the Moderator.

VII. No person shall be admitted to speak more than three times to any one subject, without liberty from the conference.

VIII. Any motion made and seconded, shall come under the consideration of the meeting, unless withdrawn by the person who made it.

IX. Every case or query presented in writing shall be twice read, if required; and before debated, shall be received by a majority of the meeting then present.

X. New churches that may hereafter be constituted, or are now constituted, lying and being within the bounds of Roanoke and Meherrin Rivers, or convenient thereto, may be admitted into this union.

XI. At the time of conference a door shall be opened for the admission of members by the ordinance of baptism.

XII. The ordinance of the Lord's Supper shall be administered at the time of each union meeting, on one of the days which the conference may appoint,

XIII. The meeting shall be opened and closed by prayer.

THESE *Union meetings* were attended with a very great blessing. At some of them three or four thousand people would meet, and sometimes fifteen or sixteen ministers attend. Great numbers were solemnly affected, and at times, we have reason to believe, many got converted. At an Union meeting at Elder Hendry's meeting-house in Bertie, June, 1803, a very worthy character, who had been *Senator* for that county, and having been solemnly impressed with a sense of his lost state by nature for some time before, under preaching on Sunday, received comfort, and hoped that his soul got converted : and when the minister concluded preaching, arose from his seat, and stood on a bench, and told the people "That he had many times been a *candidate* at *elections*, but he was now a *candidate* for the *Kingdom of Heaven.*" And being overpowered with the love of God, fell backwards off the seat, but was upholden by some of the bystanders. When he was baptized, which was a few weeks after, nearly a thousand people were present; and at the side of the water he addressed the spectators thus : "I perceive," said he, "several of my friends and old companions standing around ; and I can truly say I love you, but I cannot continue with you in the ways we have so long been in, and if you will not go with me, I must leave you;" and so bade them farewell, and went into the water.

At an Union meeting at Parker's meeting-house, August, 1803, it was supposed there were four thousand people. The weather proved very rainy on Sunday. There was a stage erected in the meeting-house yard; and at about half after eleven o'clock, Elder Burkitt ascended the stage to preach, and it was expected from the appearance of the clouds it would rain every moment, and before he was done preaching it did so. Yet notwithstanding the numerous congregation still kept together; and although every effort was used to shun the rain, by umbrellas, carriages, blankets, &c., yet we believe one thousand people were exposed to the rain without any shelter; and some crying, some convulsed to the ground, some begging the ministers to pray for them; and they composedly stood and received the falling shower without ever being dispersed.

And it is not only at particular times, but, blessed be God, these meetings are generally blessed. O! that men would praise the Lord for his goodness, and his wonderful works to the children of men! We

feel ourselves very happy, and thankful at
this time for the visitation of the Lord.
O ! that he would continue his work until
the whole world is brought into subjection
to the peaceable reign of Christ, the Prince
of Peace; and that the whole earth may
be filled with his glory. And his knowledge cover the earth as the waters do the
seas.

This gracious work in this Association,
has been differently manifested in its ope-
rations, and the effects it took on the people. Some were deeply affected under a
sense of their lost state, and their hearts
ready to burst within them, whilst reflect-
ing on their past conduct; yet under the
ministry of the Word made no noise.
Others, sensible of these things, were in
floods of tears, and at last constrained to
give vent to their passions, and cry out in
the presence of the multitude, *What must
I do to be saved?* Some were taken with a
tremor, like a fit of the ague. And others
fell to the ground like a person in a swoon,
and continued helpless and motionless for
some time ; and this power was manifest
at times, on persons at home about their
secular concerns in the house, and in the
field.

Whatever infidels may say in opposition
to the work in this Association, stubborn

reason is obliged to decide in favor of this revival. It is evident it was from GOD, from the good effects it took on the people, and the tendency it had to moralize them. Persons of the most dissolute lives, as drunkards, swearers, liars, thieves, &c., became sober, punctual, honest, virtuous persons. Surely that religion must be of *God* that makes people *godly* from *good principles;* that makes better husbands, better wives, better children, more obedient servants, better masters, better neighbors, and better citizens. This the work has evidently done. Let the politician with all his maxims of policy; the deist with all his deistical reasoning, endeavoring to invalidate the Divine authority of the Holy Scriptures; the soldier with all his arms and ammunition, see if any, or all of them together, can by all their art, sophistry, or power, or even by the force of *gunpowder*, effect such a reformation in the morals of men. Can they do what the simplicity of the *Gospel* of our dear Lord Jesus has done? Can they make those who hate God and religion, with all their hearts love him and his service? Can they make men at *variance* and *enmity* love one another? This the Gospel has done in this revival. In some neighborhoods, persons at enmity with each other, and when they met would not speak to one another, after receiving the benefits of the Gospel's gracious influence, could take each other in their arms with the greatest pleasure, and cause an unbelieving world to say, *Behold how these Christians love.*

CHAPTER VIII.

1. On the Nature of Circular Letters.—2. A Letter "On the Maintenance of the Ministry," for 1791, by Elder Martin Ross.

EVER since the second year after the minutes were first printed, which was in the year 1790, it has been customary for the Association to address the churches by way of circular letters. The custom is, to appoint some minister, the year before, to prepare one against the next Association. At first it was the practice to name a subject; but of late the minister is at liberty to choose his subject. The letter thus prepared is brought to the Association, and if approved by them is printed in the minutes.

We have thought proper to insert in this history, a few of those letters on the most interesting subjects; which will not only give our readers an idea of the nature of these letters, but, it is hoped, from the magnitude of the subjects in them discussed, will be both pleasing and profitable to the impartial inquirer.

CIRCULAR LETTER.

The Messengers of the several Baptist churches belonging to the United Baptist Association, formerly called the Kehukee Association, met at the Flat Swamp meeting-house, in Pitt county, North Carolina, October, 1791: To the several churches in union with this Association, send greeting:—

Dearly beloved Brethren :

Our Divine Lord and Master, in the course of an indulgent providence, hath favored us with another anniversary interview, by which we obtain knowledge of the circumstances of the churches that compose this convention; and we also received agreeable information concerning the interest and growth of our adorable Redeemer's kingdom in many other places. And it must give peculiar pleasure to every gracious soul to hear, "that he who sitteth between the cherubims has stretched forth his mighty arm, and is making a willing people in the day of his power."

And since Almighty God, in carrying on this glorious work, is pleased by *the foolishness of preaching* to save them that believe, it therefore becomes necessary that there should be a number of preachers or ministers of the Gospel. And according to the direction of our last Association, we proceed, in our circular letter, at this time, to make a few observations on the necessary support or maintenance of Gospel ministers; although we are very sorry that there should be the least occasion to write or speak upon that subject.

11

We apprehend that one principal reason why the churches have been so remiss in this duty is because the people have been for a number of years grievously oppressed by an ecclesiastical establishment,* in raising money by taxation for the support of ministers of a contrary sentiment, many of whom, they had reason to fear, God never sent to preach, but only preached for hire, and divined for money, and regarded the *fleece* more than the *flock*. To shun this extreme, many zealous preachers, who abhorred their works of darkness and deceit, being sensible that such men crept into the ministry for the sake of filthy lucre, have thought it their duty to bear public testimony against them. But not being careful to distinguish between *living of the Gospel of Christ*, and being *supported by the laws of men*, those zealots have injudiciously condemned the practice of receiving anything at all as a reward for ministerial labors, and so have fallen into an error on the other hand. It is therefore necessary that a just mediocrity be observed between the two extremes.

To guard against the error on both hands, it is necessary, dear brethren, we should make the Holy Scriptures the rule of our faith and practice. That ministers have a divine right to maintenance from the people is evident:

1. From the express declaration of Jesus Christ. Matt. x. 9, 10. "Provide neither gold nor silver, nor brass in your purses, nor scrip for your journey; neither two coats, neither shoes, nor yet staves; for the workman is worthy of his meat—and the laborer of his hire." Luke x. 9.

2. This *right* the apostles published throughout the world. 1 Cor. ix. 14. "Even so hath the Lord ordained, that they which preach the Gospel, should live of the Gospel." Gal. vi. 6. "Let him that is taught in the word communicate to him that teacheth in all good things."

3. This divine right of the minister's maintenance is manifested by the *law of nature:* Deut. xxv. 4. 1 Tim. v. 18. "Thou shalt not muzzle the ox that treadeth out the corn—and the laborer is worthy of his reward."

* We would not be understood to insinuate that those establishments do yet remain. They have been wholly removed, and finally abolished in this State, by the late most glorious Revolution.

4. By the *law of nations*. "Who goeth a warfare at any time at his own charges?" 1 Cor. ix. 7.

5. By the laws of farmers, graziers, vine-planters, reapers, threshers, &c. 1 Cor. ix. 7. "Who planteth a vineyard and eateth not of the fruit thereof? Or who feedeth a flock, and eateth not of the milk of the flock?" 1 Cor. ix. 10, 11. For our sakes no doubt this is written: "That he that plougheth should plough in hope; and he that thresheth in hope should be partaker of his hope. If we have sown unto you spiritual things, is it a great thing if we shall reap your carnal things?"

6. By the *Levitical law*. 1 Cor. ix. 13. "Do you not know that they which minister about holy things live of the things of the temple; and they which wait at the altar are partakers with the altar?"

Thus have we, dear brethren, clearly proven from express Scripture, that the ministers of the Gospel are justly entitled to a comfortable maintenance from the people. The ministers' support should be *sufficient* and *plentiful*, because they are enjoined *hospitality*. The matter of their maintenance is expressed in terms so general as to leave the people at liberty to pay them in *kind*, or *value*, *all good things*. The manner of paying is, *cheerfully* and not *grudgingly*. The contributors are all who "are taught in the word."

The truth of these things, beloved brethren, we make no doubt you are convinced of, but the neglect of them is too glaring to us, yourselves and others. We cannot but feel exceedingly sorry on this account. The consequences arising therefrom are very pernicious. By this sad neglect the poor ministers of the Gospel are necessarily obliged to follow their worldly avocations for the support of themselves and their families, which prevents them from reading the Holy Scriptures, meditating, preaching constantly, and giving themselves wholly to the work—which weakens their hands, dulls their ideas, cools their zeal, and of necessity they are not so profitable to the churches, nor to the cause of Christ in general. These things, in a measure, you must be sensible of. Much more might be said upon this subject, but the bounds of a circular letter will not admit of it.

Thus have we, dear brethren (pursuant to an ordinance of our last Association), endeavored to consider this

important duty; and now permit us affectionately and solemnly to call upon you to consider our adorable Master's
weighty and powerful expostulations—" Why call ye me
Lord, Lord, and do not the things I say? Ye are my
friends if ye do whatsoever I command you. If ye love
me keep my commandments. • He that saith I know him,
and keepeth not his commandments, is a liar, and the
truth is not in him. My little children, let us not love in
word, neither in tongue; but in deed, and in truth."—
Luke vi. 46. John xiv. 15; xv. 14. 1 John ii. 4. 1
John iii. 18.

Finally, brethren, those things which ye have both
learned, and received, and heard, and seen, *do;* and the
God of peace shall be with you.

Signed by order of the Association,

NATHAN MAYO, *Moderator,*
LEMUEL BURKITT, *Clerk.*

CHAPTER IX.

Circular Letters.—1. A Letter "On the Final Perseverance of the Saints in Grace," for 1794, by Elder Lancaster.—2. "On Good Works," for 1800, by Elder Gilbert.

CIRCULAR LETTER.

*The Elders and Messengers of the several Baptist churches
belonging to the Kehukee Association, met at Brother Burkitt's meeting-house, on Sandy Run, in Bertie county,
North Carolina, September, 1794—The Churches in union
with this Association send their Christian salutation:—*

BELOVED BRETHREN,

BEING favored by Divine Providence, we have once
more had a profitable and pleasing interview at the time
and place appointed. The business we have transacted
you have in our minutes, which we hope will meet with
your concurrence and approbation.

The subject of our circular letter this year, according

to a resolve of our last, is to be "*The final perseverance of the saints in grace.*" And the subject is inseparably connected with, and a concomitant of, that God-exalting, soul-reviving doctrine of particular election, and free, unmerited grace in Christ Jesus, we doubt not of its being cordially received by you, and perused both with pleasure and satisfaction.

To do ample justice to a subject of this magnitude, so copious in its nature and interesting in its consequences, would very far exceed the bounds of a circular letter. We shall therefore only offer a few reasons, supported by the best authority, in favor of it. And, first, a strong and undeniable reason in support of the doctrine may be fairly drawn from the covenant made with Noah: the tenor of which was, that God would no more drown the world by water. See Gen. ix. Now we do not, neither can we, without being guilty of the most daring and gross impiety, call in question or dispute the veracity of God in this solemn promise; neither can any call in question *the final perseverance of the saints in grace*, without being guilty of offering the most daring insults to the God of truth; for the *preservation* of the one and the *security* of the other are, in every point of view, marked with the same awful solemnity of an OATH. For the truth of which we beg leave to refer you to that memorable passage in Isa. liv. 9, 10. "For this is as the waters of Noah unto me; for as I have *sworn* that the waters of Noah no more shall cover the earth, so have I *sworn* that I would not be wroth with thee nor rebuke thee. For the mountains shall depart, and the hills be removed, but my kindness shall not depart from thee, neither shall the covenant of my peace be removed, saith the Lord that hath mercy on thee."

From the premises thus laid down by inspiration itself, the conclusion is very natural and obvious, viz: That the people of God have no more reason to doubt of their security in Christ, and *final perseverance in grace*, than they have that God, contrary to his *oath*, will send a second deluge of water and drown the world. And whoever disputes the one or the other, is so far an infidel, and deserves no better title from men.

Another authority perfectly similar to the above-quoted passage, we find recorded by that great champion of truth, and patron of the saints' final perseverance in grace, in Heb. vi. 17, 18. "Wherein God, willing more abundantly to show unto the heirs of promise the immutability of his counsel, confirmed *it* by an *oath*—That by two immutable things, in which it was impossible for God to lie, we might have a strong consolation who have fled for refuge to lay hold upon the hope set before us." Here we find the apostle speaks of the heirs of promise, who are believers; 2, of the immutability of God's counsel, *i. e.* respecting the promise and the heirs of it, which he says was confirmed by an OATH—the reason of which was, that we might have a strong consolation who have fled for refuge to lay hold on the hope set before us; which hope, the apostle saith with great propriety, is an anchor of the soul; neither does he give the least hint of any danger of this anchor giving way, so as not to answer the purpose for which it was intended, but, on the contrary, declares unequivocally, and we may add unconditionally also, that it is *both sure and steadfast.* Which shows most clearly that Noah was not more safe, when shut up in the ark, than believers are whose lives are hid with Christ in God. Again, we are informed by the same apostle, Rom. viii. 28. "That all things work together for good to them that love God"—then consequently nothing can work for their destruction. Again, Jer. xxxii. 40. "And I will make an everlasting covenant with them, that I will not turn away from them to do them good." But it is objected *they* may turn away from him, and so finally perish: To which we reply, that the same covenant provides against that also, for in the same verse God says, "I will put my fear in their hearts that they shall not depart from me." So, if God has said that he will not *turn away* from his people, and that he will never leave nor forsake them (Heb. xiii. 5), and that they shall not depart from him—then surely that man must have a front of brass, and not the fear of God before his eyes, that can dispute the point with his Maker, and say the union may be dissolved, and believers in Christ may *finally perish.*

As a further confirmation of the doctrine contended for, we offer to your consideration the following Scriptures. Psal. xxxvii. 23, 24. "The steps of a good man are ordered by the Lord; and he delighteth in his way.

Though he fall, he shall not be utterly cast down, for the Lord upholdeth him with his hand." Isa. xlii. 16. "And I will bring the blind by a way that they knew not; I will lead them in a path that they have not known: I will make darkness light before them, and crooked things straight. These things will I do unto them, and not forsake them." Mic. vi. 8. "Rejoice not against me, O mine enemy: when I fall I shall arise." 1 John ii. 19. "They went out from us, but they were not of us: For if they had been of us, they would no doubt have continued with us: But they went out that they might be made manifest that they were not of us."

Again, the blessed Jesus hath said, "All that the Father giveth me shall come unto me, and him that cometh to me I will in no wise cast out;" and further declares, "that it was the will of the Father that he should *lose nothing*, but that he should raise it up at the last day." That the water he would give his people (which is the graces of his spirit) should be in them a well of water springing up unto everlasting life. That he has given them eternal life, and that they shall never perish: And that they shall not come into condemnation, for they are passed from death unto life. And because I live (says he) ye shall live also. For a proof of which, see John vi. 36—39 ; iv. 14 ; x. 28, 29 ; v. 24.

Several authorities as much in point as those already quoted, offer their friendly assistance, but our scanty limits admonish us it is time to stop. We shall therefore beg leave to quote only two more Scriptures, and with them we close. The first we bring from Rom. viii. 38, 39. There, says that great apostle to the Gentiles, who was well acquainted with the mind of his divine Lord and Master, and under the immediate inspiration of the Spirit of God—"I am persuaded, that neither death nor life, nor angels, nor principalities, nor powers, nor things present, nor things to come—nor height, nor depth, nor any other creature, shall be able to separate us from the love of God which is in Christ Jesus our Lord." The popular objection that they may separate themselves, is too futile to merit an answer; we shall therefore treat it with silence and deserved contempt, until it shall be made appear by some unheard of arguments, that a believer himself is a nonentity, or no creature at all, which is impossible to be done.

Let the golden chain of God's decrees, and the believer's privileges, bring up the rear. Rom. viii. 29, 30. "For whom he did foreknow, he also did predestinate to be conformed to the image of his Son, that he might be the first-born among many brethren. Moreover, whom he did predestinate, them he also called; and whom he called, them he also justified; and whom he justified, them he also glorified." Here, believers, is a golden chain indeed, a chain of God's making, and therefore cannot be broken by all the sophistry of men of corrupt minds, who exceedingly err, not knowing the Scriptures nor the power of God. For here it may be observed, that those of whom it is said that they were *foreknown, pre-destinated, called,* and *justified* are identically the same people that are to be *glorified*—this being an undeniable fact, we conclude that the argument drawn from this authority is unanswerable, and therefore must be finally conclusive.

Very weighty arguments might also be drawn from the omnipotency, omniscience, and immutability of God, but we have already observed that our limits are exceeded—therefore, to conclude, we beseech you, dear brethren, by the mercies of God, to present your bodies a living sacrifice to him at all times—having had much forgiven, let the consideration thereof cause you to love much, and influence you to every good word and work. Let not this blessed soul-reviving doctrine be evilly spoken of through you; but, on the contrary, let your exemplary lives and pious conversation declare to all the world the blessed and happy influence the belief of it has on your daily conduct. Beware of thinking you have already attained, or already perfect; which would be sure to check your pious endeavors to grow in grace, and in the knowledge, not only of the doctrine here laid down, but those doctrines inseparably connected with it.

Lastly, let the consideration of your *secure standing* in Christ bear you up under all the cross-like and afflictive providence you may have to meet with in your passage through this unfriendly world: being fully persuaded that his promise of "never leaving you" stands firmer than heaven or earth ; and that, according to the prayer he put up to his father, you shall ere long be with him, not only to see him and behold his glory, but·to adore, beyond the stretch of thought, his divine perfections to all eternity, where your sorrows of every description shall be completely done away, and every divine promise meet its full accomplishment.

Now to Him who is able to keep you from *falling*, and has promised to present you faultless before the throne of his glory, to the only wise God, be glory and thanksgiving throughout all churches, world without end. *Amen.*

Signed by order of the Association.

NATHAN MAYO, *Moderator,*
LEMUEL BURKITT, *Clerk.*

CIRCULAR LETTER.

The Elders and Messengers of the several Baptist churches belonging to the Kehukee Association, met at the meeting-house near the Falls of Tar River, Nash county, North Carolina, October, 1800—To the churches in union with this Association send their Christian salutation:—

BELOVED BRETHREN,

CALLED of God to the fellowship of his dear Son, and to an inheritance amongst those who are sanctified, and beloved by us, who hope we have obtained like precious grace with you. The great satisfaction which you have expressed in, and the willingness with which you have received our former epistles; together with a desire for your good, and the glory of the great Redeemer, are motives which induce us to address you once more in an epistolary way, which we send this year on the subject of GOOD WORKS, which is highly recommended by our Lord and Saviour, together with his prophets and apostles, and ought to be carefully observed by all who profess to be followers of the blessed Jesus. Witness the following Scriptures. Ecl. iii. 17; chap. ix. 10., and xii. 14. Isa. xxiii. 17. James i. 25. Gal. vi. 4. 1 Thes. i. 3. Heb. vi. 10. Titus i. 10. James ii. 11, 21. Jonah iii. 10. Mat. xxiii. 10. 2 Cor. 11, 15. Rev. 14, 13, and xx. 12 and 32. Acts x. 35. Rom. ii. 10. These and many others abundantly testify that we were created in

Christ Jesus unto *good works*, which the Lord before ordained that we should walk in them. And as the con-
tracted limits of a circular letter will not admit of a full
investigation of our subject, we shall in a few particulars
show what we understand to be intended by the term
good works. And, first, it might not be amiss to observe,
that before works can be called, or really deemed *good
works*, it is necessary that they be the *product* of a true
and genuine faith in Christ; for as "Faith without works
is dead," so works without faith is dead also. Heb. ix.
14. The source or fountain, then, whence good works
flow is not from any expectation of merit, but purely from
a principle of love to God.

By good works, we understand works of various kinds,
as, 1. Our duty to *God*. 2. Our duty to the *Church* and
people of God. 3. Our duty to our *neighbors*. 4. Our
duty to *magistrates*, or earthly rulers. 5. Our duty to
our *family*; and, lastly, to *ourselves*. 1. Our duty to God
is, to consider him as the cause of our existence, our
great benefactor, and sole author of all our happiness in
time and eternity. To love him above any earthly en-
joyment; yea, with all our heart, soul, mind, and
strength. We should use our utmost endeavor to keep
his commandments, and have respect to all his precepts.
But, as our duty to God is inseparably connected with
our duty in other particulars, we pass on, 2. To our
duty to the Church and people of God. As our Lord and
Saviour has loved us and given himself for us, that he
might deliver us from the curse of the law and the flames
of devouring fire, and hath taken us from the wild stock
of nature, made us all to drink of the same fountain of
his everlasting love, and so tempered our spirits as to
unite us together, not by tyrannical chains, but by the
sweetest bands of love and fellowship, and declared us to
be a select body by him chosen, and set apart from the
world, it becomes our duty then to walk as people who are
not of the world, but chosen of God, and bound for the
heavenly Canaan, having given our hands and hearts to
each other, to endeavor to keep the unity of the spirit in the
bond of peace, to strengthen, comfort, uphold, encourage,
watch over, and to pray with and for one another, to bear
one another's burdens, and "so fulfill the royal law of
Christ." Our Lord has compared his church to a com-

pany of horse in Pharaoh's chariot—hence it appears that all have something to do in the church of Christ, that none should be barren or unfruitful. The Lord has made it our duty often to assemble ourselves together, and we are exhorted by an apostle not to forsake it as the manner of some was. We hope you will, therefore, endeavor as oft as possible to attend your church meetings and places of public worship. We hear of coldness among some of you—what else can be expected? When the church members so seldom see each other, they become in a manner strange and useless to one another, while some perhaps seldom, and others scarcely ever attend Conference at all. Dear brethren, pray consider the worthy name by which you are called, and the honor of that cause in which you are enlisted; you are called *the light of the world,* but how can your light be useful when many even of the people of the world are more careful to attend on worship, yea, even conferences too, than many who profess to be followers of the blessed Jesus. While thus backward or careless in attending your conferences and places of public worship, you wound and grieve your brethren, and weaken the hands of your ministers, who, after coming perhaps many miles to endeavor to comfort you, find themselves oft times under the disagreeable necessity of preaching almost to the naked walls, or not at all. The few hearers they may have being chiefly those who make no profession of religion, whilst the members of the church are busily engaged at home, and cannot take time to attend on the worship of God, and many times kept back for a small excuse even on the Lord's day.

Thirdly, our duty to love our *neighbor* is to him as *ourself,* to be kind and charitable to all whose needs may require it, be they strangers or acquaintances, without respect of persons; to visit the *sick,* the *fatherless,* and the *widow* in their afflictions, endeavoring to nourish and comfort them as far as in us lies; also to receive strangers, use them kindly, clothe the naked, feed the hungry, and to be careful to consider the poor and needy, and grant them relief according to our ability. Beware of covetousness, remember the kingdom of God is not in meat and drink, but love, peace, and joy in the Holy Ghost; therefore glorify God, and comfort your fellow creatures with what you possess.

Fourthly, we should obey *magistrates*, and all those who are put in authority to rule over us in our temporal affairs. We should not speak evil, nor reproachfully of them, but acknowledge their authority, and honor them as ministers of God, by him appointed for the punishment of evil doers, and the protection of those who wish to do well ; we should therefore show all good fidelity as patrons of *good works* and a light to the world, that we bring not reproach on the church of Christ, nor cause to be blamed that holy name by which we are called.

Fifthly, our duty to our *family*, which appears very extensive when we consider ourselves, in respect to them, not only as stewards, who have to give an account of our stewardship to God, but as it were, as *prophets, priests,* and *kings*. As a prophet, we should *teach* and instruct them ; as a priest we should *pray* with and for them, and should be careful in the order of their government. Each one to whom God has committed the care of souls, or a family, which is the same thing, should consider himself as their teacher, to whom all the family look, and from whom they all expect to receive their instruction, as it is well known that children in their tender years are naturally led to think the judgment, counsel, ways, and behavior of their parents to be superior to all others, especially when parents or rulers exercise a proper authority. Every family should have one, and only one proper head, who should take the government thereof, and in all cases endeavor to rule with justice, having a particular regard for all about him, setting forth good examples, walking in the ways of godliness and true piety, praying with and for them oft; yea, we are exhorted to "pray without ceasing," and in everything to give thanks. If we neglect public prayer, praise, and thanksgiving in our families, do we not leave them all to walk in the dark, as it were, while we suffer our light to be hidden under the bushel of worldly cares, or under the bed of sloth, while we ourselves walk unworthy the Christian name. A family should not be governed by passion; justice should be tempered with judgment and mercy. In vain does the passionate, fractious, turbulent, and inconsiderate person, after being the cause of a whole day's unhappiness and discontent in his family, at night, call on all, or any of them to join him in the worship of God, while every mind is filled with prejudice, every eye with evil, and every tongue ready to say, "physician, heal thyself," or otherwise, "thou hypocrite, first cast out the beam out of thine own eye." Therefore every ruler of a family should always remember that *example* has the most powerful influence, without which all our admonition will, in all probability, prove ineffectual. Parents should be careful to preserve and cultivate the morals of their children, they should use their authority and not gratify them in their own wicked desires, such as frolicking, vain company keeping, gaming, idle visits on the Lord's day, &c., but should on that day carry them to places of public worship, and after they return endeavor to impress upon their minds the things they heard; for, after giving too great a loose to the reins of our children's lusts, we shall find our reproofs to be in vain. Witness the sons of Eli. 1 Sam. ii. 23, 24, 25. And Solomon says, "Chasten thy son while there is hope, and let not thy soul spare for his crying." Prov. xix. 18. If we cannot command the hearts of our children and family to make them pray, and love God, we may teach and admonish them; and should all our endeavors fail, we may lastly have recourse to the example of Job. Job i. 5.

And, further, with respect to the observation of *good works* relative to *family duty*, it becomes every member of a family to practice the particular duties in the respective places our divine Lord and Master has placed us in, as *husbands* to love their wives, and be not bitter against them. Wives to submit themselves to their own husbands. Servants to be obedient to their masters, and please them well in all things. Masters to give unto their servants that which is just and equal. Parents not to provoke their children to anger lest they be discouraged; as well as for children to obey their parents. Col. iii.

Lastly, we should look to our own souls, strive to walk humbly with God, and study to show ourselves approved of him in all things, patrons of *good works*, and endeavor to keep a conscience void of offence, to check and keep under as much as possible all our unruly passions; to watch and pray, and avoid, as far as in us lies, giving any cause whereby the enemies of the Lord may speak evil of us, or blaspheme that worthy name by which we

are called. Ready at all times to reprove vice, striving
to confirm all our reproofs, counsels, or admonitions by a
regular life, pious walk, and godly conversation. We
should be careful to read and study the Scriptures, and
often to withdraw from the hurries of life to secret prayer
and meditation; for where these duties are neglected, our
case becomes very alarming, we then grow cold, backslide, and in a particular manner may give the enemy of
souls great advantage over us.

And now may the kind and good Lord strengthen, uphold, and enable you to watch and pray, fill you with
every good word and work, comfort you abundantly, and
preserve you blameless until his second appearance to
visit his sleeping saints, and to be admired by all who
love him, and long for his glorious appearance. *Amen.*

Signed by order,

NATHAN MAYO, *Moderator*,
LEMUEL BURKITT, *Clerk*.

CHAPTER X.

1. What a True Church of Christ is, the Manner of receiving Members, Constitution, Discipline, Officers, &c.
—2. History of the Seven Churches east of Chowan
River, viz: Camden, Yoppim, Cowenjock, Sawyer's
Creek, Knobscrook, Flatty Creek, and Ballard's Bridge.
—3. Memoirs of Elders Done, Cole, Harmon, Welsh,
&c.

HAVING gone through the material parts
of the History of the Association, we shall
now proceed to the history of the churches,
as they relate to the Kehukee Association.

and to the Virginia Portsmouth and Neuse Associations, which were formed out of this. And before we enter on the description of the same, it would be necessary to say something about a *church* of Christ; its *constitution, officers*, their *ordination, church government*, &c.

A church of Christ is a congregation of men and women, publicly professing faith in Christ Jesus, and being regularly baptized by immersion, who have covenanted together, given themselves up to one another in the Lord, to be governed by his word, and to be guided by a regular and proper discipline, agreeably to the Holy Scriptures. [See Preface.]

The customary way which the Baptist churches in the Kehukee Association, receive members into church fellowship is, for the person who is desirous of admission into the church to attend at church conferences; and when conference sits, to come into the church and signify his intention to the minister, or some of the members; and the church then sitting, the party who applies shall relate his experience, setting forth how the Lord awakened him, and brought him to a sense of his lost state by nature; how he had seen the insufficiency of his own works to save him : and how the Lord had revealed to him the way of

life and salvation through Jesus Christ;
and the reasons he has to believe that he
is interested in this glorious plan; and the
evidences that he has become a *new creature*. If any doubt remain, the minister, or
any of the members present, ask such ques-
tions as are necessary relative thereto; and
satisfaction being obtained, then the minister usually asks the church respecting the
life and conversation of the candidate. And
if there be general satisfaction, the minister
and members give him the right hand of
fellowship. Then a time is appointed for
his baptism; and being assembled at the
side of some convenient water, after singing and prayer, the minister takes the candidate by the hand, and leads him into the
water; and at the same time having hold
of the hands of the party to be baptized in
one of his, and the other hand holding by a
handkerchief tied fast round his head, shall
dip him discreetly backwards,* all under
water, expressing these words, or some
similar thereto: " In the name of our Lord

---

* The practice of baptizing *backwards* has been objected to by some societies; and therefore has been practiced
by dipping the person *forwards*. And some others, by
way of ridicule, say " They have no opinion of persons
going to heaven backwards." To such we reply, " The
Scriptures call baptism a *burial*, Rom. vi. 4; and we all
know that it is not customary to bury people with their
faces downward."

Jesus Christ, and by the authority of our office, I baptize thee in the name of the Father, and of the Son, and of the Holy Ghost." After the solemnity is performed, they both, coming up out of the water, join the congregation in singing,

> " Do we not know that solemn word,
> That we are buried with the Lord;
> Baptized into his death, and then
> Put off the body of our sin," &c.

At the water, the newly baptized person is met by the brethren, who sometimes salute him thus, " You are welcome to the *cross*, dear brother."

Some years past it was usual, after the party baptized was dressed and had come into the congregation, for the minister to *lay his hands* on him and pray. But of late years the practice of laying on of hands on baptized members is disused in the Kehukee Association; as it is thought the few passages which mention it in the New Testament allude to miraculous gifts being conveyed by the laying on of the hands of *inspired* men in the apostolic days.

As to the *number* sufficient to constitute a church, we do not know the Scriptures point out. Some suppose it is necessary there should be thirteen, because Jesus and the twelve apostles were present at the first celebration of the supper. Others descend-

12

ed to seven. Tertullian to three; *ubi tres
ecclesia est* Exh. *de cast*, Ch. 7. Our Lord
says, where two or three are gathered together in my name, I will be in the midst
of them ; and we read of churches being in
some houses or families, as was the case
with Aquilla and Priscilla, Rom. xvi. 5.
1 Cor. xvi. 19; also that of Philemon, verse
2. *The church in thy house.* Yet, notwithstanding, we are left at an uncertainty
to know how many were in those families;
nor can we suppose any particular number
is intended by our Lord. We judge that
where there are a sufficient number to carry
on church *discipline*, with suitable church
officers, it is sufficient to constitute a
church.

In the next place we will treat of the
manner in which a church is constituted,
according to the mode usually practiced in
our Association.

The newly-constituted churches in this
Association are such as have been constituted out of the old churches, being
branches or arms of the same. Being gathered, baptized, and received members of
such churches : and, when ripe for constitution, usually petition the body for dismission in order thereto; and having obtained
a regular dismission, a day of fasting appointed for the purpose, one or more minis-

ters present, the members all should be present, and give in a list of their names, and produce their dismission from the body. The ministers inquire whether it is their *desire* to become a church, whether their *habitations* are near enough to each cther conveniently to attend church conferences? Whether they are so well acquainted with each other's life and conversation as to coalesce into one body, and walk together in love and fellowship? Whether it is their intention to *keep up a regular discipline* agreeably to the Scriptures, to make *God's Word* the rule of their conduct in church government, obeying his ordinances, and in matters of faith, and all other things relative thereto in a church relation, and by these things distinguish themselves as a true church of Christ? These things being answered in the affirmative, then a covenant is produced, similar to that mentioned at page 34, and being read, consented to, and subscribed, the ministers pronounce them a church, in some such words as these, "In the name of our Lord Jesus Christ, and by the authority of our office, we pronounce you [mentioning their names] a true *Gospel church;* endowed with all necessary power towards becoming a complete organized body, and the due government of your

selves; and therefore stand bound to make
proper use of that power, as ye shall answer it to the Head of the church. On
whose name let us further call." Then
they pray to God for a blessing on them,
and conclude by singing his praise, and
giving each other the right hand of fellowship. The church thus constituted, have
full power to choose their *officers,* receive
members, and deal with offenders. The
last case is, when any member transgresses
and sins against God, any member or members who are acquainted with it ought to
go and charge the offending brother with
the crime; and if he make *confession* of his
sin and appear *penitent,* and the offence be
of a private nature, the *dealing* is carried
no further. See Mat. xviii. But if it be
a public transgression, he must be cited to
appear before the church; and being
charged with the crime, if he confess it,
and express *satisfactory signs of repentance,*
he is then restored to fellowship: But if he
prove *incorrigible,* he is put out of the communion of the church until he be restored
by repentance and reformation.

The principal *officers* in the church are
ministers and *deacons.* It has long been
the opinion of the Association that there is
no more to be continued in the church, or
that is sufficiently authorized from the

Word of God. The churches in the Kehukee Association, at first, had *ruling elders*. But it has a great while been the opinion of most of the churches belonging to that Association, that there are no *ruling* elders mentioned in the Scriptures, distinct from *teachers*, who are called *elders*. Therefore the practice of having *ruling* elders distinct from the ministers is laid aside. This subject has often been debated in the Association, and the only reasons which they have assigned for not having *ruling* elders, when those queries have been discussed, are, 1. The Word of God nowhere points out the *qualifications* of such officers, as is the case with *ministers* and *deacons*. 2. No *example* in the New Testament of any being called, nor the *time* when, and *manner* how they were ordained to office. 3. No work prescribed in the Word of God for them to do. The minister's work is pointed out, " To teach, rebuke, exhort," &c. The deacon's work prescribed, viz: " *To serve tables.*" But no work for a *ruling* elder. The work designed for an elder, according to Mr. Hooker and others, would be expressly to break one of Christ's commands. If thy brother trespass against thee, says our Lord, go and tell him his fault: But they say, we must go and tell the elders of it, and it is their work to try to settle it. Upon the whole, we know not anything they have to do, distinct from the minister, deacon, and what is every member's duty to do.

As we hold only these two, and as the office, call, and ordination of a minister have been treated of before, we shall only give an example of the *ordination* of a *deacon*.

It is necessary there should be two or more deacons in every church. The office of a deacon is *secular*, extending to all the secular affairs of the church. Acts vi. 2, 3, 4. His office authorizes him to require, receive, and lay out money towards answering the church's worldly necessity. The Scriptures when speaking of his office note it under the terms, *business, daily ministration, helping, caring for the poor, collecting, distributing,* and *serving tables,* viz: the table of the Lord, table of the minister, and the table of the poor. Acts, vi. 5. 1 Cor. xii. 28. Gal. ii. 10. John xii. 6. Their qualifications are expressed both negatively and positively by the Apostle Paul—*Not doubled tongued, not greedy of filthy lucre; but grave, holding the mystery of the faith in a pure conscience; approved, blameless, the husband of one wife, ruling his children and house well, men of honest report, full of the Holy Ghost and wisdom.* 1 Tim. iii.

chap. Acts vi. 3. Requisite to their ordination, it is necessary there be, 1. A meeting of the church. 2. Two ministers present at least. The ministers to inquire into their call and qualification, then lay hands on them and pray; and conclude the solemnity by a charge given, and singing God's praise, in a hymn suitable to the occasion.

The Kehukee Association at present contains thirty-one churches, viz: Bertie, Camden, Cashie, Chowan, and Gates, Cowenjock, Connoho, Connetoe, Connaritsey, Cross Roads in Edgecomb, Falls of Tar River, Fishing Creek, Flat Swamp, Flatty Creek, Great Swamp, Haywood's Meeting-House, in Franklin, Kehukee, Knobscrook, Morattuck, Mattamuskeet, Maple Spring, Pungo, Quonkey, Rocky Swamp, Reedy Creek, Sandy Creek, Sawyer's Creek, Scuppernong, Skewarky, Wiccacon, Meherrin, and Yoppim.

These churches originally took their names from some water-course near which the meeting-house stands, and if there be no water-course near, nor other noted place, they usually bear the name of the county where the churches are. And in the minutes of each Association, they are printed as they stand alphabetically. The Bertie church is the first in order, and the first in the Association on its present plan; but not the first constituted church. We shall treat of the churches, not as they stand in alphabetical order, but as they are connected in Union meetings. Beginning with those on the east of Chowan River. And first with the Camden church.

THE CHURCH IN CAMDEN COUNTY, NORTH CAROLINA.

This is an ancient and respectable church. This church (according to Asplund's Register) was constituted in the year 1757. More can be said of this than any church in our connection, with respect to her fruitfulness. She has borne nine sons, or ministers of the Gospel; and six daughters, or constituted churches. Nine ministers have been raised in this church, viz: Elder *Burges*, and his two sons, *John* and *William Burges ;* and Elders *Burkitt*, *Etheridge*, *White*, *Davis Biggs*, *Lurry*, and *Duncan*. Six churches have been constituted from this, viz: Pungo, in Princess Anne county, Virginia, Cowenjock, Sawyer's Creek, Knobscrook, Flatty Creek, and Yoppim. And the churches at Black Water, and London Bridge, in Princess Anne, may also claim affinity, being descendants from one of her children. It is believed that this church was originally gathered and organized on the Free-will plan, but has for a great many years been established on the orthodox system. Elder *John Burges* was a burning and shining light, and in his day the doctrines they held were purely Calvinistic. After the death of Elder Burges, they were attended occasionally by Elders Charles Daniels, John Moore, John Meglamre, and other traveling ministers, until Elder Abbot took the care of them. And after the death of Elder Abbot, Elder Davis Biggs took the care of that church for a few years, then resigning his pastoral charge, he left them and moved to Portsmouth.

Religion has had its ebbing and flowing in that church for many years. Sometimes it appeard at a low ebb, then it would revive. About three years since commenced a happy revival, which has continued for some time. A good many have been called in in this stir. Their meetings are holden the Saturday before the first Sunday in every month. Their yearly meetings, the Saturday before the first Sunday in September; and quarterly meetings, regularly once in three months after, throughout the year.

THE CHURCH AT YOPPIM, CHOWAN COUNTY, NORTH CAROLINA,

Is so called because the members thereof are near to, and the meeting-house stands on the head waters of Yoppim River—a small river which divides the counties of Chowan and Perquimans. This church was originally a branch of the Camden church, and was constituted a little after the Revolution at the Falls of Tar River, and was one of the ten churches that first composed our body at Sappony, in Sussex county, Virginia.

The Gospel, by the Baptists, was first preached here about 1764. Elders Henry Done, John Burges, Henry Abbot and William Cole were some of the first Baptist ministers of our order, who preached about Yoppim. Elder *Done* was born, raised, and baptized in England; came over to America, and lived not far from Edenton. He was a man of a very extensive memory, had a good acquaintance with the Scriptures, and a remarkable gift in prayer, and tolerable good in exhortation; but not extraordinary in preaching. He became a member of this church after it was gathered, and continued in it with approbation for several years. But by reason of his advanced state in life, he did not preach very frequently. He had no wife nor family; and at last finished his course with joy, being nearly 80 years of age.

Elder *Cole* was from a small boy brought up to the sea, and was miraculously converted on a voyage to Lisbon. While on the passage the Lord was pleased to show him what a vile sinner he was, and his dangerous state by nature. In his distress, never having had a religious education, and no religious book on board, except the Bible, he had no where to apply for direction but to the Lord. He searched the Scriptures, and his distress increased to such an height he was not able to perform his duty on board the vessel. He used to say, when his soul was overwhelmed in sorrow and he read how in times of old some would repent in sackcloth and *ashes*, he would go down in the vessel, and wallow and cover himself in a heap of sand, hoping the Lord would hear him, but he found no relief. But at last it pleased God to reveal his Son in him, the hope of Glory; and his soul was in such raptures and joys, he could not contain himself night nor day. Praying, praising God, and exhorting the sailors, were his chief employ. He was *mate* of the vessel, and in the absence of the captain, frequently would order the sailors in his presence, and begin to preach to them. The captain

thought him mad, and threatened to have
him put in irons. He at this time, for want
of better information, thought he could *work
miracles*, and often told the captain he could
drink poison, or walk on the water. But
the Lord through his goodness prevented
him from making the attempt. He at length
was measurably convinced that the power
of working miracles was ceased, from an
attempt he made to cut off one of his toes
with a razor, and had partly done so, but
could not heal it. As soon as he arrived at
Edenton, he began to preach to the inhabitants. The people had their attention very
much engaged, from a report which prevailed. It was said a man was to preach,
who "declared he had been dead and was
alive again; and that he should never die."
Who reported it, we know not, but take it
in a spiritual sense it might be true. He
travelled to the south and met with some
free-will Baptists, and was baptized by
Elder Winfield. He lived awhile near
Yoppim, then moved to Princess Anne,
thence to Bertie, and then into Hertford
county; and in or about the year 1785, he
left this country, master of a vessel bound to
the West Indies, and he nor any of his men
ever returned again; we expect he made
his grave in the great deep. He was a very
pious, zealous, good Christian, and we hope

he is now where winds and waves can no more distress. He left a wife and several small children behind, who some time past removed to Cumberland in Tennessee.

The first person we know of who was a resident near Yoppim, and was received into the Baptist church, was *Joseph Creecy*, a man of considerable fortune, and in much esteem amongst the people. After he had a hope the Lord had converted his soul, he went down to Pasquotank (now Camden) and was baptized by Elder Burges. And it raised the admiration of his neighbors, because when he was baptized, it was in the time of a great *snow*. But we think we can, as old experienced ministers, who have baptized hundreds, testify that we never knew a person receive any damage by going into the water at such times; no, not even so much as to take cold. After brother Creecy had joined the church, soon after Abraham Jennet, Delight Nixon, Jonathan Haughton, Thomas and Mary Burkitt, Melvin Dukes, and others were baptized.

About this time, Elder Lemuel Burkitt, son of Thomas and Mary, got awakened, and had reason to hope he experienced converting grace, and began to *read* in public congregations at his father's, near where the meeting-house now stands. He was now twenty years of age. After entertaining

the people with Whitefield's and Willison's
sermons for a while, he began to write his
own sermons and read them to the people,
and to pray with them. Some time after
he was convinced of the duty of baptism,
and was baptized by Elder *Abbot* in Pasquotank River, July, 1771, and began to
preach the Gospel in two months after.

The few members who were gathered
here, continued a branch of Camden church.
Elder Abbot used to attend them at times,
and the places he preached at, were chiefly
Joseph Creecy's and Thomas Burkitt's.
This branch kept increasing until the year
1775, when it became a *constituted* body.
The meeting-house is east of Edenton, about
five miles.

After the Constitution took place, they
were still attended by Elder Abbot for some
time, until it pleased Divine Providence to
raise up and call to the ministry Elder
Thomas Harmon, who some time after was
ordained pastor of that church, by Elders
Burkitt and Welsh. Elder Harmon continued preaching and baptizing for several
years; then applied to the church for, and
received a dismission, and moved to Cumberland, where he died. The church after
this for a while were without a pastor, until
Elder Ross came and took the charge of
them, who is now their existing pastor.

Their public meetings are holden at Yoppim meeting-house, on the Saturday before the fourth Sunday in every month. Yearly meeting in August, and quarterly in November, February, and May. On the Saturday before the second Sunday in every month, are stated meetings at Yoppim chapel. This church has had lately a comfortable revival; thirty-four were baptized here last year; and the church now contains one hundred and seventy-six members.

THE CHURCH AT COWENJOCK, CURRITUCK COUNTY, NORTH CAROLINA.

This church was also a branch of the church in Camden. The members near this place were at first received at the old meeting-house in Camden, and continued members of that church for some time, until they erected a meeting-house near Cowenjock; and conference was then holden here and communion administered. In the year 1780 (according to Asplund's Register) they were constituted into a church, but were without a settled pastor. Elders *Jonathan Barnes* and *William Lurry* were preachers in this church. They are now attended, and the ordinances administered to them by Elder Etheridge. We are encouraged by their letter to the last Association to hope that a revival is taking place amongst them. Their number of members at present is fifty.

THE CHURCH ON SAWYER'S CREEK, CAMDEN COUNTY,

WAS likewise a branch of Camden old church. The members who originally composed this church were received at the old meeting-house, and became members there, until a very commodious meeting-house was erected on Sawyer's Creek. Then a number were dismissed from that church, and were constituted into a church here about 1790, and Elder Thomas Etheridge became their pastor. The members of this and the Camden church are intermixed, and there are no natural bounds which divide the churches. There has been no great revival here, nor many members added since the constitution thereof. The church only contains about thirty-four members. There are no ministerial gifts in this church that we know of, except Elder Etheridge.

THE CHURCH AT KNOBSCROOK, PASQUOTANK COUNTY, NORTH CAROLINA,

WAS also a branch of the church in Camden. The meeting-house at which this church assembles is within two miles of Elizabeth City, the metropolis of Pasquotank. Several of the members who belonged to this church were baptized a good many years ago, and continued members of the church in Camden until about 1786, when they were constituted into a church.

The Gospel was first preached in this neighborhood by the Baptists about 1760. Elders Burges, Abbot, and Gamewell were some of the first ministers who preached here. Elder Burkitt used to attend them very frequently in 1771 and 1772. There were two brethren in the ministry, viz: *Smithson* and *Jennings*, in this branch of the church, who used to exercise their gifts in public; but they never became very popular. This church has never increased much since her constitution. They only contain, according to the accounts returned to the last Association, about twenty-five members. They have no settled pastor at present. They are attended by traveling ministers, and Elder Etheridge usually administers the ordinances to them. There are some very respectable members in this little church. Bailey Jackson, Esq., one of their members, has been a member of the General Assembly for that county several years.

13

From their last accounts we hope a revival is taking place in this church.

THE CHURCH AT FLATTY CREEK, IN THE SAME COUNTY.

THIS church is so called, because the members thereof live and the meeting-house stands near a creek so called, in Pasquotank county, to the east of Nixonton. It was formerly a branch of Camden church, and the members who were first received and baptized here belonged to that church. Elder Gamewell used to attend at Col. Lowry's, and baptized some members. Elder Abbot used to attend on Newbiggin Creek, and received some. Elder Burkitt used to attend statedly at William Freshwater's, in 1772. After a sufficient number were gathered, they were constituted into a church in 1790. There were two members in this church who used to exercise their gifts in the work of the ministry, viz: *Pendleton* and *Luten*. The church some years past were reduced to a very low ebb with respect to religion. The church got divided, and very little or no discipline was carried on in the church, and the ordinances entirely omitted, until very lately the church agreed to meet together, and come under re-examination, and such with whom the church had not fellowship to be set aside; which was accordingly done. Many of the old members died, and moved away in the time of the declension, so that the church, since her new settlement, only consisted of twenty-six members, nine of whom were baptized in a short time after. They inform us in their letter to the last Association that the Lord is carrying on a gracious work amongst them, and love and fellowship seem to abound. They have no settled pastor. Elder Martin Ross attends them, preaches, and administers the ordinances to them.

THE CHURCH AT BALLARD'S BRIDGE, IN CHOWAN COUNTY.

THE meeting-house at which this congregation assembles is about fourteen miles west of Edenton, and stands near a creek bridge, called *Ballard's* Bridge. The first Baptist minister of our order who preached near this place was Elder Burkitt. In the year 1772, he preached once or twice near Terrapin Hill. And by reason of a remarkable *dream* he had, occasioned him and Elder Dargan to preach several sermons in those regions; and we believe were attended with a peculiar blessing.

We do not place much ·confidence in dreams, but we believe that the Lord sometimes warns his people in dreams. This appears to be the case in the present instance, as related by Elder Burkitt. And from the happy effects which took place consequent thereon, and for the satisfaction of our readers how the Lord carries into effect his divine purposes, we will give a relation of the whole matter. In the year 1772, Elder Burkitt and Elder Abbot traveled together from Camden to Amelia, in Virginia, to preach the Gospel. On their return, they parted at Suffolk town; he intending for Camden, and Elder Burkitt for Edenton. It is about fifty-five miles from Suffolk to Edenton. This distance Elder Burkitt rode by himself; and, as he traveled the road, his mind seemed solemnly impressed with a sense of the *state* of that people, as there appeared to be none who professed religion, or seemed to care for their soul's concern. In the evening he took up his quarters near *Ballard's* Bridge, and the people of the house had no thought about religion. The small children were so well trained up in vice, that a small boy about nine or ten years of age had a pack of cards, and was challenging the whole company to play. Elder Burkitt being a good deal fatigued, went to bed; and that night he dreamed that an angel of God appeared to him, with a map in his hand, on which was drawn the figure of the roads, on which he said the Gospel had never been preached, viz: from Suffolk to Edenton, from Suffolk to the Great Bridge, and from Suffolk to the head of Perquimans River. This was represented in drawn lines on paper, and appeared so plainly in his view, that he drew off the figure next day in his journal. The angel of whom he dreamed, ordered Elder Burkitt, as he thought, to "Call for Elder *Jonathan Thomas*, or Elder *Dargan*, and make appointments, and offer to preach the Gospel to these people twice in each place; and if they refuse to hear, he should be clear from their blood." Accordingly, Elder Burkitt, without delay, applied to Elder Dargan, appointed, attended, and preached at the respective places. Elder *Welsh*, a resident near Ballard's Bridge, hearing that the Baptists were about to preach in these parts, and hearing of several appointments, was resolved to attend all of them, and hear all he could, as he expected to hear some strange doctrine from these *New-Light* Baptists.

Accordingly he attended; and as he often has said, the first or second sermon he was stricken with *conviction*, and never rested satisfied until he had a hope his soul was converted. He was baptized and joined the church near Wiccacon, which was a branch of the church at Cashie. Thus the work began about Ballard's Bridge. Elder Welsh became a pious zealous preacher of the Gospel. And soon after he began to preach, several others got converted in this neighborhood, and joined the same church, until a sufficient number were gathered, and then they were constituted into a church, in 1781. Elder Welsh became their pastor, and continued several years, until it was the will of his Lord and Master to call him home. The church was then a few years without a pastor. At length Elder John M'Cabe became the pastor thereof, and continues in that office to the present time. They have experienced no great revivals of late. Their yearly meeting is the Saturday before the second Sunday in August; and quarterly once in three months from that time throughout the year. Their number at present is about seventy-nine.

CHAPTER XI.

History of the five churches that compose the Bertie Union
Meeting; containing the churches belonging to the
Association between Roanoke, Chowan, and Meherrin,
viz: The Bertie church, the church at Cashie, Wiccacon, Meherrin and Connaritey.

THESE seven churches last treated of
compose the *Union Meeting* east of Chowan
river; we shall next in place give a short
description of the *Bertie Union Meeting*, and
first of the

BERTIE CHURCH.

This church was so called because it was
the first church constituted in that county,
and many of the members thereof, at the
first establishment of the same, were scattered over the country in different neighborhoods. But at present there are four
constituted churches in the country. The
church at Cashie was the next to this, and
when that church was gathered in the same
county, this still retained the name of the
Bertie Church, and that the name of *Cashie
Church*. This church was originally at
her first constitution what was then called

a *Regular Baptist* church, and we think we can boast that we have never as yet departed from our original principles. This church was the first in the *Kehukee* Association that raised a bar of communion against the members baptized in unbelief, and has ever since, in the minutes, stood the first in order on the list. The meeting-house stands in the upper end of the county, about three miles from Norfleet's ferry, on Roanoke river, and about two from Sandy-Run. The first minister of the Baptist society who preached in this neighborhood, of our order, was Elder *Thomas Pope*, and through his instrumentality the church was gathered here ; and Elder *Abington*, who was converted under the ministry of Elder *Pope*, joined this church, and at length became the pastor thereof about the year 1764, and continued until his death in the pastoral function. After the death of Elder *Abington* the church was greatly reduced. "Iniquity abounded and the love of many waxed cold." Disorders and divisions took place amongst many of the members, but there were a few who remained steadfast and orderly. The great desire these had for a reformation and revival in the church, induced them to petition the Association in 1772, for advice in this matter. The Association taking the same under consideration, ap-

pointed Elders Jonathan Thomas, John
Moore and Lemuel Burkitt to attend them,
and advise them to such measures as were
likely to regain a general fellowship in the
church, who accordingly attended, and in
conference assembled, advised the church to
relate their experiences and come under re-
examination ; and for all disorderly members, and such as with whom the church
had not fellowship, to be excluded. Which
they agreed to and accordingly put in practice, and a majority of members were received, and some were refused. The church
thus established on a new constitution made
choice of Elder Burkitt for their pastor,
who was accordingly ordained by Elders
Thomas and Meglamre, November, 1773.
The succeeding year a very considerable revival took place in this church. Many attended on the word preached, appeared
wonderfully affected, and an uncommon
power was manifest amongst the people.
Some would fall to the ground as suddenly
as if stricken by lightning, and would to appearance remain in a state of insensibility
for hours, not able to move a limb. Some
would be taken with a tremor as if they had
a violent ague. Others would be so powerfully affected, they would be exercised
nearly like a person with the hiccup. And
many were truly affected at heart who made

little or no noise. Thus the work began, increased and was carried on, so that Elder Burkitt within two years after he took the charge of this church, baptized nearly one hundred and fifty. In the time of the revival there was a branch gathered in Northampton county, N. C., on and near Pottacasy Creek, where there has since been a meeting-house built, and to which a considerable part of this church belongs, and have been a long time ripe for constitution, but will not as yet consent to it. Another branch was gathered in Bertie on Connaritsy, which is now constituted into a church, and has become a member of the Association. After a few years this extraordinary work in a measure subsided, and many of the old members died, and a considerable number moved to the western countries, and some were excommunicated for disorders, and but few added, so that the number of members was greatly reduced, and the state of religion very cold until the year 1801, when Elder Burkitt took a journey to the States of Tennessee and Kentucky, and was absent from his church on the journey nearly four months. When he returned his soul seemed full of love, and his religious exercises greatly revived at seeing the great revival in Kentucky. His church seemed very glad to see him return, and soon after a gracious revival took place again in this church. The congregation increased. Evening meetings again were appointed, and more attended them than used to attend Sunday meetings before. The word preached was usually attended with a blessing. The hearts of the people seemed open. A fast was proclaimed by the church, and the Lord heard the prayers of his church. And commonly when a revival takes place in a church, the people of God are made greatly to desire it previous to its commencement. The youth appeared to be the first imprest with a religious concern. Seldom a meeting after the revival took place but what some offered for membership—four, five, six; and as many as eleven have been baptized at a time. In about two years as many as one hundred and fifty have been baptized. Many traveling ministers visited us in the time of revival, and their labors seemed blessed. As this church was the first that experienced a revival in this part of the Association, so the work spread through the adjacent churches. Some of almost all ages, from sixteen to eighty have been called in and joined this church. Several worthy characters have been added to the church in the revival. Several in the commission of the peace, and others in office have been baptized here. And although the work was not so rapid in its progress as in some other places, and we might reasonably expect that some chaff as well as good wheat would be gathered into the garner, yet we can bless God, we have not as yet had occasion to exclude one member from fellowship since the revival commenced.

Since the first constitution of this church, a few ministering brethren have been raised up in it, and called to the work of the ministry, viz: Elders Amos Harrell, Robert Moral, M'Allister Vinson, Pitts Kirby, Frederick Futrall, James Rutland, and James Vinson. Elder Harrell has been dismissed, and is now a member of the church at Connoho, and become their pastor. Elder Moral was dismissed to the church on Meherrin, in Southampton, Virginia, and become their pastor. Pitts Kirby and Frederick Futrall are dismissed from the church militant to the church triumphant. James Vinson was a member of that branch of the church on Pottacasy, and a resident of Northampton county—he was a pious, good man. He exercised his gift several years, but never had the charge of any church. He was in the commission of the peace, and was a member of the Convention for the deliberation of the Federal Constitution. He was sheriff of the county of Northampton the year before he died. He departed this life December, 1798. The number of members at present in the Bertie church is about two hundred and twenty. Their yearly meeting is holden at Sandy Run, the Saturday before the fourth Sunday in September. And quarterly the same time in December, March, and June. And statedly at the same time once a month. Quarterly meetings at Pottacasy are holden the Saturday before the second Sunday in January, April, July, and October.

THE CHURCH AT CASHIE, BERTIE COUNTY, NORTH CAROLINA.

THE Gospel, by the Baptists, was first preached here by Elder Dargan, who was formerly a resident of South Carolina ; but by the direction of Divine Providence, he moved into this neighborhood, and settled near Cashie. Before a meeting-house was built he usually preached at a Mr. Sowell's, and at other private houses in the settlement, and was greatly persecuted by a few, who used all their influence to prevent him from preaching, particularly Capt John Campbell. But vain were his attempts ; for the Baptists were now, in a measure, like the Israelites in Egypt, the more they afflicted them, the more they multiplied.

Some of the first fruits of the Gospel here were Mrs. Hyman, Joseph Jordan, Sen., a respectable character in Cashie Neck, Prudence Maer, Margaret Read, George Davis and wife, James Yates, George Capeheart, William Fleetwood, &c. This church was first gathered and constituted on the *Separate Order*, but came into fellowship with us after the Revolution took place at the Falls of Tar River. In process of time their meeting-house was erected, about one mile east of Windsor, and by additions, is now become a commodious house of worship, being about forty-two feet square.

This church has had its revivals and declensions. Soon after its establishment a very considerable work attended the labors of Elder Dargan, and Elder Walker, and others who traveled through this church. Many souls were awakened and got converted, and joined the church, and so continued for several years. But, after some time, Elder Dargan died, the members grew cold in religion, and for several years the state of religion seemed to be languishing. The church at this time was very destitute of ministerial gifts, until it pleased the great Head of the church to raise up Elder Spivey, a man of distinguished piety and zeal in the cause of the adorable Redeemer. He was baptized in 1789, and received a member of the church at Skewarkey; and in 1790 was dismissed from this church, and became a member of the church at Cashie: and in 1794, July 6, was ordained pastor of the same, by the hands of Elders Ross and Hendry.

The church before this, being without a pastor, had become very remiss in their duty, and but little discipline was observed in the church; and of course we might expect disorders to creep in, which was the case here. But in conference, in 1790, the church was purged, and such only as had fellowship with God and their own consciences, and with one another, were continued in membership. For several years after, there were but small additions by baptism until 1802. In January, 1802, a revival begun to take place here. Elder Burkitt attended the quarterly meeting at that time. Religion appeared very cold; but few people attended, and they seemed very hard and inattentive. He preached, prayed, and sung, but no good effect seemed apparently to follow. Towards the close of worship, he told the congregation he had done all that was in his power, and his efforts were very feeble and unsuccessful; it was only the Lord that could *bless* it, and that he could do no more than pray for them, " and if there was any person in the congregation who saw himself in a lost, condemned state by reason of sin, if he would come up to the table, at the pulpit, he would pray to the Lord for him." Accordingly Mrs. *Gillam* came forward and kneeled down at the table, with one or two more. The people had never seen an instance of the like before, and beholding their great desire for the salvation of their souls so earnestly expressed, it had a very great effect on the people; and Brother Moses Gillam, the husband of Mrs. Gillam, seemed greatly affected. So that we had a happy meeting at last. About eight days before this, in Cashie Neck, another singular instance took place, which was a mean in the hand of the Lord to begin the work there. Mr. *Samuel Maer*, a very wicked man, and a ringleader in vice, was converted on his death-bed; and the solemnity of his dying speeches had a salutary effect on some. Some time after the January quarterly meeting, in 1802, Elder Spivey was again called to the precious work of baptizing. Mrs. Gillam and some others were the first fruits of the revival. Several more were soon converted and baptized; and at April meeting following, twelve related their experience and went down into the water together. And at every monthly meeting after, for nearly two years, some

were received. Sometimes ten, twelve, fifteen, twenty, and *twenty-two* at one time.
Thus the work began and increased; and
the Lord magnifies the riches of his free
grace in carrying on his work by simple
means. He is a sovereign agent; he can
and does work when and where he pleases;
and by strong means, weak means, or no
means. As was the case in this revival,
everything seemed to conspire to carry on
the work. The work of the Lord progressing at Cashie, about two hundred were
baptized in eighteen months—sundry of
whom were men of great respectability.
Three brethren, members of this church,
have been called to the work of the ministry in this revival, viz: Elders James Ross,
James B. Jordan, and Moses Gillam; who
seem promising, and we hope the Lord will
make a blessing to the people. The number of members at present is about two
hundred and twenty-one.

Their meetings are holden monthly, at
Cashie meeting-house, on the Saturday before the first Sunday. The Saturday before
the first Sunday in April is yearly meeting;
and quarterly once in every three months
after. The fourth Sunday in every month
meetings are holden at Rock-whist chapel,
in Cashie neck. And the third Sunday, at
the Indian woods meeting-house.

14

THE CHURCH NEAR WICCACON, BERTIE
COUNTY, NORTH CAROLINA.

This church was a branch of the church at Cashie. Elder Dargan's ministry was very much blessed; and the work spread down into the lower end of the county, and about Cochran's ferry, on Chowan river, at several private houses in the neighborhood, and at Capt. John Freeman's, meetings were holden, and a blessing attended; several were converted in the neighborhood, and were baptized. Some of the first fruits of the Gospel in these parts were John Freeman, Esq., a man of eminent piety, and very useful in church and State; Capt. Joshua Freeman, the sketches of whose biography were heretofore mentioned; Hardy Hunter, Elder Hendry, and others. After a sufficient number were gathered, they were constituted into a church in 1789. This church has and does contain as many worthy members as perhaps any in the union. Their meeting-house (which is a commodious building sufficient to accommodate a thousand people) stands on the lands formerly belonging to Capt. John Freeman, in Bertie county, about four miles from Colerain. After the death of Elder Dargan, this church was attended by Elder Welsh, who served them as an occasional pastor until his death ; and after his death, the church made choice of Elder *Hendry* (who was born in Ireland, and was converted and became a member of this church after his settlement in this neighborhood) to be their pastor; who continues in the pastoral function to the present time.

There are many respectable characters in this church, who have always stood faithful, zealous and orderly members of society ; and although at times the church has not increased so fast as at other times, yet the brethren have generally been lively in religion, and were not so frequently complaining of coldness as some other churches. There has been a considerable revival of late in this church. About sixty have been baptized in two years. Their number at present is about one hundred and seventy-three. Their meetings are holden the Saturday before the third Sunday in every month. Quarterly in September, December, March and June.

THE CHURCH ON CONNARITSY, BERTIE, NORTH CAROLINA.

This church was a branch of the old Bertie church; and the time it was in this state, meetings were holden at the houses of Robert Rhodes and James Jenkins.   Conferences were holden here, and the ordinances administered, until about 1797 or '98. This branch was dismissed from the body, and became a regular constituted church, and Elder Northam became the pastor, who continued in his pastoral office a few years, then removed to Guilford county, North Carolina. After the removal of Elder Northam, Elder Harrell supplied his place, as an occasional pastor. This church for some time omitted joining the Association, until the year 1803, at Connoho. This church, after constitution, increased very little for some time. They remained very cold a considerable time after the neighboring churches were blessed with a revival. But of late the Lord has visited them. Nearly fifty members have been added in a short time. The church has never as yet built a meeting-house. Meetings are holden at the house of James Jenkins on Connaritsy swamp; and at Jumping-Run chapel, which stands in the county aforesaid—not far distant from Pugh's tavern—a house of worship originally intended for the use of the Episcopal church, but now occupied by the Baptists. Their number is about seventy. Their meetings are holden the Saturday before the first Sunday in every month.

THE CHURCH ON MEHERRIN, HERTFORD COUNTY, NORTH CAROLINA.

This church was originally gathered and constituted on the *Free-will* plan. Elders Joseph Parker, William Parker, Winfield, and others of that order, frequently preached here. Elder William Parker was a resident in this neighborhood; who after being baptized, and giving himself a member of the church here, began to preach. At what time the church was constituted on this plan we are not able to say. Elder W. Parker was in the exercise of the pastoral function, as early as the year 1773. How long before we are not able to say. The customary way with him in receiving members was to baptize all who were willing and requested it. In consequence of which he baptized many, as he required no experience previous to their admission. But after a meeting-house was erected on Pottacasy, and a branch of Bertie church was gathered there, a number of the members, who before belonged to Parker's church, left that church and joined the branch at Pottacasy. This frequently being the case, the Free-will church decreased very fast until the death of William Parker. After his death the church requested Elder Burkitt to attend them, which he did and preached to them

statedly for some time. They at last concluded to come under re-examination and
be organized on the orthodox plan, and join
the Kehukee Association. It was carried
into effect. Elder Burkitt and several members from his church attended at a time appointed for that business, and a small number was received; and as a church of Christ
professing the same faith, on which our Association is established, they petitioned the
Association for admission, and their petition
was granted in the year 1794. A few of
the members who had left the church and
joined Pottacasy, returned back after the revolution; but the most continued as they
were. This caused the church to be but
few in number. They remained without
a pastor for some time; and increased but
very little. Elder Burkitt attended them
occasionally. In 1802, Elder Wall moved
from Southampton, Virginia, (who was a
member of the church in Sussex), and gave
himself a member of this church, and became pastor thereof.

*The work of the Lord increasing about
Sandy Run, Pottacasy, &c.*—The work began here in the summer of 1802, and the
Lord has carried on a most glorious work in
this church. In less than two years, about
one hundred and sixty have been baptized.
Elder Wall has baptized as many as twenty-

three in one day. Some very respectable
characters have been added to this church
in and about Murfreesborough. The meeting-house at which the church assembled
was of a small dimension before, but has
been by addition made a very commodious
house of worship, since the revival commenced. It stands about one mile south of
Murfreesborough. Their number of members at present is about one hundred and
seventy-five. Their meetings are holden
the Saturday before the first Sunday in
every month. Quarterly meetings in May,
August, November, and February.

CHAPTER XII.

History of the Flat-Swamp Union Meeting, comprehend-
ing the churches at Flat-Swamp, Skewarkey, Connoho,
Great-Swamp, Morattuck, Connetoe, Cross-Roads, and
Little Connetoe church. 2. An account of the churches
at Scuppernong, Pungo, and Matamuskeet.

HAVING given a description of those five
churches that compose the Bertie Union
Meeting, we shall next proceed to describe
the churches in the Kehukee Association
that compose the *Flat-Swamp Union Meeting,* and first of

THE FLAT SWAMP CHURCH, PITT COUNTY,
NORTH CAROLINA.

About the year 1776, the spirit of the
Lord began to breathe upon some of the
dry bones in the valley of Flat-Swamp and
the Connetoe settlements. Several persons
were seriously impressed with the importance of religion; and accordingly an invitation was given to Elder Jonathan Thomas
(pastor of the church at Tosniot) to come
and visit them. Accordingly he did so, and
preached successively for some time, and
his labors were blessed; so that numbers
embraced the doctrines of free grace. Several persons were received on experience,
and were baptized, and became a branch of
the church at Tosniot, in Edgecombe county, North Carolina.

In the year 1771, Elder Thomas informed them he thought they were ripe for constitution, prepared the plan, and set them
on the business; which was nearly effected,
when Providence put a stop to the business
by calling this great man of God out of
time, and removing him to his eternal rest.

Another circumstance happened which
greatly procrastinated the business of a
Constitution, there were two candidates for
the pastoral care of the church, viz. J. Page
and J. Stansell; but Page ultimately suc-

ceeded, who was ordained at the same time the church was constituted, with the assistance of the father and brother of the said deceased, Elder Thomas, who were both in the ministerial function at that time. The establishment took place in the beginning of the year 1776.

Elder Page being thus called to the pastoral office in this church, laboring with great zeal amongst them; and his labors were greatly blessed, the church increased, the work spread farther, and now their place for the meeting of the church was on Flat-Swamp. The meeting-house which the church meets at is in Pitt county, not far from Flat-Swamp.

This church has been very fruitful. She has become the mother of four daughters, or constituted churches, and part of another church, viz: the church at Skewarkey, the church at Great-Swamp, the church at Connoho, the church at Little Connetoe, and part of the church at the Cross-Roads. The church at Flat-Swamp had her ebbing and flowing, but to the great joy of those who wished well to Zion, she still increased and her bounds became very extensive, and her members numerous.

In 1787, a petition was handed in from a branch of this church at *Skewarkey*, requesting a dismission, in order for constitu-

tion ; and although they met with some de-
lays and difficulties, it was at length granted in 1794. Another petition was handed
from the branch on *Connoho Creek*, and obtained their request in 1795. Before this
the church at Flat-Swamp began to experience severe difficulties ; as the love of some
of her members began to wax cold, it gave
an opportunity to the enemy of souls to sow
seeds of discord amongst them, which
caused the *Arminians* and *Universalists* to
look out of their dens, where they had been
driven by the refulgent beams of Gospel
truths. The former (to wit) Arminianism,
prevailed but little amongst them, being an
old doctrine they had been very well acquainted with before conversion. But the
latter having been previously broached by
one of their former preachers, viz : *John
Stansill*, and one that was tolerable arch,
cunning, and insinuating, many of her
members were carried away with his craft,
through the subtlety of Satan. And even
to this day, some that were excommunicated
from the privileges of the church, when Satan made this havoc in her, have not been
restored to fellowship again. And although
Universalism began to haul in his horns
again, yet the church continued at ebb tide;
no ingathering for several years, even until
the death of her pastor in the year 1795,

at which time, although she had raised several useful preachers, yet was destitute of all ministerial gifts in her. In this destitute situation they raised their cries to the Lord of the harvest, to send forth laborers—to raise up, or send to them one to go in and out before them. The Lord in answer to their prayers was pleased to send them Elder Joseph Biggs, a youth eminent for his gifts, piety, and zeal; who had been baptized and received a member of the church at Skewarkey. The church gave him a call to take the pastoral care of them, February, 1796. But in answer to his request ordination was deferred until February, 1797. And as it was observed before, the church being in a cold state, abounding with disorders, no ingathering, many excommunications, and very little decorum, conferences were very thin. Often did her young pastor sit in conference with six, seven, or eight members; and the few who did attend endeavored to stir up the rest to a sense of their duty : but often did their labors prove unsuccessful. And often had their pastor reason to cry, " my leanness ! my leanness ! and who hath believed our report ?" And sometimes truly did he think of giving over the pursuit; but being preserved and supported by an invisible hand he held on his way, through many trials and sore conflicts, looking to the Lord, hoping that the time to favor Zion was not far distant. Under God he was made a means to prevail on his brethren, members of several churches, to visit each other, and pray with, and for one another, and Zion's God at last heard their cries ; and in the latter end of the year 1800, there were several added to her number, so that the work gradually progressed until the spring and summer of 1801 and 1802. The gates of Zion seemed truly to be crowded with converts ; so that in order for the church to be able to hear experiences of all that wished to relate them and offer for membership, the conference has been under the necessity of dividing into two bodies, each sitting at one time, in the meeting-house. Then, surely, the shouts of heaven-born souls were heard in Israel's camps. The congregations now crowded, and the distressed from every quarter called on the ministers to pray for them. This church, in about three years has had an addition of about one hundred and forty-two members.

There are several worthy characters in this church, who have ever adorned their profession, particularly that eminent servant of our Lord Jesus, Colonel Nathan Mayo, who has been a member of this church almost from its origin, and has been an ornament to the church and to the Baptist society in general. The members of this church, it is presumed, will never forget his usefulness as a member of their society in the execution of church discipline; and his usefulness as a member of civil society. He is now dismissed from this body and become a member in the church at Connetoe, Cross-Roads. The church at Flat-Swamp, after all her dismissions for new constitutions, contains about one hundred and thirteen members.

THE CHURCH AT SKEWARKEY, MARTIN COUNTY, NORTH CAROLINA.

This church was once a branch of the Flat-Swamp church; and was attended as such by her pastor John Page for several years. Conferences were holden, discipline kept up, and the ordinances administered to them as a branch of that church for some time; and by his labors the work seemed to flourish. At length they became too numerous to continue a branch; and as they had a young man raised amongst them of promising talents, they concluded they were ripe for exercising church discipline; therefore petitioned the body to which they belonged, for a dismission, in order to become a constituted body; the petition being granted, they were constituted, and their young preacher, Elder *Martin Ross*, came under examination, and the laying on of hands of the Presbytery, in the year of 1787, by Elders Lemuel Burkitt and John Page.

This church experienced some additions for several years. But like the rest of the churches, in a time of coldness she experienced a share; although her pastor served her, as also in traveling and preaching elsewhere, with indefatigable labors.

In the year 1791, a petition was received from a number of her members, at a remote distance, for dismission, in order to become a constituted church at *Morattuck;* which was granted them. And in the year 1796, Elder Martin Ross, their pastor, moved for a *dismission* from them to join the Yoppim church. And at the same time Elder Joseph Biggs also petitioned for *dismission* to join the Flat-Swamp church. With reluctance they were both granted; and she now was stript of all ministerial gifts. She therefore groaned under her affliction, until the kind hand of Providence favored her in raising up Elder *Luke Ward*, a member of that church, to the work of the ministry, who in the year 1799 was ordained pastor of this church, by Elders Joseph Biggs and Amariah Biggs.

The Lord has been pleased to raise up and call to the ministry a number of ministers in this church. As many as eight who were, and now are members of this church, viz: Martin Ross, Aaron Spivey, Joseph Biggs, Luke Ward, Abraham Tice, Hartell Cherry, John Bennet, pastor of a church in Anson county, North Carolina, and James Daniel, who was a very respectable member of this church nearly three years, and departed this life September, 1803. Having great faith, rejoicing in the Lord to the great surprise and satisfaction of all who attended him in his last illness. The Skewarkey church was the last, in the Flat-Swamp Union Meeting, that experienced a revival. The work seemed more gradual and appears to continue. In the year 1803, thirty-four members were dismissed to be constituted into a church on Smithwick's Creek, which was expected to be done in November last. Their number of members at present is about one hundred and thirty-nine. The meeting-house at which this church assembles is about one mile from Williamston.

THE CHURCH ON CONNOHO, MARTIN COUNTY, NORTH CAROLINA.

This church was formerly a branch of

Flat-Swamp church; and obtained a dismission in the year of 1794, in order for a
constitution. And she became a constituted body accordingly the same year, and
called on Elder Amos Harrell, a member
of the church at Sandy Run, to take the
pastoral charge. Elder Harrell had been
before ordained on the itinerant plan. He
obeyed the call, became the pastor of said
church, and continues to serve them in
that capacity. Connoho church, like others,
is well acquainted with a cold, wintry state
in religion. Yet she has, with her sisters
in the same union, experienced in some
good degree the late revival, so that she became numerous by its effects; and therefore,
in the year 1803, she received a petition,
and granted a dismission to some of her
members, who, with some dismissed from
the Flat-Swamp, were constituted at the
Cross-Roads. The place where this church
assembles is at a house called the Log
Chapel, which stands on Connoho Creek,
about six miles from Taylor's Ferry, on
Roanoke. Their number of members at
present is about sixty-six; and the time of
holding their meetings is the Saturday before the third Sunday in every month.

THE CHURCH ON GREAT-SWAMP, PITT COUNTY, NORTH CAROLINA,

Was formerly a branch of Flat-Swamp church, which was called the Tar River branch; but obtained a dismission from the body in the year of 1795, in order to become a constituted church, which was done in a short time after; and called Elder Noah Tison to take the pastoral care thereof; who was ordained on the itinerant plan, and a member of the church at the Red Banks, on Tar River. He obeyed the call, and serves them in that capacity (when able), until the present time. The Great-Swamp church being the last of the branches in the Flat-Swamp church that was constituted in the time religion was at its low ebb, she of course has not felt so much coldness as the rest, and in this revival has experienced very considerable additions; and, as she has not dismissed any for constitution, her number at present is greater than any church in the Flat-Swamp union, and still appears to be in a prosperous state. Although the pastor is a man much afflicted, yet the church is not neglected among the families of Israel; for by the zeal of the pastor, and the Lord's raising up two young preachers in the church, and the friendly visits of others,

15

she has the Word preached, and the ordinances administered, as duly as any of the
churches in union with her. Their meeting-house stands in Pitt county, on the
north side of Tar River, within eight or
nine miles of Greensville. Their number
is one hundred and thirty-nine.

MORATTUCK CHURCH, WASHINGTON COUNTY, NORTH CAROLINA,

Was first gathered through the instrumentality of Elders Silas Mercer and John
Page, who were succeeded by Elder Martin Ross. A few were connected in a church
relation; but, like many other churches,
they had some unworthy characters among
them, which were very troublesome, and
proved to be a fatal stroke towards their
downfall; so that the church in a little time
became extinct. But a few of her members,
who delighted in church fellowship, became
members of the church at Skewarkey (although at a great distance), and endeavored
to attend there once in three months, for
some time, until 1791, when they petitioned
the body to which they then belonged for a
dismission, in order to become a constituted
body again at the same place; which they
obtained, and were again united in a small
body; and through the long, tedious night

of coldness and spiritual darkness, this church had, to appearance, only a *name to live*. She was attended by Elder Martin Ross until his removal from Skewarkey to Yoppim ; and afterwards, very generally, by Elder Amariah Biggs; but each attended them, and served as an occasional pastor. But, in the latter end of the year 1801 and beginning of 1802, the church became more lively, and also experienced some additions, which stirred them up; so that, in 1802, they gave Elder Amariah Biggs a call to take the pastoral care of them, which call he accepted, and is now considered their existing pastor. Although this church, in the beginning of 1803, had some severe trials and difficulties; yet she appears at present to have surmounted them all, and seems to be in a flourishing state. Her pastor is very attentive to her, and very industrious in his labors elsewhere. The meeting-house at which this church assembles is within about two or three miles of Plymouth. Their number, at present, is about sixty-five.

THE CHURCH AT CONNETOE CROSS-ROADS, EDGECOMBE COUNTY, NORTH CAROLINA.

Part of the members of this church formerly belonged to the church on Connoho, and part belonged to the church at Flat-Swamp,who obtained dismissions from their respective bodies, and embodied in a church at the Cross-Roads. They were constituted a church the Saturday before the second Sunday in July, 1803, with the assistance of Elders Joseph Biggs and Jonathan Cherry. On the same day, they gave Elder Cherry a call to take the pastoral care of them (who had some time before been ordained on the itinerant plan); which call he accepted, and was received, and continues pastor of the said church. The church being constitued in the time of a revival of religion, and composed mostly of young members lately converted, has many pleasing prospects before it ; and seems possessed with great confidence at present. They have some very useful lay-members. Their number at present is sixty-eight.

THE LITTLE CONNETOE CHURCH

Was formerly a branch of Flat-Swamp church, and had quarterly meetings held in that branch for several years, attended by the pastor of Flat-Swamp church. But in 1803, they obtained a dismission from the body, in order for constitution at Little Connetoe Creek meeting-house; which accordingly took place on the Saturday before the fourth Sunday in July, 1803, assisted by Elders Joseph Biggs, Jonathan Cherry and Joshua Barnes. And at the same time, the church gave Elder *Thomas Ross*, one of her members, a call to take the pastoral care of them; and although the call was not at that time accepted, yet on Saturday before the fourth Sunday in September following, he obeyed the call, and was ordained by Elders Joseph Biggs, Jonathan Cherry and Luke Ward, and was received as pastor of said church. Their number at present is about forty-three. These two churches were received members of our Association at their last sitting.

There are three more churches to the east of these, which, by reason of their distance from other churches, and other inconveniences attending them, are not connected with any Union Meetings as we know of; but as they belong to the Kehukee Association, we think it our duty to give a few sketches of their history. And first,

THE CHURCH AT SCUPPERNONG, TYRREL COUNTY, NORTH CAROLINA.

Some of the first ministers of our order, who preached near Scuppernong river, were Elders Page, Stansill and Mercer. Their labors were blessed; several were admitted to the ordinance of baptism, and after there was a competent number received, the church was constituted about the year 1785. Elder Amariah Biggs took the care of the church, and continued in that office several years; but is, at present, pastor of the church at Morattuck. The labors of Elder Biggs have been blessed here. A revival has taken place in some parts of the church, and within two years a considerable number have been added. Their meeting-house stands a few miles from Scuppernong river. Their number is about fifty-eight.

THE CHURCH AT PUNGO, BEAUFORT COUNTY, NORTH CAROLINA.

Near this place was a church of the Free-will order, of whom Elder Winfield was pastor. But it was the will of divine Providence that the Gospel of the free grace of God in Christ Jesus should be preached here; and sundry persons hearing, embraced the truth, and were constituted into a church; and the church is now under the care of Elder James M'Cabe. This church has experienced but little of the late revival. Their number at present is about thirty-two.

THE CHURCH AT MATTAMUSKEET, HYDE COUNTY, NORTH CAROLINA.

From the remote distance that this church is from us, we have but a small acquaintance with her state and standing. The local situation of the church, as it is environed with swamps, deserts, creeks, rivers, &c., renders it very inconvenient to get at. This church has several years been a member of our Association; but she seldom attends at our annual appointments. Her number of members, according to the last accounts, was about sixty. They are now under the pastoral care of William Carrowan.

CHAPTER XIII.

1. The Swift-Creek Union Meeting—Falls of Tar River, Reedy Creek.—2. Biographical Sketches of Elder Walker.—3. Fishing-Creek Church, Elder C. Daniel, Kehukee, Rocky-Swamp, Quonkey, Sandy-Creek, Maple Spring, and Haywood's meeting-house Churches. Memoirs of Elder Mercer, C. Daniel, &c.

In this chapter we propose to give an account of those churches belonging to the Kehukee Association which compose the

Swift-Creek. Union Meeting. The churches belonging to this union are between Roanoke and Tar river, west of Flat-Swamp Union Meeting. This meeting took its name from the place it was first holden at, which was on Swift-Creek, Edgecombe county, at Prospect Chapel. We shall first begin with the

CHURCH AT THE FALLS OF TAR RIVER, NASH COUNTY, NORTH CAROLINA.

This is an ancient and respectable church. According to the best accounts we can get, this church was constituted on Swift Creek, by Elders C. Daniel and John Moore, in the year 1757. Whether the church was constituted on the *Free-will* or *Regular* Baptist order we are not able to say. Elder John Moore was their pastor a number of years, while the church was on the regular plan. But in 1780, he took a dismission from the church and moved out of the neighborhood. After this, *Emmanuel Skinner*, a worthy member of this church, being an ordained minister, and raised up in the church, supplied the place of a pastor, but was never appointed by the church to that office. In September, 1797, he took a dismission from the church and moved to Cumberland, in Tennessee. August, 1795, Elder Nathan Gilbert (a respectable character), who was an ordained minister, joined this church by a letter of dismission from Scuppernong church, who supplied the place of a pastor after the removal of Elder Skinner. In 1798, the church by unanimous vote, requested Elder Gilbert to take charge of the church as pastor, but his mind was not to do it at that time. In 1802, he accepted the call and is now the existing pastor.

After the revolution in the Association, this church continued in the regular Baptist Association (viz: that part of the Kehukee Association that refused to accede to our measures) until March, 1781, when this church, being dissatisfied with the proceedings of that Association, withdrew from them, and was in communion with no other church until November of the same year, when she joined communion with the church on Fishing Creek, at Daniel's meetinghouse, under the care of Elder Silas Mercer. Soon after this she joined our association again. We do not learn that there have been any great revivals in this church, since her constitution, until lately. The ingatherings have been gradual. At the Association in 1801, the number in fellowship was only fifty-nine. Soon after this a glorious revival took place here, and by the Association in 1802, there were eighty members added by baptism. And from that to the

Association in 1803, seventy-four more were received.   Eighty members were dismissed this year for constitution ; and are now constituted on Town Creek, and appear to be in a flourishing state.   This constitution has increased already to one hundred and twenty-two, and is under the care of Elder Winstead.   The meeting-house at which the church assembles is a very commodious house, sufficient to accommodate a large assembly of people, and stands on the north of Tar river, a small distance from the Falls.   There are, at present, four preachers in this church, viz : Nathan Gilbert, pastor, Jordan Sherred, an ordained minister, and Lewis Wells and John Atkinson who are young preachers.   The number of members at present is about one hundred and thirty-four.   There have been, and still continue to be, several respectable members of society here ; who have a long time adorned the profession they have made ; and their memory will always be dear to this church and to all their acquaintance.

THE CHURCH ON REEDY CREEK, WARREN COUNTY, NORTH CAROLINA.

Doctor Josiah Hart was the first preacher of the Baptist persuasion who preached here.   He came about the year 1750, and preached and baptized.   Soon after him,

Wm. Washington, James Smart, Samuel Davis, William Walker, and others joined in the work of preaching and baptizing, all upon what is called the *Free-will* plan, and numbers came and were baptized. But nothing like a church constitution. Wm. Walker was chosen from among the rest, and was called their pastor. Things went on thus until 1755. In May, that year, Elder John Gano, from the north, visited this place, and seeing the situation of affairs, probably represented the case, on his return, to the Philadelphia Association, who, the fall following, delegated Elders Peter Peterson Vanhorne and Benjamin Miller to attend, and settle churches upon the doctrines of Free Grace, and according to Gospel order. They attended accordingly, and received all the baptized persons that in a judgment of charity were born again. And of the great numbers baptized only about ten more were received. William Walker was received as a member, but not admitted as a preacher. The members thus received were then constituted, and joined in covenant, adopted the confession of faith, and were declared a Gospel church of Christ. At the departure of the aforementioned brethren, the oversight of the church was committed to Elder Thomas Pope; who attended at times, and preached and administered the ordinances

to them.   Elder Thomas Tully also visited
here occasionally.   The impressions that
William Walker professed to have with
respect to preaching the Gospel still continuing with him, he began again to exercise.   The church approved of his gifts,
and was solemnly called upon to take the
oversight of them.   He accepted the call
and went to Charleston, accompanied by
some of the brethren here, and was there
(probably) ordained in the year 1756.   He
returned, took upon him the pastoral
charge, and continued in that appointment
until his death, which was in the year
1784.

There were several preachers raised up
in this church, viz: Elders Charles Daniel,
Thomas Daniel, and William Lancaster.
After the death of Elder Walker, Elder
William Lancaster supplied the place of a
pastor until February, 1786.   At which
time, after mature deliberation and prayer
to God for direction, the church agreed to
call *Lewis Moore,* a resident of Johnston
county, to take the pastoral care of them.
He accepted the call, and was ordained to
office by fasting, prayer, and laying on of
hands; and continued in that office until
1798, when he removed to Kentucky.

The same year the church made choice
of Elder Moses Bennet (a preacher of promising talents, who had been raised up in

this church) for their pastor, who still continues to hold that office. Elder Pemberton who had been in the exercise of his gifts in this church, was ordained at the same time.

Elder Philemon Bennet was raised up in this church and ordained in 1801. There have been several happy revivals of religion in this church, but chiefly under the ministry of Elder Walker. It is true there have been happy times, and considerable additions under the subsequent ministers, but they were only as the gleanings of the vintage in Elder Walker's day. Their number of members at present is about seventy. Their meetings are holden the Saturday before the third Sunday in every month.

BIOGRAPHICAL SKETCH OF ELDER WILLIAM WALKER.

The time and place of his nativity to us are unknown. He settled in Warren county, between the years 1750 and 55. He at first became a Free-will Baptist preacher, as was mentioned before. After he embraced the doctrines of grace, and was regularly authorized as a Gospel minister, he was very zealously engaged in preaching, and his labors were very much blessed.

His labors in the ministry were not confined to Reedy Creek only, but he traveled and preached in a number of places, and was an humble instrument of bringing many precious souls to the knowledge of the truth. After he was established in the truth of the doctrines of the Gospel, he was never known to court the smiles or fear the frowns of any man. God's free electing, everlasting, unchangeable love through Christ to poor sinners was his favorite theme; whilst he pressed the necessity of the new birth, in consequence of our fallen, degenerate state by nature. He was loved and esteemed by all ranks of people. The labors of his life which closed his ministry here on earth, were Saturday and Sunday, October the third and fourth, 1784. On Saturday he attended a funeral at Mr. Honorias Powell's, and preached from Deut. xxxii. 29. *O! that they were wise*, &c. In the first part of his discourse he seemed much engaged, but a sudden weakness affected his mortal frame, and he concluded the labors of the day after going through his second head of doctrine. He retired to the house of one of the brethren, dined heartily, but in conversation seemed incoherent, and at times inclined to be wild and startish. He rested but very little that night, and was in a great hurry to get to the meeting-house next morning—more so than was ever known before—and said he wished to go and do what he had to do. He went to meeting and took his text in the eighth chapter of Paul's epistle to the Romans; but could not distinctly read it before he was stricken with the dead palsy, and fell in the pulpit, and was heard to say, "Blessed be God, I have fallen in a good cause." He was put into a chair and conveyed to the house where he lodged the night before; his reason left him and returned no more. He was carried to his house in Franklin county, on Wednesday following. It was observed that he scarcely ever slept from the time he received the stroke of the palsy. A physician was consulted who gave him a sleeping dose; it operated, and put him to sleep, and he never awoke more in this world, but breathed out his soul into the bosom of his Redeemer, on Wednesday, the 13th of September, 1784, much lamented by all who knew him.

There were two other brethren in this church, who, for their eminent piety, zeal and usefulness, merit a place in this history, viz: *Samuel Thompson* and *Charles James.* Samuel Thompson was baptized August, 1770, and Charles James, January, 1776. The great advantage (under God) that these servants of Christ were to this church, will never be forgotten by numbers. Their extensive knowledge of church government, their godly, pious, exemplary lives, their quickness of apprehension and unshaken faithfulness in the discharge of their duty, reflect honor on their memory. Samuel Thompson was dismissed, in August, 1786, to Elder Lancaster's church, at Poplar Spring, and was killed by a tree falling on him, in the beginning of the year 1800. Charles James, after a long and singularly useful life, died in the fall of the year 1794

THE CHURCH ON FISHING CREEK, HALIFAX, NORTH CAROLINA.

This church was originally gathered through the instrumentality of Elder Chas. Daniel. According to Asplund's Register, it was constituted in 1755. If so, we may suppose it was at first established on the orthodox plan; as we judge it was formed after the regulation took place, on the visit of Elders Vanhorne and Miller. Charles Daniel was the first pastor of this church, who was a man of considerable abilities; and in the former part of his life was very pious; but in his latter days did greatly backslide.

But from the account we have received of his exercises when he came to die, we hope he died in faith. About the year 1783, Charles Daniel, who then lived in Warren county, was taken with a complaint in his head, which in about two months ended his life. In the time of his illness, he greatly lamented his backsliding state. About two weeks before his death, his wife despairing of his being restored to health, she desired to know the exercise of his mind. She asked him if he thought the Lord had pardoned his sins and restored peace to his soul? He told her he hoped he had. He further added, "The pain is so sharp that I must die; I shortly must leave you; but my soul has an interest in Christ."

Thomas Daniel, brother of the deceased, was the next who had the care of this church; until a division arising amongst them, he separated from them. And after him, Elder Silas Mercer took the charge of the church, who was an instrument in the hand of God to reconcile matters, and settle the church again on a regular plan.

Elder Silas Mercer was a great man of God. He was a remarkably zealous, orthodox preacher of the Gospel; and, perhaps, possessed as extensive an acquaintance with the mysteries of the Holy Scriptures as any in this Association. He was very indefatigable in his labors; and, we suppose, for a few years, no minister in our connec-

16

tion traveled and preached more than he.
He was pastor of this church for a few years,
then removed to Georgia, where he ended
his course with joy, the first of August,
1796, in the 52d year of his age.

After the removal of Elder Mercer, Elder
Joshua White, who had been a member in
the Camden church and called to the ministry there, moved into this neighborhood,
became a member of this church, and took
the pastoral care thereof; who continued
that office a few years, then removed to
Cumberland, in Tennessee. After his removal, Elder Holloway Morris, who had
been raised in this church and called to the
ministry here, was ordained, and became
their pastor; who continued but a short time
in that office, before he moved likewise to
Cumberland.

After the removal of Elder White, the
church labored under great coldness and
barenness until about 1801, when the church
consisted of not more than twenty members
in full fellowship. About this time, Elder
Burkitt on a circuit of meetings attended
this place. He preached, prayed, and sung,
but no good effect seemed to attend his labors. At the close of the meeting, he at
last told them, " that if there was any person in the congregation who desired to go to
heaven or be converted, if he would come

up to the pulpit, he would pray to the Lord for him." No person came for some time. At length a young man came, with tears in his eyes, and requested his prayers.—Some months after, this young man was converted and related his experience at a Union Meeting, Warren, Ready Creek, and declared this was a mean in the hand of the Lord for his conviction and conversion ; and said he was a thousand times obliged to the man for praying for him ; and ten thousand to the Lord for putting it in the mind of his minister to do so. Soon after this a revival took place in this church, since which about one hundred have been baptized ; and sometimes as many as twenty-four at one time. The church now contains one hundred and twenty members.

Since the removal of Elder Holloway Morris, the church has made choice of Elder Philemon Bennet, a respectable minister of Jesus, for their pastor, who taking a dismission from the church on Reedy Creek, whereof he was a member, and joining this church, he now acts in that capacity. Their meeting-house stands about one mile from Wyatt's bridge, on Fishing Creek ; and their meetings are holden the Saturday before the second Sunday in every month. Their yearly meeting is in August; and quarterly once in three months.

THE CHURCH AT KEHUKEE, HALIFAX COUNTY,
NORTH CAROLINA.

This church, at first, was gathered and
constituted out of some members who had
been received and baptized on the Free-will
plan. On the visit of Elders Vanhorne and
Miller, they were established on the regular
order, and joined in covenant in the year of
1755; and were under the care of that eminent servant of our Lord Jesus Christ,
Thomas Pope. After the death of Elder
Pope they were under the care of Elder
Meglamre for some years. Elder Meglamre removing his residence from this neighborhood to Sussex, Virginia, he resigned
his pastoral concern to Elder William Burges; who was raised in Camden, and called
to the ministry in that church, and brother
to the famous *John Burges* of that place.
Elder Burges continued a few years in that
office, after which he was called home to
rest from his labors. The church had
now grown very cold; and by reason of
deaths, excommunications, and removals,
the church was greatly decreased in number.
Elder Mercer used to attend at times; after
his removal to Georgia, was statedly attended by Elder White for several years. After
his removal to the westward they have been
attended by Elder Burkitt. This church

has gone through sundry revolutions, as may
be seen in the minutes of the Association;
and although she has been blest with many
pious members, some able ministers, and the
place where the Association was first holden
and has been holden many years, and from
which the name of the Association took
place, yet she is so greatly reduced that
they are at present hardly able to hold conferences or keep up church discipline.
Amongst the few who belong to this church
is William Vaughan, of singular piety, and
a preacher of the Gospel; but has not as
yet been ordained: and Mrs. Sally Smith,
consort of Capt. James Smith, a woman of
unparalleled virtue, piety and charity.

We have a flattering hope of a revival
here. A few have been added in the late
revival.

There is a connection between this
church and one on Fishing Creek, at the
new meeting-house, as it is called, which
was originally gathered by Elder *Tanner*,
but was never constituted a church as we
know of. This congregation and the old
Kehukee church became one body; and
the minutes of the Association have been
considered as such, and the members on
Fishing Creek have by the Association
been deemed a branch of that church. But
at present this branch has become more nu-

merous than the body. A very considerable revival has taken place here lately. They are attended monthly by Elder Gilbert, and meetings holden, beginning on the Saturday before the fourth Sunday in every month. Meetings at old Kehukee meeting-house are, Saturday before the third Sunday in every month. Yearly meeting in August.—November, February and May, are quarterly meetings at this place. There were forty-four members added to this church last year, but chiefly at the meeting-house on Fishing Creek. Their number at present, in both branches, is about one hundred and twelve.

THE CHURCH ON SANDY CREEK, FRANKLIN COUNTY, NORTH CAROLINA.

This church came out from the church at Reedy Creek, and was constituted in 1774. The number of members constituted we cannot ascertain. William Walker was chosen pastor, and continued till his death, in 1784; then Elder Lewis Moore took the charge thereof, and continued until 1798. This church being left destitute, made choice of Elder John Pemberton; he continued but a short time. They then chose Elder Jacob Crocker, Jr., who soon after left them, and moved to Broad River, in South Carolina.   After the removal of Elder Crocker, they called on Elder Moses Bennett, in 1801, who served them as an occasional pastor, and continues so to the present.

This church adopted the confession of faith and joined in Covenant, and has been a prosperous church; although at present there are not more than twenty-five members in fellowship.   The time of their meetings is the Saturday before the second Sunday in every month.   This church is not connected with any Union Meeting as we know of.

THE CHURCH ON ROCKY SWAMP, HALIFAX COUNTY, NORTH CAROLINA.

In the year 1767, Elder Jesse Read (who is now the pastor of this church) was convinced of the necessity of speedily reforming his life; which he undertook with great engagement, but soon was reduced by affliction to a low state; so that his friends despaired of his recovery.   In this tedious spell of affliction he endured great pain of body, and much distress of soul; but the Lord had mercy on him, and restored him again.   He was then brought to discover the sinfulness of his nature, his own weakness, and the impossibility of being saved by his own obedience to the law of God.   He was greatly distressed and grievously tempted, and could obtain no relief until he was enabled by grace to believe in Christ Jesus, as the Saviour of his soul. He then could feed on the sincere milk of God's word ; and when he met with the writings of George Whitefield and John Bunyan, they gave him great consolation. He then desired the happiness of mankind, and wanted them to know the way of salvation through Christ. He, therefore, undertook to appoint meetings, and in public read Whitefield's sermons. At that time there were no Baptists in the neighborhood. Some time after, Elder Charles Daniel, a regular Baptist minister, came into those parts to preach ; and, not long after, Rocky-Swamp meeting-house was built on the land Elder Read gave for that purpose. There were several people who made profession of their faith in Christ, and were baptized by said Daniel, and they were considered a branch of the church on Fishing Creek (Daniel's meeting-house). Elder Read was not quickly convinced that it was his duty to be baptized ; and when he was satisfied that it was his duty, he embraced the sentiments of those who were then called Separate Baptists, and accordingly was baptized, in the year 1773, by Elder Jeremiah Walker, a minister of that order. Not long after this, Elder John Tanner came into the neighborhood and baptized several others; and, on the 11th of July, 1774, the church was constituted, with the assistance of Elders Walker, Tanner, and Joseph Anthony. The church, at her first constitution, consisted only of eight members : but there is reason to hope the Lord planted this little vine, and directed several ministers to visit and water it. This church, the same year, sent a letter and delegate to the Separate Association, holden in Amelia county, in Virginia, and was there received. On this journey, the impressions on the mind of Elder Read to preach the Gospel of salvation to sinners increased; so that, on the Lord's day after his return, he made an attempt to preach in public. He was encouraged by the members to continue in the work ; and on the 5th of May, 1775, the church unanimously called him to the pastoral care thereof. Elders Samuel Harris and Joseph Anthony assisted at the ordination. After the division took place at the falls of Tar River, as heretofore mentioned, this church joined the Kehukee Association, and was one of the ten churches at her first establishment on the present order. Notwithstanding this church was constituted with only eight members, yet the Lord has greatly added to her number, and smiled upon her. Since that time, two hundred and sixty have been baptized; but by deaths, removals, and dismissions for constitution, the church consists at present of about one hundred members in fellowship.

There is a branch of this church at Davis's meeting-house, which is not far from Connicannary, in Halifax county. The yearly meeting at Rocky Swamp begins on the Saturday before the fourth Sunday in August; and the quarterly and monthly meetings in course. Meetings are holden at Davis's meeting-house the first Sunday in every month.

THE CHURCH ON QUONKEY, HALIFAX COUNTY, NORTH CAROLINA.

This church was formerly a branch of the church at Rocky Swamp; and for some years exercised discipline with the assistance of Elder Read, who generally attended at Quonkey Chapel, two days in every month. But on the fourth Saturday in July, 1799, they sent a petition to the body of the church at Rocky Swamp for a dismission, in order to become a constituted body.

Their petition was heard, and accordingly thirty members were dismissed, and on the 7th of August following, they had to their assistance Elders Burkitt and Read, and by mutual consent they were constituted a church. Since that time there have been thirty-six added to the church. But by deaths, removals, &c., they now contain only fifty-four members.

They have no pastor, but at their request are attended by Elder Jesse Read as formerly; and Elder M'Allister Vinson, who was ordained on the itinerant plan before their constitution, and is a member in this church, also assists them in word and doctrine. The yearly meeting begins on the Saturday before the third Sunday in October; and monthly and quarterly meetings in course..

HAYWOOD'S MEETING-HOUSE, FRANKLIN COUNTY, NORTH CAROLINA.

This church is thus named because the meeting-house at which the congregation assembles is so called in honor of *Judge Haywood*, who gave for the use of the society the piece of ground on which the meeting-house was erected. This church, we believe, was originally a branch of the Sandy-Creek church, gathered through the the instrumentality of Elder Walker. After some time it pleased the Lord to convert and call to the ministry Elder Jacob

Crocker, who laboring amongst the people in this neighborhood, and a blessing attending his labors, a church was gathered and constituted here. But, since, it hath pleased Almighty God to call Elder Crocker to his eternal home, and they are now without a settled pastor; but Elder William Lancaster supplies them as an occasional pastor. Their number at present is only about thirty-five. Their yearly meeting is holden the first Sunday in August; monthly and quarterly meetings in course.

MEMOIR OF ELDER JACOB CROCKER, THE FORMER PASTOR OF THIS CHURCH.

Elder Jacob Crocker attended a meeting at his meeting-house, the first Sunday in November, 1791, and was greatly engaged in exhorting the people, at which time he said to his auditory that he believed it would be the last time he should ever address them, which eventually proved to be no chimera, for he never attended a meeting after that time. The same evening he said to his beloved wife, "Many lonesome hours you have seen in my absence, but comforted yourself with the hope of my return; but now I am going from whence I shall no more return." Some days after this his wife asked him if he thought he should die:

he answered (with a smile), " I hope I shall ;
I have no desire to stay here any longer."
Some time after, he desired that she might
resign to his death, saying " it would be but
a short time before they should meet again."
The day before he died, one of his daughters being by his bedside a weeping, he said
to her, " Do not weep for me; I hope God
has converted your soul, and if so, we shall
soon meet again in a better world." One of
the brethren asked him a few hours before
his death how it was with him ; he answered, " A few more struggles, and it will
be eternally day with my soul." Thus that
faithful servant of the Lord bid this world
adieu. He was greatly lamented by his
pious acquaintances in general, and his
church in particular.

THE CHURCH AT THE MAPLE SPRING, FRANK-LIN COUNTY, NORTH CAROLINA.

This church was at first composed of a
few members, who obtained a dismission
from the church at Sandy Creek, in order
to become a distinct body, and accordingly
they were constituted a church, July 27th,
1793 ; and Elder William Lancaster took
the oversight of them ; who, as a minister
of the Gospel, is eminent for his clearness
in the doctrine of grace, as you may see by

the circular letter which was written by him on the perseverance of the saints in grace, page 164.

The number of members in this church at present is thirty-eight. Their yearly meeting is holden the fourth Sunday in July, and their monthly and quarterly meetings in course. Their meeting-house is a tolerable roomy building, and stands near the road, about four miles from Louisburg.

THE CHURCH AT THE POPLAR SPRING MEETING-HOUSE.

Elder William Lancaster was instrumental in gathering and planting this church, which was constituted in November, 1793, and he continues to serve them as a pastor. Their number at present is fifty-seven. When the Neuse Association was formed, Tar river was considered the boundary line, and this church being on the south side of said river belonged to that association, but their minister living on the south side of said river, they have obtained a dismission from the Neuse Association in order to join the Kehukee Association. Their yearly meeting is holden the second Sunday in October. Their monthly and quarterly meetings in course.

CHAPTER XIV.

IT was promised that a brief account of the churches in the Virginia Portsmouth Association should be inserted in this history; inasmuch as the greater part of these churches once belonged to the Kehukee Association. The Portsmouth Association was dismissed from the Kehukee in 1790, and became an established Association in 1791. Their first meeting was at Portsmouth, in Virginia. And for that reason, and from the polite treatment of the gentlemen of that town, it took the name of the *Virginia Portsmouth Baptist Association.* The bounds of this Association are from James' River to the State line; from the sea to Petersburg, and lower end of Dinwiddie and Mecklenberg counties in that

State; and at present contains twenty-three churches, viz: Black-Creek, Southampton county; Black-Water, Princess Anne county; Cut-Banks on Nottoway, Dinwiddie county; Davenport's meeting-house, Prince George county; London Bridge, Princess Anne; Fountain's-Creek, Greensville; Genito, Mecklenberg; High-Hills of Nottoway, Sussex; Meherrin, Southampton; Mill-Swamp, Isle of Wight; Otter-dams, Surry; Portsmouth and Norfolk; Pungo, Princess Anne; Rowanty, Dinwiddie; South-Quay, Southampton; Shoulder's-Hill, Nansemond; Raccoon-Swamp, Sussex; Reedy-Creek, Brunswick; Sappony, Sussex; Seacock, Sussex; North-West River Bridge, Norfolk county; Western-Branch, Nansemond; Hayes's-Creek, Brunswick county. All these churches, except four, were once members of our Association. We shall begin with the church at Pungo, which appears to be the first constituted church in the Portsmouth Association.

THE CHURCH ON PUNGO, PRINCESS ANNE, VIRGINIA.

This church was a branch of the church in *Camden* county, North Carolina; and in 1762, they petitioned the body for a dis-

mission in order to become a constituted
church, which they obtained, and at the
time of constitution were forty-five in number. They were constituted by Elders
John Burges and Charles Daniel. Elder
James Gamewell now became their pastor,
and he made application to the Governor
of Virginia, who granted him license to
preach; and a place for a meeting-house
was procured, and recorded in the general
court at Williamsburg. This church, at
first, was founded on the Calvinian principles, and has continued in the same faith
until now. They used to associate with
the Kehukee Association, at Kehukee,
North Carolina. In the year 1766, Elder
George Plummer took the care of them,
who some time after was suspended for
marrying his wife's sister. Elder Abbot,
from Carolina, then served them as an occasional pastor. In 1774, Elder Joshua
Lawrence was sent for to take the care of
said church; and in 1775 they came under
a new examination, and May 14, 1775, he
was ordained their pastor by Elders Dargan and Abbot. Elder Lawrence for some
years was in great repute amongst them,
until a matter of difficulty happened in the
church; which occasioned the Association
in Portsmouth, in 1791, to appoint Elders
Barrow, Armistead, and Mintz to attend the

17

said church and endeavor to conciliate matters, the result of which was the excommunication of said Lawrence. No facts of any
importance were supported against him.
The committee left him to clear or con-
demn himself by an appeal to God, in presence of them, with a declaration of his in-
nocency, which he refused, leaving it to
his accusers to support the charge brought
against him. After he was excluded, he
continued to preach, and publicly declared
before God and his congregation, his inno-
cence of the charge brought against him.
The people erected a meeting-house for
him, in which he preached for several
years. The church was then without a
settled pastor, being only supplied by traveling preachers, until the first Sunday in
October, 1803, at which time, we understand, Elder Lawrence was restored to full
fellowship again. The time of holding
their monthly meetings is the Saturday before the first Sunday in every month.
Their yearly meeting is in April; and
quarterly in July, October, and January.

THE CHURCH ON BLACK-WATER, PRINCESS ANNE, VIRGINIA.

This church was once a branch of the
church at Pungo. They were constituted

a church in 1784. Several ministers of the Gospel were instruments (under God) to begin and carry on the work of God here. Beside the ministers who used to come from Camden to Pungo, and preached here on their journey, were Elders Thomas Armistead, William Cole, Daniel Gould, George Plummer, and others, who used to labor statedly, in and near this place. They are now under the pastoral care of Elder *Sorey*. Their number at present is about fifty-seven.

THE CHURCH AT LONDON BRIDGE, PRINCESS ANNE, VIRGINIA.

This church is so called, because the congregation assembles at a meeting-house which stands not far distant from a bridge called by that name, east of Norfolk, in Princess Anne county. Some of the members of this church formerly belonged to the church at Pungo, and were a branch of said church. They were constituted in May, 1784, by Elders Daniel Gould and William Morris. At the constitution, Elder Morris delivered a sermon, introductory to business, from Songs ii. 15. *Take us the foxes, the little foxes, that spoil the vines; for our vines have tender grapes.* The church at the time of her constitution consisted of fifty-five members. On the same day, the church made choice of Elder Morris for their pastor. A sermon introductory thereto was delivered by Elder Gould, from Acts xx. 26. *I am pure from the blood of all men.* A few years before the constitution of this church, there was a great stir of religion amongst the people; many on the right and left might be seen and heard crying for mercy. About this time, Elder Isaac Totewine was raised up, and began to preach, whose gifts were approved. He is now in the western country. About the time of constitution, the church seemed to be in a colder state. Only about seven were added in one year. Isaac Jacob, Thomas Norris, John M'Caul, and Henry James were chosen and ordained deacons. From the year 1785 until '87, there were but small additions. In 1787, about August, there appeared a small revival again; thirteen were received in one day. The work seemed to go on until November 1788, by which time thirty-five were received. Through various changing scenes, this church passed until the year 1802, when Elder Morris, the pastor, petitioned for a letter of dismission, informing the church of his intention to move to Kentucky. The letter was granted, but a great uneasiness was created in the minds of the members, they being loth to part with their pastor. It not only caused an inquiry in their minds, but a cry in their mouths—"What shall we do for one to go in and out before us?"   Accordingly application was made to Elder Jeremiah Ritter, a member of the church at Shoulders's-Hill, and he granted their request, and has attended them monthly, and administered the ordinances to them ever since.   From the time Elder Morris left this church, there was no revival until the 27th of March, 1803; at which time, being that of their quarterly meeting, just at the time of dismission, the brethren appeared to be much engaged, and were bidding farewell to each other, up stepped a little lad who wished to tell the church what the Lord had done for his soul. In so doing, the whole house appeared to be in floods of tears; and within a few months after twenty-three were baptized.   It is hoped the Lord is about to revive his work in this place.   Their number at present is about one hundred and thirty-four.   Their monthly meeting is the Saturday before the last Sunday in the month.   Their quarterly meetings are in November, February and May; and August meeting is their yearly meeting.

THE CHURCH IN PORTSMOUTH AND NORFOLK, VIRGINIA.

In the year 1789, there were a few members in Portsmouth and its vicinity, who were of the Baptist society, but were members in the church at Shoulders's-Hill. Through the instrumentality of Elders Elijah Baker, Thomas Armistead and others, there were several added in Portsmouth and Norfolk. After which, the members petitioned the Association, then held in the Isle of Wight, to send helps to constitute them into a church. Whereupon Elders John Meglamre and David Barrow were sent; who, when attending, called to their assistance Elders Elijah Baker, William Morris, Thomas Armistead, James M'Clenny and Etheldred Lancaster. A covenant being formed by a committee appointed for that purpose, was read in conference, consented to and subscribed by the members. They were constituted on the principles of Free-grace. Elder Thomas Armistead took the care of this church, and his labors were blest for a season.

In the year 1791, there came from Europe a certain Mr. *Frost*, in the habit of a Baptist preacher, who at first seemed to be approved of, but soon began to deny the faith of the church, and preach the doctrines of *free-will*, supposing man had power to work himself into a state of favor with God. This man caused great uneasiness in the church. The brethren appointed a committee to wait upon him and try to gain him over to embrace the principles of the church; but he remained incorrigible.

The church appointed another committee to go and try to silence him, but could not prevail. He said he had a meeting to attend the Wednesday night following; and he *should* preach. But the Lord interfered in behalf of his distressed church, for when *Frost* went to preach again, and took his text, which was, *He shall thoroughly purge his floor, and gather his wheat into his garner;* and coming to the words "purge his floor," his tongue failed; he cried, " Let us pray," but sunk on his knees, and spoke not another word. He was dead in less than three hours. Thus did God avenge his suffering church in these towns, for this fox was spoiling the tender grapes.

On Saturday, the 9th of June, 1792, in conference, Elder Armistead requested the church to look out another pastor to go in and out before them, as he was much indisposed in body, and not able to serve them as he ought, or wished to do. But no person supplied his place for some time. In 1794, Elder Armistead moved into King and

Queen county; and in 1795, there came a
black preacher from Northampton county,
in Virginia, whose name was *Jacob Bishop.*
The brethren and friends in that county
gave him money to buy his freedom, which
he did; and soon after bought his wife's.
And when he came to Norfolk he bought
his eldest son's freedom. His preaching
was much admired both by saints and sinners, for some time wherever he went. As
a stranger, few received an equal degree of
liberality with him. After Elder Armistead
moved away the church fell into a cold
negligent state for several months; no conference business done; some of the members did backslide: yea, the state of church
seemed at a low ebb, until October, 1796, at
which time the church seemed stirred up to
try to get together again. They called for
helps from the neighboring churches to sit
in council and give them advice,—who advised them, that whereas the black brethren
in the church seemed anxious for a vote in
conference, that it would be best to consider
the black people as a wing of the body, and
Jacob Bishop to take the oversight of them,
as this church at that time consisted of a
number of blacks. The black people at
first seemed pleased with the proposition,
but soon repented and came and told the
deacons they were afraid that matters might

turn up disagreeably to them and dishonor-
ing to God, and said they would be subordi-
nate to the white brethren, if they would
let them continue as they were ; which was
consented to. The church now applied to
Elder Thomas Etheridge, who served them
awhile ; and soon after there came over from
Africa, and settled here for awhile, Elder
Jacob Grigg, who had been on a mission
from England to Africa. While in this
church he exercised a public gift, but soon
married and moved to North Carolina, and
took the care of a church at N. W. river
bridge, and in 1802 moved to the State of
Kentucky. In 1799, Elder Davis Biggs
moved near to Portsmouth, and took the
care of the church in these towns ; and a
few have been baptized every year since.
The brethren have been very attentive to
conferences, and have been careful to maintain a good discipline. In 1802, there came
from Europe, and took up here a man
named *Ralph Mather*, who called himself a
Christian minister. He preached once for
the Methodists in their meeting-house in
Portsmouth ; and expected to preach a second time, but some other preacher was in-
troduced in his stead, which very much dis-
pleased him. He then came to the Baptists
with a very smooth tongue, and got in favor with many of them, and began to rail

at the Methodists from the pulpit and from
the press. And by some he was answered
again. In order to invalidate their doctrine,
he said that *good works* could not add anything to the creature, nor to the praise and
glory of the Creator. And that there was an
intermediate state where all the world, except a few, must go into when they left this
life. He was discovered to be of the Swe-
denborg profession, who suppose that particular characters were sent into this intermediate state to preach to spirits there imprisoned ; in which state the spirits there
might be instructed and prepared for heaven:
or by disobedience be sent to hell. Also
those women who loved little children here
would go into this intermediate state after
death, and there nurse and bring up little
children and prepare them for heaven,
and sundry other wild and enthusiastic no-
tions. Elder Biggs wrote him, that he
must acknowledge his error, and make public recantation for two particulars, as charges
against him, viz: 1. For holding with an
intermediate state in order for the preparation, and 2. *denying good works*, which does
most surely advance the glory and praise of
God amongst men. Which acknowledge-
ment, if not made, he must not expect to
preach any more in the Baptist meeting-
house. He wrote Elder Biggs several ill-

natured letters, which were answered. He
then applied to one of the principal members in Norfolk for leave to preach in the
Baptist meeting-house on that side of the
water, but was wisely told that their members on each side were one body. He then
appeared to try to draw a party away with
him, speaking evil of their present pastor,
trying to bring him into disrepute amongst
the citizens in general. But his zeal for
preaching quickly abated, and he turned
into speculation, and soon died.

Saturday, the 16th of October, 1802, was
set apart as a day of fasting and prayer to
the Lord to revive his work. The brethren
seemed to engage heartily in the work, and
the Lord heard the prayers of his church.
A revival commenced in December: the
second Sunday a mate of a ship was baptized. In February, eighteen were baptized; and by the 15th of September, 1803
(about fifteen months), eighty were added
by baptism. Their present number is
about two hundred and forty.

In March, 1803, were ordained to the
work of the ministry in this church, Elders
Benjamin Ashley, *Peter Lugg*, *Henry Keel-
ing*, and *James Mitchell*. Since which time
another young man has begun to exercise
his gift, and appears likely to be profitable.
Their yearly meetings are holden the Sa

turday before the second Sunday in December; quarterly in March, June, and September.

THE CHURCH AT SHOULDERS'S-HILL, NANSEMOND COUNTY, VIRGINIA.

Some of the first Baptist ministers who preached in the neighborhood of Shoulders's-Hill, were Elders Barrow and Mintz. They first began to preach at, and near to Sleepy-Hole, on Nansemond River. As the Lord had a work to do in this place, so the Devil and his emissaries began to try to impede the work. So it was when Paul and Silas were at Philippi, and their labors were blessed. The Devil stirred up the mob and the magistrates to persecute and imprison the innocent apostles, in order to stop the work. Acts xvi. So it was on Nansemond River with Elders Barrow and Mintz; after preaching a few times, and their labors being blessed, the Devil influenced some wicked and ungodly men to persecute them. And at a certain meeting when they were going to preach, these impious men went to the meeting and dragged Elders Barrow and Mintz from the place where they were standing to preach, down to the water, not far distant from the place of worship, in order, they said, "as they

loved *dipping,* to give them enough of it."
And carried them down into the water and
plunged them into it. Elder Barrow said
they almost drowned him. They dipped
him two or three times, and held him under water nearly one minute at a time, and
when they raised him up, would ask him
" If he *believed?*" He at last replied, " I
believe you will *drown* me." They at last
desisted and let them go. Afterwards
these two innocent sufferers never sought
any recompense, but submitted to it as persecution for Christ's sake.

It may be observed that the *dissenters* in
Virginia, before the Revolution, were persecuted more than they ever were in North
Carolina. In the county of Chesterfield
several Baptist ministers were imprisoned
for preaching in that county ; and the people were so desirous to hear preaching that
they would attend at the prison, and the
ministers would preach to them through
the grates of the prison. And in order to
prevent their hearing, Colonel Cary had a
brick wall erected ten or twelve feet high
before the prison, and the top thereof fixed
with glass bottles set in mortar, to prevent
the people from sitting on the top of the
wall to hear the word. But if persecutors
did but know it, they take a wrong step to
prevent the progress of religion by persecu-

tion: for persecution always whets the edge of *devotion*. Col. Cary and others in Chesterfield argued that the act of *toleration*, in the statute of William and Mary, did not extend to the colony of Virginia. But Elder Jeremiah Walker, a Baptist minister, was imprisoned for preaching in that county, and he was permitted to plead in his own defence; and after he had pleaded his own cause, and explained the act of *toleration* before the court in Chesterfield, they allowed his arguments were conclusive; and so discharged the prisoners.

But blessed be God, all scruples now are removed by the glorious Revolution, which gives all, under its auspicious government, equal and impartial liberty.

After the persecution of Elders Barrow and Mintz, the work of the Lord progressed about Shoulders's-Hill, several got converted and were baptized; and about the year of 1785, they were constituted a church. They continued under the care of Elder Mintz until his death; then Elder Jeremiah Ritter took the care of them. Their number is about one hundred and sixty-one.

THE CHURCH AT THE N. W. UPPER BRIDGE,
NORFOLK COUNTY, VIRGINIA.

This church is supposed to be constituted (according to Asplund's Register) in the year of 1782. Elder Mintz used frequently to attend this place, and preach and administer the ordinances here. After him they were attended by Elder Etheridge and others. Some time after, Elder Jacob Grigg became a member of this church, and took care of them; but is now moved to Kentucky. They are at present without a pastor. Elder *Dempsey Casey* is a member of this church, and exercises a public gift in the church, and is approved of. There are some very respectable characters in this church; amongst whom is *James Grimes*, Esq., who has a long time been a member of this church great in repute. Their number at present is about fifty-two.

THE CHURCH ON THE WESTERN BRANCH,
NANSEMOND, VIRGINIA.

This church was constituted about 1779. Elder Edward Mintz first took the care of this church, and continued in the pastoral function for several years. Since him, we believe the church has been without a settled pastor. They are supplied by traveling preachers, and lately by Elder Thomas Bunting statedly. Elder James M'Clenny, a man of respectability (who was an officer in the military and civil departments) used to exercise a public gift in preaching in this church. But it has been the will of the Great Head of the church to call him to the church triumphant. His usefulness has been a blessing to the church; and his labors are much missed. There has not as yet been any great revival in this church. The number of members in the year 1802 was only thirty-six.

THE CHURCH AT SOUTH-QUAY, SOUTHAMPTON COUNTY, VIRGINIA.

About the year 1774, the ministers of the Gospel of Jesus Christ of the Baptist order, commenced preaching in the neighborhood of South-Quay. Several people in that neighborhood, about that time, made profession of faith in Christ, and gave themselves members of the Baptist church in the Isle of Wight. But in consequence of the distance they lived from the body of that church, and for the purpose of preserving order and decorum amongst themselves they formed a distinct society; held meetings regularly once a month; met frequently in conference; admitted to baptism and membership such as offered, with a good account of a work of grace upon their souls; watched over one another in love; dealt with disorderly members, &c.

The first conference held by this society is dated the 1st of March, 1775, when the necessary officers were chosen; and so from time to time conferences were holden as stated above: but was nevertheless considered and held a branch of the Isle of Wight church, until October 1, 1785; at which time, having first obtained a regular dismission from that church, this society was constituted a church under the denomination of the "*Baptist church at South-Quay.*"

This church has never had a regular qualified pastor; but from the first formation of the society she had the ministerial aid of Elder David Barrow, until his removal with his family to Kentucky, which took place in the year 1798. From that period Elder John Bowers, who was a member of the church at Black-Creek, and who had for some time exercised a public gift, waited on the church as a preacher once a month, at the time of her public meetings. Since his ordination he has served this church as their minister. Their meetings are holden the Saturday before the first Sunday in every month. Quarterly in

18

March, June, September, and December; and their stated conferences the Saturday of each quarterly meeting, after preaching.

No extraordinary event has taken place in this church since she was first planted. She has, like other religious societies, alternately experienced the various vicissitudes of seasons. This is a church, in the composition of which there have been several shining professors, and some useful and active members of society; but the most of them are called home, and we believe are receiving the reward of their labors at the right hand of God, through Jesus Christ. The piety, zeal, and usefulness of *Holland Darden*, *Elisha Darden*, *John Lawrence*, and others, who were once members in this church, will ever reflect honor on their memory. The number of members at present in this church is about forty-one.

THE CHURCH ON BLACK-CREEK, SOUTHAMPTON COUNTY.

The first minister of the Baptist society who preached on Black-Creek was Elder James Dupree. Soon after him Elders Meglamre and Barrow attended, and preached in this neighborhood. The labors of these servants of Jesus Christ were blessed; several were converted and baptized. Elder Barrow was the first who baptized any by immersion in this place; and they were received members of the church in the Isle of Wight, whereof Elder Barrow was their pastor. When a sufficient number were received, they were constituted into a church in 1786. At the time of constitution, their number was seventy. Elders Barrow and Abraham Marshall attended. A sermon, introductory to business was preached by Elder Marshall from Songs, ii. 15. There a covenant was brought forward, read and consented to and then subscribed by all the members. This took place on the 27th of May, 1786. Elder Barrow took the care of the church and settled in the neighborhood. His labors were blessed; and his usefulness in this church and others, we think, will never be forgotten. Since the removal of Elder Barrow to the westward, this church has been supplied by the labors of Elders John Bowers and Henry Jones, who, being regularly called to the ministry and ordained, appear useful in the ministry. There appears of late to be a revival taking place in this church. Their number last year was about eighty-seven.

THE CHURCH ON MILL-SWAMP, ISLE OF WIGHT
COUNTY, VIRGINIA.

In the neighborhood wherein this church
was gathered, were formerly some free-will
Baptists, but they had no minister. S. Jones
was the first in this place who was baptized
by a minister of our order. After he got
converted, he went out to Bute, in N. C.,
and was baptized. Then Elder Meglamre
went down into those parts and preached,
and baptized several members; they were
received members of the church on the Raccoon-Swamp, Sussex county; and were
considered a branch of that church. When
a sufficient number were added they were
constituted a church the 2d of July, 1774;
at the same time Elder David Barrow, a
member of the church in Brunswick county,
under the care of Elder Zachariah Thompson, was called on to take the pastoral care
of said church, who accordingly did, and
served as pastor until December 15, 1797, at
which time he was dismissed, on his request.
Since the removal of Elder Barrow, the
church has had no settled pastor. Elders
Jesse Hollimon and John Gwaltney, members of said church, have been called to ordination, which took place June 6, 1801.
They both continue members in this church.

Benjamin Bell, James Gwaltney and Lemuel Wombwell are deacons in this church.

There are some very respectable members in this church ; and for a regular discipline, and good decorum in church matters, they are not excelled, if equalled by any church in that Association. There appears to be a revival taken place of late in this church, about eighteen were added last year. This church now consists of above one hundred and fifty-six members. Their yearly meeting is holden on the Saturday before the first Sunday in September. December, March, and June, quarterly meetings ; and monthly, at the same time of the month, in every other month throughout the year.

THE CHURCH ON SEA-COCK, SUSSEX COUNTY, VIRGINIA.

Elder Elijah Baker was the first Baptist preacher of our society who preached near Sea-Cock. Soon after he was succeeded by Elder James Bell and Elder Burkitt. As some of the first preachers were itinerants, some people in this place, by way of derision, gave them the name of the running Baptist. About this time Elder Meglamre preached here, and received those he baptized, and some who were baptized by the itinerant preachers, as members of the church on the

Raccoon-Swamp, and they were called a branch of that church. The church was constituted in 1787, consisting only of eighteen members. There has been a comfortable revival here lately. As many as twenty-three members were added in a few months last year. They have no settled pastor. Elder Brown attends this church occasionally.

THE CHURCH ON THE RACCOON-SWAMP, SUSSEX COUNTY.

Elders John Meglamre, John Rivers and Benjamin Bell were the first Baptist preachers of our order who preached in Sussex, which was about the year 1770. Elder Rivers was a minister of the separate order, who was a resident in Sussex county, on Sappony-Creek; a very pious and zealous minister of Jesus Christ. He preached frequently, not only in the neighborhood where he lived, but in several places in that county, and his labors were wonderfully blessed. Elder John Meglamre was at that time pastor of a church at Kehukee, North Carolina. He used to preach frequently at the house of Henry Bailey and Henry Andrews in said county; and his labors were also attended with a blessing. Some of the first fruits of the Gospel here were John Fort and wife,

Richard Johnston, Richard Marks, Nathaniel Tatum and others. Soon after, Elder James Bell (who had been a leading man in that county) had a hope the Lord had converted his soul, and was baptized by Elder Meglamre. After the work began to progress, Elder Meglamre resigned his pastoral charge at Kehukee to Elder Burges, and moved into Sussex. In the year 1772, June 13, the church was constituted in that place by Elders John Moore and William Walker, consisting of eighty-seven members, and Elder Meglamre took the pastoral care thereof. Several ministering brethren have been raised up and called to the ministry in this church, viz: James Bell, Zaddock Bell, Balaam Izzell, John Wall, Randolph Nusam and William Browne, the last of whom is a man eminent for piety, gifts, and zeal; and acted in the pastoral function after Elder Meglamre resigned on account of inability. The church for some time past has been in a declining state; but of late the work of the Lord seems to revive. Sundry members have been received here within twelve months; and we hear the work is still going on. The yearly meeting in this church begins on the Saturday before the second Sunday in August, and continues three days. Quarterly meetings in November, February, and May.

CHAPTER XV.

1. History of the Church on Meherrin, High-Hills of Nottoway, Fountain's Creek, Reedy-Creek, Geneto, Cut-Banks, Sappony, Rowanty, &c. 2. Persecution of Elder Elijah Baker.

THE CHURCH ON MEHERRIN, SOUTHAMPTON COUNTY, VIRGINIA.

THE members who originally composed this church were members of the church on the Raccoon-Swamp, in Sussex, and the first of them were received and baptized at that place. After a considerable number were received, the ministers began to hold meetings at John Sturgeon's, on Meherrin, and the ordinances were administered : and the members were called a branch of the church in Sussex. At length a meeting-house was erected near to said Sturgeon's, which was called *Sturgeon's meeting-house;* and in, or about the year 1788, they were constituted into a church. Elder John Meglamre (who had been an instrument of gathering this branch) continued to serve them as an occasional pastor for awhile; then application was made to Elder Murrell, who was a member of Elder Burkitt's church, to take the pastoral care of said church ;

and he now continues to serve them in that capacity.

This church has a branch in Northampton county, and the congregation assembles at a place called Smith's church, not far from Northampton court-house, North Carolina. This was a house of worship, built, at first, for the use of the Episcopal church; but, for several years, was chiefly occupied by the Methodists, of which order a considerable class was gathered here, until the preaching of the Baptists. Of late, the Baptist interest prevails; several have been baptized at this place; amongst whom were seventeen or eighteen of the Methodist Society. Quarterly meetings, on Meherrin, are holden the Saturday before the fourth Sunday in December, March, June, and September. And at Smith's church, monthly, the third Sunday in every month.

THE CHURCH AT THE HIGH-HILLS OF NOTTO-WAY, SUSSEX.

This also was a branch of the church on the Raccoon-Swamp. The greatest part of the members here, before the constitution of the church, were received and baptized at the meeting-house on the Raccoon-Swamp. That church being numerous, and its limits extensive, it was thought best for a consti-

tution to take place here, which was effected in the year 1787. Elder William Browne
took the pastoral care of the same, and continues in that office to the present time.
There have not as yet been any great revivals in this church, notwithstanding they
have been statedly attended by that eminent servant of Jesus Christ, Elder Browne.
Their number of members, in the year 1802,
was only twenty-two.

THE CHURCH ON FOUNTAIN'S-CREEK, GREENS-
VILLE COUNTY.

Some of the members who at first composed this church were baptized by Elder
Zachariah Thompson, and were under his
care for several years; and about this time
there was a considerable revival of religion
in these parts. After some time, a church
was constituted here, and Elder William
Garner took the pastoral care of the same;
and became a member of the Kehukee Association, and continued so until the division
took place between the Kehukee and the
Virginia Portsmouth Associations, and then,
of course, this church became a member
of the Portsmouth Association, because
she fell within the boundaries of the same.
This church, like others, has experienced
her different seasons; both of declensions

and revivals. For some years past, religion seemed cold; but of late, a considerable revival has taken place. We learn that in this late revival, several of the Methodist Society have submitted to the ordinance of baptism.

There is a branch of this church in Northampton county, North Carolina. The congregation assembles at a meeting-house, called Vasser's meeting-house, about ten miles above Northampton court-house. The church on Fountain's-Creek was constituted about the year 1787.

THE CHURCH ON REEDY-CREEK, BRUNSWICK COUNTY, VIRGINIA.

This church was originally gathered by Elder Zachariah Thompson. He used to preach here, and attend them statedly; and a few members were baptized. In the year 1776, they were constituted into a church; but had no settled pastor; nor have had to the present time. Elder Thompson attended them for awhile. Since, they have been supplied by the labors of Elder Browne and others, who have attended them at convenient times. There are some members in this little church, famous for virtue, piety, and usefulness. Amongst whom is Joseph Saunders, who generally serves the Association as clerk. The number of members in the year 1802 was only thirty-three.

THE CHURCH ON GENETO-CREEK, MECKLEN-BURG COUNTY.

This church was constituted in the year 1771. The ministers who attended at the constitution were Elders Elijah Baker, John Williams, and James Shelborne. The number of members were few at the first institution of the church. The first preacher who attended this church as pastor was Elder Elijah Baker, who some time after moved from this church to Northampton, on the eastern shore of Virginia, where his labors were abundantly blessed. He suffered great persecution in his first attempts to spread the Gospel in the lower parts of Virginia. He was once seized by a giddy set of ruffians, where he was preaching, who took him by violence and carried him on board of a vessel, informing the captain he " was a *disturber of the peace*," and wished him to make him work for his passage over the seas, and leave him in some of the European countries as an exile. It was on Saturday night he was carried on board; and was put to work and continued till late at night. Next morning

he came before the captain, and begged
liberty, as it was the Lord's day, to go to
prayer amongst the people on deck. He
was gratified; and he exhorted and prayed,
and the captain heard him. He thought
Elder Baker a good man, and was determined not to humor the spiteful mob, but
ordered his people to put him on shore. In
the mean while his friends despatched a
messenger to the governor, stating facts, in
order to prevent Elder Baker's banishment.
But when the messenger returned with the
governor's orders to the captain to release
Baker, behold it was done. He was often
threatened to be mobbed; and sometimes
apples thrown at him while preaching; but
of it all, the Lord delivered him; and by
his labors a glorious work of God was begun and carried on, on the eastern shore of
Virginia.

After Elder Baker moved from Geneto,
Elder John King took the care of the
church, and after some years he moved to
the westward, near the mountains. After
which, Elder Balaam Izzell attended the
church for a few years. He then moved
high up in Mecklenburg. Elder William
Creath has since attended the church at
this place, once a month. The number of
members in 1803 was forty-one.

THE CHURCH NEAR THE CUT-BANKS ON NOT-TAWAY, DINWIDDIE COUNTY.

The church near the Cut-Banks was constituted in 1789, by Elders Read, King, and Lee. The number of members was about nineteen. Elder Lee served them while he lived; after his death they have been attended occasionally by Elder Wynn. The number of members in 1803, was about thirty-eight. Their meetings are holden on the Saturday before the third Sunday in every month.

THE CHURCH ON SAPPONY, SUSSEX COUNTY, VIRGINIA.

About the year 1770, a work of the Lord began in this neighborhood. Elders John Rivers, Isaac Robinson and others got converted, and went up into the county of Amelia, about fifty miles distant, and were baptized by Elder Jeremiah Walker; these members were received as members at Harper's meeting-house, in Dinwiddie. But the work progressing about Sappony, at length there were a considerable number added, and then they were constituted into a church, in 1773. Elder Rivers, who was a man eminent for piety and zeal, and raised up in this neighborhood, and called

to the ministry here, took the charge of
this church ; who, laboring amongst them
a few years with great success, was at last
taken with the consumption, and his Lord
called him home to rest from his labors.

The church was first established on what
was then called the Separate order.   After
the death of Elder Rivers, Elder James Bell
joined this church, and in a short time became their pastor.   Elder Bell continued
but a few years, and he was called away by
death.   The church then for a considerable
time remained without a pastor.   Elders
Robinson and George Parham, exercised a
public gift in the church.   They have for
some time been attended by Elder Browne.
For several years she bemoaned her widowed state, after the death of her pastors, and
when religion was on the decline.   But
blessed be God, he has heard their mourning voice and has granted them a revival of
late, and we hope the Lord will continue
his work.

THE CHURCH AT ROWANTY, DINWIDDIE COUNTY.

This church is supposed to be constituted
in 1775.   Elder Jesse Lee had the care of
this church for many years.   It was a small
church when first constituted, and there

never have been any great revivals here; and not many added. In the year 1790, this church consisted only of forty members; in 1791 she contained thirty-six members, and in 1792 only thirty-four members. Elder Lee continued pastor of this church for several years; but was removed to the world of spirits a few years past. Since his death we don't know that the church has had any settled pastor.

There are three more churches in the Portsmouth Association, viz: Davenport's in Prince George, Otterdam's, in Surry, and Hayes's Creek, in Brunswick county, that we have but a small acquaintance with; and as we have never received proper documents from those churches, we are not able to give the history of the same. It may suffice to say, that it appears from their minutes of 1802, that the church at Davenport's consisted of one hundred and sixty-five members that year. This church is supplied by the ministerial aid of that worthy servant of Jesus Christ, Elder James Wright. And the Otterdams by Elder Beverly Boothe.

CHAPTER XVI.

1. History of the Church on Tosniot, Little Contentney, Rock-Spring, Town-Creek, Winstead's, Bear-Marsh, Town-Creek, Edgecombe; Naughunty, Saddletree-Swamp, Muddy-Creek, Coor-Creek, &c.—2. Biographical Sketches of Colonel Nathan Bryan. 3. Conclusion.

As the Neuse Association came out from the Kehukee Association, and the greatest part of the churches now in that Association were formerly members of our Association, we propose to give a brief account of such churches as are within our knowledge, or from whom we have received intelligence.

In a short time after the Virginia Portsmouth Association was dismissed from us, the churches increasing, it was thought best to divide again, which was accordingly done; and their first meeting was on Bear-Marsh, in Duplin county, October, 1794. This association is bounded on the north by Tar river; and extends to the South, nearly to the southern boundaries of North Carolina. As this Association consists of churches on both sides of Neuse river, it was therefore called the *Neuse Baptist Association*.

The names of the churches, and the coun-
19

ties in which they lie, are as follow : Durham's Creek, Beaufort ; Livingston Creek and Lockwood's Folly, Brunswick ; Hadnor's Creek, Newport and North river, Carteret county ; Coor-Creek, Goose-Creek, and Swift-Creek, Craven county ; Cape Fear, Cumberland ; Bear-Marsh, Duplin ; Muddy-Creek, Duplin ; Tosniot, Town-Creek, and Winstead's meeting-house, Edgecombe ; Little Contentney, Green county ; Mill-Creek and Rocky-Spring, Johnston ; White Oak, Jones ; Bear Creek, Lenoir ; Beaver-Dam, Lenoir ; Bull-Tail, New-Hanover ; New River, Onslow ; Red Banks, Pitt ; Ashpole and Saddle-Tree, Robeson county ; Cowhairy, Mingo and Seven miles, Sampson county ; Cross-Roads, Wake ; Black-Creek and Naughunty, Wayne county.

THE CHURCH ON TOSNIOT, EDGECOMBE COUNTY, NORTH CAROLINA.

This church was one of the first constituted churches in the Neuse Association. This church was constituted in the year 1756. Some of the members who first composed this church were baptized on the Free-will plan, but before the organization of the church they embraced principles of free and sovereign grace—and were established on the orthodox plan. They received and strictly adhered to the Baptist Confession of Faith. About the time of the first formation of the church, there were three preachers in it, viz: Elders John Thomas and his two sons, Jonathan and John Thomas. The memorable *Jonathan* was an instrument in the hand of God of gathering this church in its various branches. After his death the church was in a languid situation for many years, being without a pastor. At length Elder Reuben Hayes took the care thereof, and continued in that office for some time, but he has resigned, and Elder Jordan Sherrod has taken the oversight thereof. From the latest accounts we have received, there has a considerable revival taken place of late in this church.

THE CHURCH ON LITTLE CONTENTNEY, GREEN COUNTY, NORTH CAROLINA,

Was a branch of the church on Tosniot. This church was constituted the 10th of August, 1785; and has been generally known by the name of the Meadow meeting-house. There were only twenty-four in number at the time of constitution. Their number at present is about sixty-two. As they had no pastor, they called on Elder Joshua Barnes, who serves them at present as an occasional pastor.

THE CHURCH AT ROCKY-SPRING, JOHNSTON COUNTY, NORTH CAROLINA.

In the year 1776, John Killingsworth, who was baptized in Wake county by Elder John M'Cabe, moved into this county. At this time, there was no other Baptist in the neighborhood, and he, in the year 1788, requested Elder Jacob Crocker, of Franklin county, to come into the neighborhood to preach the Gospel. He did so, and his labors were blessed. Several were baptized, and gave themselves members of the church under the care of said Crocker, in Wake county, at the Cross-Roads meeting-house. In 1790, John Gulley, one of the members, began to preach the Gospel; and after the death of Elder Crocker, he and eight more petitioned the church at the Cross-Roads for a dismission in order to get a constitution, which they obtained; and, on the 16th of November, 1793, Elders Reuben Hayes and John Thompson were called to their assistance, and they were constituted a church; and the same day, Elder Gulley was ordained pastor of said church. Soon after, several were added to the church. Their number in 1803 was thirty-seven. Their monthly meetings are holden every month, on the fourth Sunday, and Saturday before. Their yearly meeting begins the Friday before the fourth Sunday in August.

THE CHURCH ON TOWN-CREEK, WINSTEAD'S MEETING-HOUSE, EDGECOMBE.

There were a few members in this neighborhood belonging to the church at the Falls of Tar River. Elder Francis Winstead, who was born and raised to the northward of Virginia, moved into this neighborhood, and, in the year 1794, began to preach the Gospel. When Elder Winstead first came into this place, there was a very small appearance of religion. Many were his sorrows and afflictions of mind on account thereof. In 1800, he was received a member of the church at the Falls of Tar River, and continued preaching in these parts. The Lord blessed his labors; and several were baptized near him, by Elder Jordan Sherrod, a member of the church at the Falls, before Elder Winstead was ordained. As many as forty-four were received and baptized by 1802, and became a branch of the church at the Falls. In September, 1802, Elder Winstead was ordained; and, in December of the same year, this branch was constituted into a church by Elders Gilbert and Sherrod. Since that time, this church has had an addition of one hundred and one

members.   A glorious work of God has been
carried on, and is carrying on in this church.
On last Christmas day, Elder Winstead
baptized a Mr. Shepherd and all his house-
hold (like the Jailor was), which contained
three in family.   In this church, there has
been raised up, and called to the ministry,
Hillary Morris, who continued preaching in
this church for some time with approbation ;
who since has removed into Hertford county, and become a member of Elder Wall's
church, on Meherrin.

THE CHURCH ON BEAR-MARSH, DUPLIN COUN-
TY, NORTH CAROLINA.

Near this place were ten persons, five
males and five females, who requested some
Baptist brethren in Pitt county to visit them.
Accordingly Elders Jeremiah Rhame and
John Nobles came about the 25th of February, 1763, who examined into their principles, and finding them sound in faith, and
orderly in life and conversation, they were
on that day, by the said ministers, constituted a church, under the care of Elder
Rhame.   Some time afterwards, there were
added five more members.   William Goodman, who was a preacher, moving into the
neighborhood, became a member.   After
exercising his gift in word and doctrine, and

being approved of, about the year 1775 he was ordained, and took the pastoral care of this church. He continued in the pastoral function until about the year 1781 ; he then removed southwardly. Elder Charles Hines then took the care of the church, and his labors were blest, and a number were added to the church. Some time after, the work increasing, and Elder Hine's charge appearing too great, having the charge of several branches, Elder Francis Oliver, who had been exercising his gift in the ministry, was called, ordained, and took the care of Bear-Marsh church, and Elder Hines was dismissed on the 17th of May, 1792. The labors of Elder Oliver have been greatly blessed, and several branches gathered. One branch is at Naughungo in Duplin, another at Pleasant Plains in Wayne; and at each of these meeting-houses they enjoy all church liberties and privileges. Their number is about one hundred and twenty. Yearly meeting at Bear-Marsh begins on the Friday before the third Sunday in August, and quarterly in course. Quarterly at Naughungo, the Saturday before the second Sunday in September, &c. At Pleasant Plains, quarterly meeting begins the Saturday before the fourth Sunday in August, and so in course.

THE CHURCH ON TOWN-CREEK, EDGECOMBE COUNTY, NORTH CAROLINA.

This church was gathered by means of Elder Joshua Barnes, whose labors have been abundantly blessed in these parts. This church was constituted with the assistance of Elders John Thomas and John Page, on the 17th September, 1780. The state of this church appears at present something promising. Their number now is sixty-one. The yearly meeting in this church begins on the Friday before the second Sunday in August, and continues three days. And quarterly and monthly, regularly in course.

THE CHURCH AT NAUGHUNTY, WAYNE COUNTY, NORTH CAROLINA.

The work of the Lord began near this place about the year 1781. Elder Hayes and others used to attend and preach here, and their labors were blessed. The church at Naughunty was constituted in September, 1791, with the assistance of Elders Hines and Hayes. This church is now under the watchful care of Elder John Thompson. The church at present appears to be in a cold state. Their number at present is only twenty-five. Their yearly meeting is the Saturday before the third Sunday in September in every year, and quarterly meetings in regular rotation thereafter.

THE CHURCH ON SADDLE-TREE SWAMP, ROBESON COUNTY, NORTH CAROLINA.

This church was constituted with the assistance of Elders Thomas Browne and Benjamin Mosely, of South Carolina, and left under the pastoral care of Elder Jacob Tarver, previous to the date of 1788. At the time of constitution, she consisted of about thirty members. They continued under the care of Elder Tarver for seven or eight years; then he moved to the State of Georgia; but the number of members increased to seventy-six or eighty while he continued with them. They were then left for some time without a pastor; but about the year 1798, it pleased the Lord to hear the cry of the church in her widowed state, and grant them their present pastor, Elder William Hawthorn, who was raised in that church under the ministry of their former pastor. The increase of the church, from the ordination of their present pastor unto the year 1801, was one hundred and fourteen. There were forty members dismissed and constituted under the care of Elder Isham Pitt-

man.   Their number at present is about
eighty-nine.

THE CHURCH ON MUDDY-CREEK, DUPLIN COUNTY, NORTH CAROLINA.

Elder Job Thigpen moved into this neighborhood in the year 1781.   At that time,
there were none of the Baptist society in
these parts, only himself and his wife.   He
had then just begun to preach a little more
than one year, and it appeared that the Lord
blessed his labors, insomuch that a considerable number was brought to the knowledge of the truth, and by him was baptized.
But as he was a minister of the *Free-will*
order, and the members received on that
plan, it was thought advisable for the church
to come under re-examination; accordingly
helps were called for, who were Elder Robert Nixon and others, and the members in
this place were received into fellowship with
the *particular* Baptist churches, and came
under the care of Elder Nixon, and continued
so for five or six years, in which time very
few were added.   Through various revolutions this church passed, until· the year
1792, February 25, at which time this
church was constituted of thirty members,
and the same year joined the Kehukee Association.   In the year 1793, Elder Thig-

pen was called to the pastoral office in this church, and was ordained in May the same year, by Elders Nixon, Dillehunty and Oliver. The church remained without any great addition until the year 1802; she then in two years, received fifty-seven members by baptism; but by reason of deaths and removals, the church contains only ninety-five members. Their yearly meeting begins the Friday before the fourth Sunday in November, quarterly once in three months, and monthly the same days of the month.

THE CHURCH ON COOR-CREEK, CRAVEN COUNTY, NORTH CAROLINA.

This church was originally a branch of Swift-Creek, in the said county, under the care of Elder William Phipps, and continued under his care until December, 1791; then she was constituted, and in 1792 joined the Association. At that time her number was fifty-one. Elder Phipps continued to attend them until he removed to the State of Tennessee, in 1797. At the same time John Beasley was exercising his gifts in the ministry, and on the 29th September, 1798, he was ordained and received pastor of this church. Their number at present is about forty-nine. Their yearly

meeting commences the Friday before the
fourth Sunday in September.

THE CHURCH ON WHITEOAK RIVER, JONES COUNTY, NORTH CAROLINA.

This church was formerly a branch of
the church on New-River, under the care
of Elder Nixon. Elder Robert Nixon was
a remarkably pious, zealous minister of
Christ. He was of the *Separate* order at
first, but joined the Kehukee Association
some years after the revolution in that Association. After a long and very singular
useful life, it was the good will of his Lord
and Master to call him home the 4th of
December, 1794. After the death of Elder
Nixon, this church was constituted into a
body the 21st of March, 1795. From this
time till the 15th of November, 1800, they
were without a pastor. On that day Elder
Caleb Smith was ordained pastor of this
church. Their number in 1802, was forty-
five. Their yearly meeting begins on the
Friday before the fourth Sunday in July,
and their quarterly meetings the Saturday
before the fourth Sunday in January, &c.

THE CHURCH AT THE CROSS-ROADS, WAKE
COUNTY, NORTH CAROLINA.

Elder Jacob Crocker, pastor of a church in Franklin, was requested to preach in these parts. Several professed faith in Christ, and soon after were baptized. After some time a meeting-house was erected at the Cross-Roads, near Rogers's Ferry, on Neuse River. The members gathered here were considered a branch of Elder Crocker's church in Franklin county. He continued to attend them as long as he was able, but they were not constituted in his lifetime. On September 22, 1792, the church was constituted of fifty-three members, with the assistance of Elder Lewis Moore. Soon after they called Elder Zadock Bell to take the pastoral care of them, who was ordained to office by Elder William Lancaster, &c. Their number in 1802 was thirty-nine. Their yearly meeting begins on the Friday before the third Sunday in August, and other public meetings regularly in order.

THE CHURCH AT THE RED-BANKS, PITT
COUNTY, NORTH CAROLINA.

This church was constituted the 20th of November, 1758, consisting of about twenty

members, assisted by Elders Thomas Pope
and Joseph Willis. Elder Jeremiah Rhame
was received pastor of the church. There
was a considerable increase in the church,
but no records of church conferences kept.
Their list of members contained ninety-five
in number. Elder Rhame moved away
about the year 1771 or '72, and a declension took place in the church, and matters
lay very unsettled until the 24th of September, 1773, when, through the goodness
of God, and the instrumentality of Elder
John Thomas, a reformation took place,
and the church came on a more regular
plan. William Travis and John Moye
were considered principal members in the
church. William Travis used to exhort
and teach in the church, and continued
until November, 1784, when he was dismissed, and moved to Georgia. John Moye
continues a member yet. June 8, 1782,
Elder Abram Baker took the pastoral care
of the church, and there was a considerable
increase for several years, and the limits of
the church became very extensive. May,
1789, Elder Baker resigned the pastoral
care of this part of the church in Pitt
county, consisting of one hundred and four
members; and in or about the year 1792,
there were three ministers in this church,
viz: Noah Tison, John Vinson, and George

Granberry; and the church agreed to cast lots for one of them to serve them in the office of a pastor, and the lot fell on John Vinson: and notwithstanding he was at that time approved by the brethren generally, yet because his wife would not live with him, some in the church were dissatisfied, and got dismission, and some others refused to come to the Lord's Supper, for which they were excluded, and the church became very few in number. George Granbery moved to Georgia, and Elder Tison took the care of the church at the Great-Swamp; and in August, 1796, Vinson was excommunicated. James Hancock has been a teaching member in the church some time, but has never as yet become their pastor, and they are still without one. There has been a revival of late in this church. There have been twenty-seven baptized in one year. Their number at present is about seventy-nine.

THE CHURCH AT LOCKWOOD'S FOLLY, BRUNS-WICK COUNTY, NORTH CAROLINA.

About the year 1757 or '58, Nathaniel Powell and James Turner came into that quarter, preaching the Gospel, whose ministerial labors the Lord blessed to the conversion of some souls. In about 1762, came

Elder Ezekiel Hunter, who was pastor of the Baptist church on New-River in Onslow county, and received and baptized some members here, and were considered a branch of his church. James Turner settled amongst them, and continued to preach with zeal and success. Thus the church stood until the death of Elder Hunter, which took place about 1772, and said Turner died shortly after. Then they were visited frequently by that worthy old servant of the Lord, Robert Nixon, from New-River, and Samuel Newton, and others, who supplied them with ministerial aid till Elder William Goodwin, who had been pastor of a church in Duplin county, N. C., moved into the county of Brunswick, and took the pastoral care of them about the year 1788, and continued in that office till his death, which was in 1793. Shortly after his decease, Abram Baker, who formerly resided on Neuse, and exercised the pastoral care of a church situate in the counties of Pitt, Dobbs, and other counties adjacent, moved into the county of Brunswick, and attended their meetings for several years; but finding the principal part of the old and most pious members deceased or moved away, and the remainder being scattered through a large and extensive county, living remote from each other, and so much coldness prevailing amongst them, that they could not be collected even to hold conferences, he refused to take the pastoral care of them in that situation, but recommended them to collect together, and renew fellowship by relating their experience, and renewing their church covenant, to which they consented, and accordingly Saturday, the 11th of February, 1797, was appointed, and helps sent for; the worthy Francis Oliver attended; the business was entered upon, at which time no more than six members were received, besides Elder Baker; when, upon their entering anew into church covenant, he consented to take the pastoral charge. Since that time about five or six have been received, who were formerly members; but the Lord has been pleased to add to the church, until the number returned to the last Association was sixty-seven. Since which five have been received, which makes the number seventy-two. In March, 1801, a meeting on the west side of Waccamaw River was first appointed for the reception of members on the Seven-Creeks, near which two or three members lived. The Lord has so blessed the work there, that they dismissed upwards of thirty members on that side of the river, who were constituted into a church on the 25th of November, 1803,

20

and Elder Job Goodman ordained their pastor.

THE CHURCH ON LIVINGSTON CREEK, BRUNS-WICK COUNTY, NORTH CAROLINA.

This church contains two branches, viz : one on Livingston creek, the other on the White Marsh in Bladen county. About the year 1765, it pleased the Lord to send the Gospel into Bladen by Elder Ezekiel Hunter. The Lord was pleased to bless his labors, and there was a church gathered, and William Bryan being one of that number, in a short time after it pleased the Lord to call him to the ministry. He was approved by the church, and exercised his gift, but was never ordained. Elder Hunter soon died after he began to preach, and the church was left as sheep without a shepherd. William Bryan labored amongst them many years through afflictions and difficulties, until the 26th March, 1797 ; when he died.

About this time it pleased God to work effectually upon the soul of his son Ezekiel Bryan, and bring him to the knowledge of the truth, and also to call him to the work of the ministry ; and at the time he was baptized, two more were baptized with him. These three and four old members first composed the church, and the Lord in about one year and eight months added to the church till their number increased to twenty-one, and then they were constituted. Elder Bryan was chosen pastor, and on the third Sunday in November, 1801, was ordained. There appears to be a great work of God carrying on here. Their quarterly meetings at Livingston creek are on the first Sundays in February, May, August, and November; and at the Marsh the first in September, &c.

THE CHURCH ON NEAL'S CREEK, CUMBERLAND COUNTY, NORTH CAROLINA.

This was formerly a branch of the church on Swift Creek, but they obtained a dismission from that church and became a constituted body, and chose William Taylor to be their pastor, who continued to serve them several years, until 1798, and then he moved away. The church from that time continued without a pastor until November, 1803, at which time Elder Nathan Gully took the pastoral care thereof. There has lately been a considerable revival of religion in this church. Their number in fellowship at this time is fifty-seven.

We shall close this treatise with a biographical sketch of Colonel *Nathan Bryan*, who was formerly a member of the Kehukee Association, until the division took place between the Kehukee and Neuse Associations, and then of course, on account of his local situation, he became a member of the Neuse Association.

COLONEL NATHAN BRYAN,

Of Jones county, and state of North Carolina, was a very useful man both in church and State. And although the Scriptures have abundantly testified that the *poor* receive the Gospel, and that God hath chosen the *poor* of this world, rich in faith; and that not *many* wise men after the flesh, not *many* mighty, not *many* noble, are called, &c. (Matt. xi. 5; James ii. 5; 1 Cor. i. 26), yet the Scripture does not say not *any* of such characters, but not *many*. To answer His divine purposes he calls some of all ranks to be witnesses of his grace, and to advance his glory among men. Col. Bryan was a man of reputation. He was possessed of an independent fortune, was a person of considerable talents, and in great esteem amongst men of the first character in this country : yet it pleased the Lord to bring him to an experience of his grace, through faith in Jesus Christ, and that at an early period of his life. He was baptized at eighteen years of age, and became a member of the Southwest of Neuse, under the care of Elder M'Daniel, succeeded by Elder Dillahunty. Being a promising youth, he was called upon to represent the county in the General Assembly. He served them in that capacity for a number of years, and although he was usually opposed, yet he always obtained his election when he offered as a candidate. Notwithstanding he was a man of abilities, and worthy to fill posts of honor and profit in the State, yet it is well known to his constituents that he sought no lucrative office; but from that patriotic spirit with which he was possessed, the good of his country was his general aim. His public and private life were so regular and agreeable to a Christian character, that he clearly manifested to all his acquaintance the sincerity of his heart in that profession he had made of Christ Jesus the Lord. His countenance was grave yet commanding; and he was very affable in his addresses, and inferior to none of his age and learning. He was very careful to contribute to the relief of the poor saints and ministers of the Gospel. He was careful to fill his seat at the house of God on Conference days, and other days of preaching. In the year 1791, at the house of God, he said, " Brethren, what lies before us to-day?

I see nothing but good. We are all at peace and in love with each other. This is joy to me. Brethren, be strong in the Lord. The days may come when we shall desire to see one of these days, and shall not see it. Brethren, in my childhood, in the Gospel, I often feared and doubted my saving interest in Christ, but in so doing it was no honor to my Lord; but through the goodness of God I have been kept from the base pollutions of the world, and have no reason to doubt, for I know I shall stand in my lot."

He was a man of so much philanthropy that he wished well to all, and strove for peace amongst religious professors of every denomination, and amongst all men. From his respectability, and the great desire of the people, he was elected a member to represent the district of Newbern in the Congress of the United States, in the year 1794, by a majority of twelve hundred. In 1796, he was re-elected for the same district. But his promotion to honor did not make him look with contempt on a poor brother, or ever divert his mind from religion and the fear of the Lord; but true piety and holiness were his aim, by which he distinguished himself to be a servant of the meek and lowly Jesus.

In the year 1796, from Congress, he wrote

to Elder Koonce on Trent, in Jones county, as follows, viz :—

Philadelphia, Saturday Night, 10 *o'clock,* *9th April,* 1796.

DEAR BROTHER KOONCE,

Although at the distance of five hundred miles, my mind is often with you, thinking of my religious brethren on Trent, and sympathizing with you. I expect you and the rest of the brethren with you feel weak under the loss of your pastor, but you are set as a watchman in Israel; you are to support the weak, and say unto Zion, "thy God reigneth." I expect there are many sons of God in our church. I call it *our church,* for I must say of it as David did of Goliah's sword, "there is none like it" with me. And whatever part of the globe I may be in, or whatever station I may be in, my right hand would much sooner forget her cunning than I could forget my brethren who are with you, or cease to pray for you and the prosperity of Jerusalem. Farewell in the Lord. **NATHAN BRYAN.**

In the year 1797, before he went to Congress the last session, he said to his children, "I have no expectation of surviving this year—for none of my family ever sur-

vived fifty years." He went to Congress,
where he served the public until the year
1798, and the same year he died in the fif-
tieth year of his age—and was buried in the
Baptist meeting-house yard, in Philadelphia.
His funeral sermon was preached by Elder
Ustick. And although this great, good man
of God is gone to receive his crown of life;
yet he *speaketh* by his past pious life and
undoubted character, which will render his
memory dear to thousands, and reflect immortal honors on his name.

Finally, to conclude. We have great
reason to praise the Lord for his goodness
and wonderful works to the children of men.
About ninety years have rolled round since
the first Baptist Association was established
in America, which was in the city of Philadelphia; and now at this time there are between forty and fifty Associations in the
United States, with about twelve hundred
churches, and nearly one hundred thousand
members.

The Baptists in North Carolina, as well
as the rest of their brethren in the United
States, hold it their duty to obey magistrates,
to be subject to the law of the land, to pay
their taxes, to pray for all in authority.
They hold with lawful oaths, and are willing, when required, to take an oath of God

upon them to testify the truth before a court or magistrate, but reject profane swearing. Their religion allows them to bear arms in defence of their life, liberty and property. This Society have manifested themselves to be true friends to civil liberty ever since the commencement of the war ; and, generally speaking, in their politics they are strict republicans.

We shall, by way of conclusion, add a sentence from General Washington's answer to the address of the Baptist committee of Virginia, in the year 1789.

" When I recollect with satisfaction that the religious society of which you are members have been, throughout America, uniformly, and almost unanimously, the firm friends to civil liberty, and the persevering *promoters* of our glorious *revolution*, I cannot hesitate to believe that they will be the faithful supporters of a free yet efficient general government. Under this pleasing expectation, I rejoice to assure them that they may rely on my best wishes and endeavors to advance their prosperity."

A LIST OF SUBSCRIBERS

To the First Edition, Printed at Halifax, North Carolina, 1803.

A.

John Anderson, Caroline, Virginia
James Askew, Hertford.
David Askew, Bertie.
John Askew, Bertie.
Alexander Arquehart, Bertie.
Baldy Ashburn, Bertie.
James Allen, Bertie.
Hardiman Abington, Northampton.

B.

Elder Richard Broaddus, Caroline.
Elder Andrew Broaddus, Caroline.
Mrs. Mary Brame, Caroline.
Elder William Brame, Richmond,   2 copies.
Epaphroditus Butler, Isle of Wight,   2
Jacob Battle, Edgecombe,   30
Wyatt Ballard, Edgecombe,   12
John Berry, Pasquotank,   13
Anthony Burroughs, Martin,   12
Elder Joseph Biggs, Martin,   12
Jesse Bazemore, Jun., Martin,   12
Elder Davis Biggs, Portsmouth,   12
Elder Abram Baker, Brunswick, N. C.,   12
Samuel Buston, New Hanover,   2
Abraham Beasley, New Hanover.
William W. Billops, Currituck,   4

Abraham Baum, Currituck.
Timothy Brogdon, Currituck.
Green W. Burge, Prince George.
John Butler, Prince George.
Joseph Browne, Dinwiddie.
Elder John Bowers, Southampton.
Dr. Willis Bowers, Southampton.
Arthur Bowing, Southampton.
Jesse Bracy, Southampton.
Richard Barden, Hertford.
William H. Boyce, Hertford.
Benjamin Browne, Hertford.
Arthur Byrd, Hertford.
Jeremiah Browne, Esq., Hertford.
Edmund Barrow, Murfreesborough.
Dr. B. Bunbury, Murfreesborough.
William Burdin, Bertie.
Blake Baker, Bertie.
Benjamin Baker, Bertie.
Michael Britton, Bertie.
William Byrum, Bertie.
John Bond, Bertie.
William Burlinghame, Windsor.
Joseph H. Bryan, Windsor.
Rhoades Barclay, Northampton.
Joseph Britt, Northampton.
Thomas Banks, Northampton.
Benjamin Banks, Northampton.
Matthew Beck, Northampton.
William Best, Northampton.
Jeremiah Bunch, Northampton.
John Branch, Esq., Halifax.
Wm. Burt, Esq., Halifax.
Lewis Barlow, Halifax.

C.

Elder Jonathan Cherry, Martin,   14 copies.
Nathaniel Chambles, Sussex,   12

Elder John Courtney, Richmond.
Thomas B. Coleman, Caroline.
Samuel Coleman, Caroline.
John Chiles, Caroline.
John Crumpler, Jun., Southampton.
Shadrack Cobb, Southampton.
Matthew Crumpler, Southampton.
Mills Carr, Isle of Wight.
Crutchins Council, Isle of Wight.
William B. Cheatham, Murfreesborough.
Godwin Cotten, Hertford.
James Cherry, Hertford.
Jeremiah Cale, Hertford.
Isaac Carter, Jun., Hertford.
David Coffield, Bertie.
George Cox, Bertie.
Andrew Collins, Bertie.
William Crutch, Bertie,   2 copies.
Solomon Cherry, Bertie.
Cullen Carter, Bertie.
William Clements, Windsor.
William Cottle, Northampton.
Jesse R. Cross, Northampton.
Gen. Stephen W. Carney, Halifax.

D.

Isham Davis, Halifax,   12
Lemuel Deberry, Pitt,   20
Israel Decoudrey, Petersburg,   6
Robert Duncan, Louisa.
Jacob Darden, Southampton.
Jethro Darden, Hertford.
Thomas Deans, Hertford.
Mrs. Sally Davenport, Prince George.
William Dickerson, Northampton.
David Dickerson, Northampton.
Lawrence Daughtrey, Northampton.

William Deans, Northampton.
Edward Dunstan and John Dewer, Bertie.

E.

Elder Ed. Eley, Culpepper, Vir.,	2 copies.
James Etheridge, Currituck,	12
Thomas Etheridge, Sen., Camden,	12

John Edmunds, Isle of Wight.
Kinchin Edwards, Southampton.
John Edwards, Northampton.

·F.

Elder Reuben Ford, Hanover.
Jackson Fraysar, Henrico.
John Figures, Southampton.
Shadrach Futrell, Northampton.
John Futrell, Northampton.
Thomas Futrell, Northampton.
James Farmer, Bertie.
William Farmer, Bertie.
Carney Freeman, Bertie.
Jeremiah Freeman, Bertie.
Jacob Freeman, Bertie.
Joshua Freeman, Bertie.
Charles Freeman, Bertie.
Jesse Freeman, Bertie.
James Freeman, Bertie.
Benjamin Folks, Bertie.
William Freeman, Bertie.
Enoch Fly, Hertford.
Arthur Foster, Hertford.

Richard Figures, Hertford,	2

G.

James Grimes, Norfolk,	12
Thomas Guion, Tarborough,	24

Miss Edny Gillam, Southampton.

B. Griffin, Southampton.
Micajah Griffin, Southampton.
John Gornto, Onslow.
Lewis Guion, Hertford.
Pat. Gatlin, Hertford.
Thomas Gill, Hertford.
Jonathan Gay, Northampton.
Nathan Gums, Northampton.
William H. Green, Bertie.
Jacob Garret, Bertie.
Moses Gillam, Bertie.

H.

Amos Harrell, Martin,	22 copies.
Charles Hooks, Esq., Duplin,	12
Jesse Hassell, Chowan,	12
Josiah Holliman, Isle of Wight,	18
Luke Howard, Hertford,	12

John Harrell, Hertford.
William Hill, Hertford.
Robert Hide, City of Richmond.
Doctor Peter Hawkins, City of Richmond.
John Haddon, Prince George.
William Hawthorn, Prince George.
William Horne, Jun., Northampton.
Kinchin Hayes, Northampton.
B. Hardy, Bertie.
Samuel Haste, Bertie.
James House, Bertie.
Joel Hyman, Bertie.
Josiah Holley, Bertie.
Thomas E. Hare, Bertie.
Joseph Horne, Bertie.
Lemuel Harrell, Bertie.
Henry Harrell, Bertie.

J.

William James, Fredericksburg.

Abner Jackson, Washington,   12 copies.
John Jones, Bertie.
Abraham Jenkins, Bertie.
James Jenkins, Bertie.
James B. Jordan, Bertie.
Elder Henry Jones, Southampton.
Thomas Jones, Bertie.
Amos Joyner, Southampton.
William Johnson, Southampton.
Benjamin Joyner, Southampton.
Joseph Jones, Hertford.
John Jones, Hertford.
Grafton Ireland, Hertford.
James Jones, Hertford,   2
Benjamin Jenkins, Northampton.
Guilford Jones, Esq., Halifax.

K.

The Ketockton Association subscribed
    by Elder William Fristoe and Tho-
    mas Buck, in behalf of that Asso-
    ciation,   125
John Key, Sussex,   12
Edmund Kidd, Caroline, Virginia.
Job Kail, Bertie.
John Knott, Bertie.

L.

Willis Langfort, Isle of Wight.
Mills Lawrence, Isle of Wight.
John Lee, Southquay.
Benjamin Lanier, Duplin,   177
Sarsfield Leonard, Prince George.
Shelly Lee, Dinwiddie.
William Lane, Hertford.
Adamant Liverman, Hertford.
Elisha Lawrence, Hertford.
Edwin Liles, Hertford.

William Lurry, Bertie,	3 copies.
Alexander Legate, Bertie.	
Frederick Lawrence, Bertie,	2
William Lurry, Currituck,	12
Reuben Lawrence.	
Jesse Little, Edgecombe,	14
Frederick Luten, Chowan,	12
James Lawree, Northampton.	
Elias Langford, Northampton.	
William Lightfoot, Northampton.	

M.

Gideon Moye, Pitt,	26
William H. Murfree, Murfreesborough.	
William Moore, New Hanover,	2
John M'Christy, Portsmouth,	12
Parrot Mewburn, Lenoir,	12
Thomas Mason, Halifax,	12
Eli M'Mullen, Halifax.	
Ephraim Miller, Bertie,	12
Demsey Modlin, Bertie.	
Nathan Modlin, Bertie.	
Lewis Miller, Bertie.	
Moses Morriss, Bertie.	
Cader Minton, Bertie.	
William Mitchel, Bertie.	
William Maer, Bertie,	6
John Mhoon, Bertie.	
John Miller.	
Peter Moore, Southampton.	
Elder Robert Murrell, Southampton.	
Moses Manning, Duplin.	
James Moore, jun., Hertford.	
William Moore, Hertford.	
John Moore, Hertford.	
Edward Murphey, Hertford.	
Hilary Morris, Hertford,	12
Randolph Maddry, Northampton.	

21

William E. Moore, Northampton.
Theodorick Mann, Northampton.

N.

Thomas Nelms, Southampton.
Elisha Newcomb, Petersburg.
Demsey Nowel, Bertie.
John Nowel, Bertie.
Willis Nickins, Hertford.
William Negus, M. D., Wayne.

O.

Col. John Overton, Louisa.
Henry Obery, Southampton.
Elder Francis Oliver, Duplin,   12 copies.
David Outlaw, Hertford.
John Oliver, Bertie.
Joshua Outlaw, Bertie.
William Outlaw, Bertie.
Aaron Outlaw, Bertie.
Wright Outlaw, Bertie.
Lewis Outlaw, Bertie.
Micajah Oliver, Bertie.
Edward Outlaw, Bertie.
George Outlaw, Bertie.
George Outlaw, jun., Bertie.

P.

Augustine Pugh, Bertie.
Cader Powel, Bertie.
Henry Pugh, Bertie,   2
James Pugh, Bertie.
Josiah Perry, Bertie,   4
William Powel, Bertie.
Thomas Parker, Bertie.
Reuben Parker, Bertie.
Jethro Pender, Hertford.

Cader Powell, Jun., Hertford.
John Parker, Hertford.
Silas Parker, Jr., Hertford.
Silas Parker, Sr., Hertford.
Robert Parker, Hertford.
King Parker, Hertford.
Peter Parker, Hertford.
William Parker, Hertford.
John H. Pugh, Hertford.
Micajah Powell Hertford.
Samuel Powell, Halifax.
Jesse Powell, Halifax,   12 copies.
Henry Peebles, Northampton.
Lemuel Parker, Northampton.
John Pipkin, Esq., Northampton.
Lemuel Parker, Northampton.
William Pethross, Caroline.
Elder John Poindexter, Louisa,   3
William Pope, Southampton.
Jeremiah Plummer, Princess Anne,   12

R.

James Robbins, Edgecombe,   2
Nathan Ross, Martin.
Thomas Ramsay, New Hanover.
Joseph T. Rhoades, Duplin.
Frederick Rances, Petersburg.
Robert Rhoades, Bertie.
Moriah Rawls, Bertie.
Joshua Rayner, Bertie.
Samuel Rayner, Bertie.
Zadok Rayner, Bertie.
Elijah Rayner, Bertie.
William Rayner, Bertie.
John Rowan, Bertie.
James Rian, Bertie.
Thomas Rhoades, Bertie.

Enoch Rayner, Bertie.
Jonathan Rhoades, Bertie.
Capt. John Rhoades, Bertie.
James Rutland, Bertie.
John Rascoe, Bertie,   6 copies.
Miles Rayner, Colerain.
Elder Martin Ross, Perquimans,   24
Benjamin Roberts, Esq., Murfreesborough, 2
Abednego Rutland, Northampton.
Watson Rutland, Northampton.
James Ruffin, Northampton.

S.

Jonas Shivers, Pitt,   24
Jacob Sawyer, Currituck,   12
Elder Aaron Spivey, Bertie,   12
J. E. Sumner, Bertie.
Richard Spivey, Bertie.
Nathan Sessoms, Bertie.
Lanier Smithwick, Bertie.
William Spivey, Bertie.
David Spivey, Bertie.
Thomas Sutton, Bertie,   2
Henry Speller, Bertie.
Thomas Speller, Bertie.
John Skiles, Bertie.
Luke Smithwick, Bertie.
Humphrey B. Smithwick, Bertie.
Irijah Simmons, Nansemond.
John Saunders, Nansemond.
Robert Southerland, Duplin.
Philip Southerland, Sr., Duplin.
John P. Saunders, Hertford.
George Sowel, Hertford.
Thomas Spiers, Hertford.
Adam Spires, Prince George.
John Shelly, Prince George.

Jeremiah Scoggin, Prince George.
James Skinner, Northampton.

T.

Robert Tucker, Dinwiddie,	20 copies.
Elder Henry Toler, Westmoreland,	2
Elder John Thompson, Wayne,	12

John Turner, city of Richmond.
Joseph Turner, Southampton.
Jacob Turner, Southampton.
Elder Job Thigpen, Duplin.
Douglas Turner, Prince George.
Epps Temple, Prince George.
Reuben Tucker, Prince George.
John Tart, Bertie.
James Thompson, Bertie.
James Taylor, Bertie.
Mrs. Elizabeth Turner, Bertie.
R. Tunstall, Bertie.
James Tunstall, Bertie.
Thomas Taloe, Bertie.
Absalom Tadlock, Bertie.
Nicholson Thompson, Northampton.
Isaac Tignor, Northampton.
Donaldson Turner, Greensville.

Charles Tull, Lenoir.	12

W.

Elder F. Winstead, Edgecombe,	12
Spilsby Woolfork, Caroline,	2
William Wells, Duplin,	18
Levin Watkins, Duplin,	12
Aaron Williams, Duplin,	12

Nathan Waller, Duplin.
George Williamson, Richmond.
Elder Absalom Waller, Spotsylvania.
Charles Wortham, Caroline.

John Winn, Hanover.
James Wright, Nansemond.
James Wilson, Isle of Wight.
Elder James Wright, Prince George.
Micajah Webb, Prince George.
George Wair, Bertie.
Timothy Walton, Bertie,   4 copies.
James Ward, Bertie,   2
William Watford, Bertie.
Francis Williams, Bertie.
Joshua Ward, Bertie.
John Wynns, Bertie.
Peter White, Bertie.
Jesse Williams, Bertie.
Mrs. Ferebe Ward, Bertie.
William Ward, Bertie.
George White, Bertie.
Demsey Welch, Bertie.
George Wynns, Bertie.
William Wilson, Bertie.
James Warren, Bertie,
John Warborton, Bertie.
Thomas Worley, Bertie.
William Watford, Jr., Bertie.
John Watson, Bertie.
George West, Bertie.
Thomas West, Bertie.
James Wilkes, Bertie.
Micajah Wilkes, Bertie.
John Wade, Northampton.
Jonas Wood, Esq., Northampton.
Demsey Winborne, Northampton.
Henry Wheeler, Northampton.
William Winborne, Northampton.
William Winborne, Sr., Northampton.
John Wheeler, Murfreesborough,   12
James Wynns, Hertford.
Solomon White, Hertford.

James Wynns, Hertford.
Matthew Wynns, Hertford.
Elder John Wall, Hertford,   12 copies.
Thomas Weston, Hertford.

V.

Alexander Valentine, Hertford.
John Vandiford, Hertford.

APPENDIX.

BIOGRAPHY OF ELDER LEMUEL BURKITT AND HIS FAMILY, BY DR. WM. P. A. HAIL.

As Lemuel Burkitt is so nearly connected with this work, the reader will not expect a lengthy biography. He was the son of Thomas and Mary Burkitt, and was born near Edenton, N. C., on the 26th April, 1750. He joined the Baptist Church, was soon after called to the ministry, and commenced preaching at the early age of twenty years; and continued a true, faithful, and unchangeable servant of Christ until the day of his death.

He was a meek and goodly man, and a great favorite among all his brethren and acquaintances. Nature seemed to have formed him for the pulpit. He possessed a pleasing address, fluent speech, and surpassing eloquence. He was a useful member and shining light in the Kehukee Association, and served as clerk of that body for about thirty-two years; and his absence from the Association in 1802 (occasioned by indisposition) was so much regretted by all the members, that they passed a resolution expressive of their sorrow, and entered it upon the minutes of said Association. [See page 137.]

This exceedingly pious and venerable man, though caressed and honored by all classes and sects of the people for the space of thirty-six years, never became giddy or puffed up with popularity, as is too often the case with such characters; but still remained at the zenith of popular favor until his death, which took place A. D., 1806, in the fifty-seventh year of his age.

His almost irreparable loss was greatly regretted by all his numerous acquaintances, and he yet lives in the memory of many of his brethren.

He was the author of several religious works, one of which (a Collection of Hymns) was of unusual popularity. During the Revolutionary War, when the issue with us was liberty or death, his voice was often heard in moving and eloquent accents from the pulpit, exhorting his brethren and countrymen to embrace the cause of Liberty : and it seems that his progeny imbibed the same noble spirit, as will be seen below. [See the sketch of his two grandsons, James and Joseph.]

He married and settled in Northampton county, N. C., where he resided the greater portion of his life. His first wife was Hannah Bell (daughter of Captain James Bell, of Sussex county, Virginia, and sister to Elder James Bell, whose biography is given in another part of this work), by whom he had many children ; but those who reached the years of maturity were few, and are as follows, viz : three daughters, Mary, Nancy, and Sally ; and three sons, Lemuel, Jr., William, and Burges. The maiden name of his second wife was Prudence Watson, also of Virginia, by whom he had one son, who died in infancy.

His oldest daughter, Mary, married a man by the name of Halsey, by whom she had two children—a son and daughter. The latter is dead ; the former, whose name is Lemuel, is living. Halsey died, and his widow married John Nixon, by whom she had three sons, John, Henry, and James ; all of whom are now (1850) living near Edenton, N. C.

Nancy married Abednego Rutland, by whom she had three daughters, Mary Burkitt, Hannah Bell, and Lucy ; and two sons, William Creth and James Bell ; all of whom now reside in Wilson county, Tenn., except Hannah, who resides in Tuscumbia, Alabama.

Sally married a man by the name of Thatch, by

whom she had one son, and called him Joseph. After the death of her husband, she married a man by the name of Long; and after his death, she again married another man by the same name. She raised a family of children, all of whom, when last heard from, resided near Edenton, N. C.

Lemuel Burkitt, Jr., married, and raised up a family of children near his father's former residence, and died there; but as to the particulars of his family the writer is uninformed.

William Burkitt married in the year 1814, and removed to Sumner county, Tenn., where he resided many years. He now lives in the State of Illinois. I am entirely unacquainted with his family, except his son, William, who has visited this place, and now resides near his father, in Illinois.

Burges Burkitt (the youngest son of Elder Lemuel Burkitt) joined a company of volunteers, was elected sergeant of the company, and marched to Norfolk, in Virginia, where he was stationed during the war of 1812. In August, 1812, he married Mary Hardin, daughter of Richard Hardin, of North Carolina. After he was discharged from the army, he located in Halifax county, N. C., where he remained some years, living in the height of wickedness; and, as he often expressed it in after life, rolled sin under his tongue as a sweet morsel. But God was pleased to convince him of the error of his way, and he was baptized by Elder Joshua Lawrence, in company with his worthy consort, at Kehukee meeting-house, in the year 1817. He soon after, like his venerable father, felt a desire to declare the Gospel to the world, and commenced preaching to the people. He continued a pious and worthy minister of Christ the remainder of his days. In his last illness, he was asked what he thought of death and eternity.

"O! "said he, "my faith is the same that it has ever been since I had a hope in Christ!"

He was a man of quite an ordinary education, but of a bright genius, a quick and penetrating mind, and extraordinary memory.

In the year 1819, he removed to Tennessee, and settled in the cane on the head-waters of Indian Creek, in Giles county, eight miles east of Pulaski; where, from misfortune and disease, he was reduced to *extreme* poverty, and was compelled to sell his last horse to purchase provisions to supply the wants of his distressed family. He was taken with what the physician pronounced a disease of the liver, and nearly all he could make for six or seven years was consumed in the payment of *doctors' bills.* Of course, he remained very poor.

In the fall of 1828, he removed to the north-west corner of Giles county, and settled on Big Creek, two and a half miles north of the little villlage now called Campbellsville, and one mile south of the Spring Mill, where he enjoyed some better health, and gathered means sufficient to purchase a small farm. He remained there eight years. In the winter of 1836–37, he removed to Lawrence county, Tenn., and settled within two miles of this place (Lawrenceburg), where he died, February 15th, 1844, aged fifty-three years.

A few days before he was taken with his last illness, he was sitting by his fireside in quite a pensive mood, and being surrounded by his family, he said to his wife, " If the Lord has called me to his work in this world, I have performed my task. I feel acquitted before God, as though my work was ended upon earth." True and fatal foreboding ! For in three weeks thereafter, he slept beneath the sod of the valley ; and that arm which had been lifted up to declare Christ and his Gospel, and which had been for so many years *honestly* and *faithfully* engaged in the support of his *people* and his *country,* has *long since fed the worms of the dust.* His loss was regretted by all who knew him. His sermons were plain but evangelical. Though

they were not ornamented with the rhetoric of his pro-
genitor, yet they abounded with scriptural truth. His
gravestone now stands two miles north-east of this
place, and but a short distance from where his widow
now lives.

He had six children by his wife, (all of whom are
now living, save one), viz: two daughters, Lucy Caroline and Mary Hardin; and four sons, Henry
Lemuel, James Bell, Joseph Burges and John Bunyan.
The latter is but a youth, and yet remains with his
mother. James and Joseph were both born on Indian
creek, in Giles county; the former on the 3d December, 1822, the latter on the 6th July, 1828. In May,
1846, our government was at war with Mexico, and
called upon Tennessee for troops. There was then
formed at this place a company of volunteers called
the Lawrenceburg Blues. They responded to the call
of their country, were accepted by the Governor of
the State, and directed to march to Monterey, in
Mexico. There, on the 21st September (a day so
fatal to many of Tennessee's bravest sons), they were
literally cut to pieces; so much so, that after the battle
there could be mustered but *thirteen* of the Blues,
when near one hundred, in good health, and *high
spirits*, and with hearts beating full of hope and expectation, had marched from this place but a few months
before. But many of those brave hearts were destined
soon to beat no more. When the company were pre-
paring to leave this place, there stood at their head
Capt. A. S. Alexander and Lieutenant James B. Burkitt—the latter about twenty-four years of age, and
in the vigor of manhood. There was some dissatis-
faction expressed by some few individuals of the company in relation to the officers who commanded it
(arising perhaps from a difference in political sentiment),
which resulted in the immediate resignation of the
captain and first lieutenant, and their re-election by the
company. At this time there was seen advancing to

join the company, with a firm step, and musket in hand, a youth in his eighteenth year, with comely form and pleasant features, of a mild and lovely disposition, and pleasing address, through whose veins gently flowed that pure and patriotic blood which he had inherited from his worthy ancestors; and in whose breast, filled to overflowing with *patriotism* and *love* of *country* not surpassed in the bosom of the valiant Jasper, beat a young hero's heart. He was chosen sergeant of the company, and notwithstanding his youth and inexperience, discharged the duties of his office to the entire satisfaction of all until the hour of his death. That extraordinary gravity and genius which he possessed would seem to say that the day was not far distant when he would be an *honor* to his country, and one of the foremost citizens of society. But, alas! how often do we see the axe applied to the root of the tallest cedar of the forest, just as it begins to tower above the surrounding grove. This was ere long to be his fate. For on that bloody 21st September following, he was swept away by a cannon ball, while braving the storm of battle, with the firmness, gallantry, and heroism of a Croghan or a Gwinn. The name of this extraordinary youth was JOSEPH B. BURKITT, whose name I cannot write without my eyes inevitably turning upon that beautiful and noble structure (the monument) erected of late upon the public square of this town by the grateful countrymen of the fallen brave—*high* upon whose column *stands forth in bold characters, speaking to the world and to posterity,* and *pointing* to the *heavens as if to show where this gallant* and *youthful spirit now rests,* the name JOSEPH BURKITT.

The ashes of this heroic youth have been scattered over his country, and will enrich the soil of *patriotism,* and cause it to produce an abundant harvest.

He is dead! but he stands high on memory's page, and yet lives in the breasts of all who knew him.

His name will adorn history's page, and children yet unborn will read with *admiration* his daring deeds and dying words upon the battle field of Monterey. [His last words are given below, in a letter from Lieutenant Burkitt to his brother Henry after the battle.]

I will now make a few remarks in relation to the officers under whom this company marched.

They had advanced as far as Lometo, in Mexico, when the same dissensions which caused the resignation and re-election of the officers before they commenced their march, again made their appearance in the company. So the captain and first lieutenant resigned voluntarily a second time (as appears from Col. Campbell's letter), and each took his musket and retired to the line. This they were not compelled to do, being at liberty after resigning to return home, if they chose. But they had left their homes, their wives, children and friends, to fight the battles of their country, and this they intended to do, and this they did. And never did the Spartan show more daring and less fear than did these two patriots upon the battle field.

William B. Allen being placed at the head of the Blues, they proceeded on to Monterey, where Captain Alexander was severely wounded early in the action, but still remained upon the field, aiding the wounded by giving them water, &c. Lieut. Burkitt, who had seen his younger brother swept from his side by a cannon-shot, when within about six hundred yards of the enemy's works, pressed forward in the front rank with an impetuosity not surpassed by the famous M'Donald himself : while the very *elements* seemed to rain canister and grape shot around him, often piercing his clothes and accoutrements. And when the charge was sounded, still remaining unhurt (with the exception of a slight wound on the hand, of which he never complained) he led the van, and was by the side of the

first man that charged over the mouth of the enemy's
cannon, and stood upon the walls of the captured fort.
These officers were not selfish men ; they labored
more for the general good than for their own aggran-
dizement. Such disinterestedness, patriotism, and love
of country are seldom found recorded upon the pages
of history, since the days of Fabius and Cincinnatus.
We first see them at the head of the company laying
down their commissions at the feet of a minority, and
again, resigning upon the first notice of the least discontent, retiring to the ranks, and there performing all
the duties of private soldiers until discharged from the
army as such. As to the above facts, I do not speak
at random, for I was a member of the company my-
self.*

Lieut. Burkitt to his brother:—

MONTEREY, *Mexico, Oct.* 1, 1846.
DEAR BROTHER—I seize a few spare moments to
write to you. The great storm is over. Monterey
is taken, and the Mexican army is defeated. The
Tennesseeans have won laurels that will never fade so
long as honor dwells amongst men. But many of them
now sleep in their cold, bloody graves; amongst whom
are Capt. Wm. B. Allen, F. Glover, Wm. Rhodes,
J. Wilson, J. Campbell, J. B. Burkitt, and several
others who were attached to our company from Lincoln county, Tenn. Oh, the horrors of battle ! never
shall I forget that day, the 21st of September. When
we were advancing on the enemy, I looked upon that
tender youth,† and what should I see but that lovely
face all lighted up with the joy of battle, and proudly
facing the enemy as though he was an experienced
hero, when, with six others, he was swept from my

* The reader will pardon me for my digressive remarks in relation to my fellow-sufferers in arms, when he remembers the
partiality which one soldier has for another.
† His brother Joseph.

side with a cannon ball. We soon made a charge on the fort, and it was carried instantly. I then returned to my brother and had him carried to camp, where he soon after died of his wound. He talked to me, and told me he was dying ; his last words ran somewhat thus: " Brother, I am almost gone ; we gained the day, and I am dying satisfied, for I fell at my post. Tell mother how I died, and not to grieve after me." He paused for breath. He then said, " Get the money due me and give it to mother, and tell her to use it." He then turned his face towards mine (for he was in my arms), gave me one farewell look, folded his arms across his breast, and expired.

We had three days' hard work in capturing the city. In addition to six strong forts, every house was fortified, and every street a battery. They made a gallant defence, but were unable to withstand American courage. We charged into fort after fort, battery after battery until we had them completely surrounded, and on. the 24th, Gen. Ampudia surrendered the place. The force of the enemy was between eighteen and twenty thousand; ours amounted to something over six thousand. The loss of our troops amounted to three hundred and forty, whilst that of the enemy was one thousand three hundred and fifty. I was in the hottest of the battle, and saw many gallant friends fall on every side, but I remained unhurt, and had the honor of being one of the first men on the walls of the first fort that was taken from the enemy. I am now attending on the wounded at the hospital in this city. * * * * * * *

JAMES B. BURKITT.

To HENRY L. BURKITT, ESQ.,
    Lawrenceburg, Tenn.

By the request of the present editor of the foregoing work, I have not given his biography ; but the

22

following letter from the editor of the *Middle Tennesseean* ought not to be omitted.

LAWRENCEBURG, *Feb. 4th*, 1850.

DEAR SIR—Having learned that you have in course of preparation a series of biographical sketches in reference to the descendants of the Rev. *Lemuel Burkitt*, a distinguished Baptist divine, who, some half century ago, published a comprehensive History of the Kehukee Association which flourished in North Carolina, and which is now under course of re-publication by Henry Lemuel Burkitt, Esq., of this place, I have thought it not improper to embrace this method in offering you such facts identified with the history of the present editor of the work as may not have been presented in the progress of your researches as the biographer of the families which have descended from the venerable patriarch and author alluded to. I am aware that the editor of the forthcoming edition has signified his unwillingness to become the subject of the least prominence in your pages, and it is with extreme reluctance that I transcend, in the least measure, this reasonable injunction, by directing your attention to a few of the many worthy points in his career which deserve a place beside the histories of those of his kindred whom you have doubtless noticed more fully. It will not, I hope, be deemed a breach of courtesy to that worthy gentleman, or an act of violence to the system you have been pleased to adopt, to proceed as I propose, while it can but facilitate, in a greater or less degree, the success of the work in regions where the book is unknown, and where some knowledge of the character and motives of the new publisher will be indispensable to its ready sale.

HENRY LEMUEL BURKITT needs no eulogy at my hands, yet I may aver that he boasts much in his eventful history of which he could well be proud—

much from which could be deduced a solid and practical example for humble youth. Its uniformity and consistency throughout are not among the least of its merits—while the whole may be said to embrace a career at its meridian, which has been quarried from the gloomiest realities of life. Having been born under the evil star of adversity, he boasts no pyramid of honor won by the immortal dollar. Penniless he began life's uneven task, coveting only the virtues of an honest and upright citizen ; and, buoyed on by such impulses, he has mastered many " an ill to which flesh is heir," and overcome obstacles at which many would have cowered and fallen.

> " Honor and shame from no condition rise :
>   Act well your part, there all the honor lies."

Truths are these which seem never to have been lost sight of in the framing of his destiny. Of earthly privations and vicissitudes, his cup has indeed been filled to the brim, though of these it is not my purpose to speak further than to bestow some fit tribute to the energy which has surmounted them.

The subject of this sketch was born in the native State of his venerable grandfather, on the 28th October, 1818, and may, in a word, be termed a " *self-made man*." He cherishes yet the *characteristics* of the humble born of his good old native State, where the dignity of human labor has never sunk to reproach, and where honest toil is respected as the solid stamina of life, and the sure passport to comfort and true independence. I mean that he is a man who is not afraid to soil his hands, if necessary, with the plough or the axe, and to abandon his books when needs be for the coarser labors of the field or the workshop. Although born, as it were, to be " a hewer of wood and drawer of water," he has made such progress in the business of life as to be rendered independent of such means of subsistence, in the elevation of his ambition to more exalted employment. At the age of nineteen, without learning, and unskilled in the artifice of the world, he left the roof of his parents to try the colder realities of an unfriendly world, taking with him the paltry contents of his purse, which amounted to six and a quarter cents, as the beginning of his fortune in a land of strangers. The future indeed was dark, but the hope of a better day was anchored in the youthful ambition of his bosom, as he prosecuted his solitary journey. He had received from his father, as the basis upon which he was to conduct himself through life, this advice : First, *To be honest in all his dealings with mankind.* Secondly, *To be industrious;* and Thirdly, *To be faithful to every promise.* A legacy this, which combines the noblest elements in the *chart of life.* Loyal to these injunctions, he entered the great arena of life in the dawn of his manhood to be " a hero in the strife." This first adventure of his youth was crowned with reasonable success. By the " sweat of his brow" he procured a handsome little sum of money in the State of Georgia, which, upon his return to Tennessee, he expended toward acquiring an education. Having exhausted his funds thus, he became a teacher for a short time as a means of prosecuting his studies. At this period, or thereabouts, he married a most amiable lady, whose industry and fortitude formed a happy and efficient auxiliary toward the accomplishment of future comfort and independence in life. With a mind well stored with practical knowledge, and an ambition which shrunk not at the reverses and difficulties which challenged his energy at every step, he entered the study of the legal profession under one of the most gifted members of the bar of this place, WILLIAM DAVIS, Esq., whose memory is yet green in the bosoms of his admirers, and whose virtues and example have survived the decay and crumbling of his mortal remains. By that assiduous application and unyielding diligence for which he has always been remarkable, Mr. Burkitt acquired *the profession* sought. He is still a resident of the scene of many of his reverses and struggles, and bids fair by his proverbial economy and industry to become independent in the "goods of this world," as he has already become a prominent and useful citizen of the section in which he resides.

It may not be improper, in conclusion, to relate a little incident, which exhibits the patriotism and liberality of Maj. Burkitt in more significant beauty than any words which I could use in portraying them. In 1846, while he was acting as proprietor of the "Farmer's Inn," in this place, a way-worn veteran soldier of the Revolution, who fought at Savannah, took lodgings at the Inn, and being in ill-health, in addition to the natural infirmities of his great age, he remained several days, and was favored with marked hospitality. When the palsied old soldier was about to depart, he drew out his purse and tremblingly asked the amount of his bill. "*Your bill was paid, sir*," replied the landlord, "*when you fought by the side of Jasper.*"

I have, sir, with all freedom, and in some haste, made the foregoing rather elaborate, but still imperfect and brief statements in reference to the character of Major H. L. Burkitt, which are submitted to your consideration with the hope that you may cull something from them which will facilitate you in the completion of a sketch, which I conceive demanded by the relationship of the editor of the work to the public at large.

Yours, truly,
WM. P. HORNE.

To Dr. W. P. A. Hail.

To conclude this biographical sketch, permit me to say that it is true as stated by Mr. Horne in the foregoing letter, that H. L. Burkitt may be justly styled a *self-made man*, having obtained his education principally since he arrived at the years of maturity. He is now a respectable member of the bar, and advancing in learning and wealth.

He often expresses his gratitude to the public for that liberal patronage which has been extended to him by generous hearts who reached out a helping hand in the hour of need.

Providence has smiled upon his labors, showered blessings upon his pathway, and crowned his industry with success.

WM. P. A. HAIL.

NAMES OF SUBSCRIBERS

To the Second Edition.

TENNESSEE.
Lawrenceburg.

Gen. R. H. Allen
F. C. Allen, *Clerk of the Circuit Court.*
Isaac W. Alford
Col. A. S. Alexander
Samuel L. Arrington
P. G. Austin
W. J. W. Alexander
Robert Black
Col. John H. Beeler
Dr. Gab. Bumpass
Charles Barnett
R. G. Bolin
Milton L. Benlley, Esq.
F. Buchanan, *late Speaker of the House of Representatives, Tennessee Legislature.*
W. G. Buchanan
Capt. Jas. B. Burkitt
John Bunyan Burkitt
Robert J. Black
Leonidas M. Benlley, Esq
Rev. J. N. Bradshaw, *Tutor in the Jackson Academy.*
Josiah Bostian

S. A. Carroll, *Clerk of the County Court.*
J. R. Carroll
P. H. Carstarphen
John Campbell
Shadrach Chapman
H. H. Dotson
James Dial
Henry N. Estes
Samuel H. Edmiston
Ja. W. Edmiston
John Fondran
J. G. Fuller
Simon B. Foster
Buford Foster
J. J. Gibson, M. D.
Samuel B. Garrett, Esq.
R. C. Green
Wm. P. Horne, *Editor of the " Middle Tennesscean."*
L. L. Higdon
Dr. W. P. A. Hail
Wm. H. Hensley
Joseph Haynes
A. W. Hogwood
C. L. Herbert, M. D.
Frank Hughs, *Sheriff*
Isaiah Joy

Larkin Jackson
Samuel W. Johnson
Wm. F. Kirk
James Kelly
James B. Kozure
J. J. Kelly
J. J. Kidd
Major J. W. J. Kidd
John J. Lacroix
Wm. H. Lanier
Rev. Wm. McKnight
Samuel McBride, Esq.
Ja. F. McCracken
Elder Isaac Morris
Shadrach Morris
Lewis Miller
Charles McLean, *Deputy Sheriff*
Jeptha Newton
Redin B. Owens
Isam Pullen
John W. Parks
Robert H. Powell
Jesse Pullen
George Park
Thomas Pullin
William Pullen
Joseph Powell
Wm. P. Rowles, A. M.
William Rhea
Amos Richardson
Thos. A. Richardson, Esq.
Franklin Richardson
George W. Richards
Ananias Oliver Richardson
T. C. Ramsey
J. P. Rider
Solon E. Rose, Esq.

Robert H. Rose, Esq.
Elias Rider
Elder J. P. Richardson.
G. F. Simonton, *Cashier Lawrenceburg Bank of Tennessee.*
Lewis Smith
Jacob Springer, Esq.
John B. Stribling
G. Tucker Simonson
James Sykes
John L. Smith
Archibald L. Smith
Col. Ja. L. Stribling
Col. J. O. Tarkington
J. C. Thomas
W. P. H. Turner
Col. J. W. Tarkington
John A. Tinnon, C. M.
George Taylor
Thomas Vaughan
Benjamin Williams, *Chairman of the County Court.*
Robert Williams, Jr.
Wm. B. Wright
Benjamin Weaver.

Rossborough.

R. L. Pearce
Robert B. Williams
Wm. F. Williams
J. C. R. Williams
Daniel A. Goff.

West Point.

Charles J. Herin, Esq.

Lawrence County.

J. W. Barnett
S. P. Bramlet
G. N. Brackenridge
Samuel Caldwell
James T. Guthrie
Nicholas Welch
Wilson B. Norman, Esq.
J. H. Chronister
Zadoch Williams
Allen Eves
Johnston Craig
Joseph E. Wisdom, Esq.
J. H. Wisdom
Lawson Williams
J. W. Curtis
Wm. B. Chaffin
Jacob Copeland
Thomas Spencer
Elder Allen Hill Bryan
Joseph Cook
John Moody
Joseph Boren
John T. Eves
S. W. Eves
Elder John Bryan
Wm. K. Lindsey
M. D. Watson
Jacob Bryan
H. J. Bumpass
W. R. McGee
Sidney S. Paine
Nicholas Gower
Thomas Crews
Jesse A. Houser, 2 copies
Lemuel M. Emerson
John Glover
Ephraim Grissam

Thomas J. Moody
Willis Briant
Martin H. Moody
W. M. McCluskey
Francis Smith
James F. Gordon
James M. Powell
Robt. Newton, Esq., 2
  copies
Wm. Comer
Benj. Powell
Elder G. B. Mitchel
Obadiah S. Williams
John E. Williams
Rolen Hull
Capt. H. P. Walden
Elizabeth Ratliff
E. H. Bell
Wm. Brock
Col. Jacob H. Pennington
W. J. Hale
F. L. L. Carroll
Capt. James Curtes.

Waynesborough.

Robt. A. Hill, *Atty. Gen.*
Lemuel B. Askew
John M. Atkinson.

Wayne County.

Elder Levi Hurst
Wm. J. Henry
Wm. M. Horton
James Horton
Nathaniel Horton
George S. Horton
Isaac Horton
Isaac W. Horton

Samuel M. Cypress
John H. Gray, Esq.
John L. Fielder, Esq.
Andrew M. Smith
John F. Fielder, Esq.
Thomas Adams
Jesse T. Hurst
James M. Hurst
Solomon Philips
Timothy L. Wallis
James B. Anderson
F. W. Loyd
Ruth Wallis
Zachariah Cypret
Thomas Morrison
A. Montgomery
Eli S. Grimes
George C. Huckabey
Wm. D. Copeland
Wm. M. Gallogly
John Grimes
Brinkley Hopson
Solomon Brewer
Joseph Brewer
Miles Jordan Durbin
John G. Durbin
Wm. G. Grisham
Charles Liles
Solomon Brewer, Jr.
Mark Bradley
Mordica Thompson
Marcus B. Fowler.

Nashville.
Elder Philip Ball
Wm. L. Nance
Josiah C. Nance
Susan Paul

Angeline Nance
R. B. C. Howell, D. D.,
    Pastor 1st Bap. Church.

Franklin.
Jesse Cox, 30 copies
James King
John W. Harvey
E. K. Moore
R. H Harvey
W. C. Cox
Price Gray
M. D. Stanfield
Wm. A. Gilliam
M. P. Montgomery
C. Burch
Gilford Read
David Read.

Hardin County.
Reese White
Thomas Huggins
Daniel Davis.

Perry County.
Elder David H. Mikel
Wm. Ward
Jesse Simmons
James Simmons
Nepthali Tracey
Samuel Denton
Isaac Dickson
J. H. Brown
Daniel Starbuck
Asa Huse
William H. Campbell
A. J. Cragg
Robert Booker

Smith Mettock
William Young
Lawrence Lamberson
G. W. Shelton
Josiah Shelton
Isaac Pace
Westley W. Lucas
A. D. Goodman
T. R. Shepard.

Lindon.

Thomas Lancaster
Pleasant Whitwell
Cooper B. Land
Gardner Kelly
Thomas Lancaster
James Hopper
John Cates
Stephen Ledbeter.

Lewis County.

William P. M'Makin
Eli Pogue
James Pogue
Samuel Balsh
William Cox
Wills H. Johnston
Berry Brashears
P. H. Nichols
J. N. Bailey
Jefferson Brown
John Weaver
Charles Y. Hudson
R. H. Grimes
S. H. Holmes
Jabez Leftwick
J. W. Byrum
Nancy M. Duke

Nancy Gordan
T. Noles
Thomas R. Wood
N. O. Smith
W. A. Rickets.

Palestine.

James Harder
J. O. Harder
James Campbell.

Hickman County, Sulphur Springs.

Allen Jones.

Pleasantville.

Elder Gabriel Lancaster
William Whitwell
Lewis Durning
Michael Smith
Eli Dyer
Alexander Joice
Thomas Kelly
James M. Ray
William Larnax
John Duncan.

Mount Pleasant.

D. G. Grimes
David Craig
William Lindsey
J. W. Grimes
Sabrey Pickard
Thomas Brown
William Blackwood.

Williamsport.

William R. Archer.

Giles County.

John Bass
Elder Allen Jones
William L. Willsford
Anuel Atkinson
William Cotham
Joseph Parsons
Garner M. Parsons
J. A. Heald, M. D.
Abram Appleton.

Pulaski.

Elder Albert Moore
Thomas J. Wilkinson
E. W. Overstreet
John C. Walker, Esq.
A. W. Willeford
Thomas S. Webb
Amasa Ezell
John M. Kenclow.

Campbellsville.

Martin Jones
John W. Harwood
John Compton.

Lindville.

John Hickman
Hardy Willeford
Thomas C. Compton.

Maury County.

J. D. Mitchell
Michael Lancaster
Nicholas Rice
T. M. Thompson.

Lincoln County.

James Randolph

N. W. Watson
Philomon Higgins
Willis C. Higgins
Joel Higgins
M. Higgins
John Williams
E. B. Osborne
S. M. Hampton
W. J. Briant
T. H. Silvester
J. Stovall
C. C. Bryant
Hugh Randolph
Arthur Randolph
Martin Towery
Philip Faggin
Ervin Stephens
J. W. Holmon.

Winchester.

Thomas H. Garner
Wm. Duncan
Hendon Green
Wm. Hendon.

Bedford County.

T. B. Ussery, Sr.
John Bramblet
F. H. Keller
Zephaniah Roberts
James Green.

Hillsboro.

Hosed Jones
Elijah Turner
Wm. Lowry.

Decatur.

Elder James Lillard

Daniel Cate
Wm. L. Adams
John Sevboum
Wm. Benson
Allmon Guinn
Wm. Lillard, Sr.
Martha J. King
Nancy F. Davis
Robert Elder
Pleasant Snow
Demsey Sikes
John Huff
Hiram Gibeson
Benjamin Blalock
Prior Neil
George Keenam
Wm. Buster
Coffield T. Tellerry
Wm. T. Newton
James Buckner.

Robertson County.
James Moxey
Thomas Harrow
Isaac Sherron.

Henry County.
Elder Richard Lea Tho-
mason
Joseph Thomason
A. A. Thomason
John Dunn
James A. Lawrence
Calvin Fowler
Daniel Atkins
Wm. Blackshir
James H. Howard
A. Middleton
Wm. Crawley

J. W. Page
Bryant Dearmose
Joel S. Tyson
Nelson Walton
Jesse Nix.

Weakley County.
Elder Reuben Ross
Stephen Smith
James Powers
Benjamin Dunlap
Wm. Lawrence
Jeremiah Arnold
Nathaniel Orsburn
W. H. Hubbard
George W. Ellis
T. Parker
Andrew Wallice
J. Tompkins
Wm. C. Porter
C. Curlee
J. Wiggins
Amos Webb
James McWherter
Walter W. Buckley
Reuben W. Biggs
W. R. Mitchel
James R. Turner
Ephraim C. Baker
Wiley Todd
Samuel L. A. Wheeler
E. P. Satham
John R. Parish
S. R. Wheeler
V. H. Wheeler
Samuel Morris
Edmond Reed
W. L. Dunn
Willis J. Price

Smith Brooks
Wm. Stow
Hogan Edmiston
J. Terrell
Jesse H. Parrish
James H. F. Atkins
Wm. Todd
Samuel Baker
J. B. M. Allen
John Fields.

Rhea County.
Thomas Smith
David F. Ward
Jefferson J. Carr.

Hamilton County.
Elder Charles A. Wallard
Jordan Smith
Robert Quals
Thomas Rutchledge
John Wilson
Stephen Wilson
Daniel Plumley
Walter M. M'Gill
William H. Douglas
Robert Douglas
Charles Witt
John M. Jasper
Oston Shipley
William Varner
Hyram Montgomery
William Varner.

Clarksville.
N. B. Whitfield.

KENTUCKY,
James Wallice

Morgan Chandler
W. A. Bowden
A. H. Willingham
Benjamin M. C. Nott.

NORTH CAROLINA.
C. R. Hendrickson,
*Pastor Baptist church,
Elizabeth city, and edi-
tor Baptist Messenger.*

ALABAMA.
Huntsville.
Elder R. W. Crutcher, 25
copies.

Madison Cross-roads.
Joseph Hollaway
Allen Walls
Samuel J. Hunts
James A. Stovall
Charles Ward
Jacob P. Holloway
Martha Atkins

Limestone County.
Elder James Shelton
William Legg
Andrew C. Legg
Samuel Bradley
Charles Perver
Nicholas Long

Landerdale County.
Anderson Cox
Leonard W. Stutts
George B. Martain
John M'Murtrey
T. B. Stutts

William Stutts
Robert Carr
James Waits
A. F. Harwill
Jesse Oakley
Permelia Roads
Thomas Hassel
John Seargeant
Abner Beard
William Howell
James Hill
Jane Brewer
William M'Murtrey
Henry Simmons
William C. Heston
Elias Cranford
B. D. Todd
Isaac C. Whitaker
H. N. Poteel
A. B. Hammonds
William Fielder, Esq.
John Parker
Elder John Rachels
Walter Danley
Carroll Tucker
Elder Jordan Ham
Isham Richardson, *Deacon*
Dr. M. T. Griswell
Martin Hill
Henry Clemones
James Canada
Joseph E. M'Donald
William Waldrop.

MISSISSIPPI.
Van Buren.
Elder Charles Hodges,
30 copies.

Tishamingo County.
William Williams
Henry Rogers.

Tippah County.
William Hopkins
H. Berry
Joseph Thomeson.

Penola County.
John W. Simmons
James S. Petty
A. M. Crofford
John James
David Brackenridge
Noah Foster.
A. J. Lettlefield
R. W. Wooten
C. Hauson.

Lafayette County.
Michael Waldrip
R. E. Simmons
L. M. Moncrief
A. L. York
C. Gandy
James Waldrip
L. V. Nance
Jesse W. Elmore
Benjamin Allen
W. W. Harrell.

Desoto County.
Jesse M. Langston.

Adamsville.
A. Adams.

THE BAPTIST TRADITION

An Arno Press Collection

Asplund, John, **The Universal Register of the Baptist Denomination in North America.** 1794

Bacote, Samuel William, **Who's Who Among the Colored Baptists of the United States.** 1913

Baker, J.C., **Baptist History of the North Pacific Coast.** 1912

Baker, Robert, A. **Relations between Northern and Southern Baptists.** 1954

Baptist Ecclesiology. 1980

British Baptists. 1980

Burkitt, Lemuel and Jesse Read, **A Concise History of the Kehukee Baptist Association from its Original Rise to the Present Time.** 1850

Colonial Baptists. 1980

Colonial Baptists and Southern Revivals. 1980

Dagg, John Leadley, **Manual of Theology.** 1858

Dawson, Joseph M., **Baptists and the American Republic.** 1956

Freeman, Edward A., **The Epoch of Negro Baptists and the Foreign Mission Board.** 1953

Gaustad, Edwin S., **Baptist Piety.** 1980

Gaustad, Edwin S., ed., **Baptists: The Bible, Church Order and the Churches.** 1980

Guild, Reuben A., **Early History of Brown University, including the Life, Times, and Correspondence of President Manning, 1756-1791.** 1897

Howe, Claude L., Jr., **The Theology of William Newton Clarke** (Doctoral Dissertation, New Orleans Baptist Theological Seminary, 1959). 1980

Jeter, Jeremiah Bell, **Recollections of a Long Life.** 1891

Jordan, Lewis G., **Up the Ladder in Foreign Missions.** 1901

Knight, Richard, **History of the General or Six Principle Baptists in Europe and America.** 1827

Lambert, Byron C., **The Rise of the Anti-Mission Baptists** (Doctoral Dissertation, University of Chicago, 1957). 1980

Lewis, James K, **Religious Life of Fugitive Slaves and Rise of the Coloured Baptist Churches, 1820-1865, in what is now Ontario** (Bachelor of Divinity Thesis, McMaster Divinity College, 1965). 1980

McBeth, H. Leon, **English Baptist Literature on Religious Liberty to 1689** (Doctoral Dissertation, Southwestern Baptist Theological Seminary, 1961). 1980

Macintosh, Douglas C., **Theology as an Empirical Science.** 1919

McKibbens, Thomas R., Jr., and Kenneth L. Smith, **The Life and Works of Morgan Edwards.** 1980

Morris, Elias Camp, **Sermons, Addresses and Reminiscences and Important Correspondence, with a Picture Gallery of Eminent Ministers and Scholars.** 1901

Olson, Adolf, **A Centenary History as Related to the Baptist General Conference of America.** 1952

Pitman, Walter G., **The Baptists and Public Affairs in the Province of Canada, 1840-1867** (M.A. Thesis, University of Toronto, 1957). 1980

Powell, Adam Clayton, Sr., **Against the Tide.** 1938

Purefoy, George W., **A History of the Sandy Creek Baptist Association, from Its Organization in A.D. 1758, to A.D. 1858.** 1859

Seventh Day Baptist General Conference, **Seventh Day Baptists in Europe and America.** Two volumes. 1910

Shurden, Walter B., **Associationalism Among Baptists in America, 1707-1814** (Doctoral Dissertation, New Orleans Baptist Theological Seminary, 1967). 1980

Smith, Elias, **The Life, Conversion, Preaching, Travels, and Sufferings of Elias Smith.** 1816

Stealey, Sydnor L., ed., **A Baptist Treasury.** 1958

Stiansen, P., **History of the Norwegian Baptists in America.** 1939

Taylor, John, **A History of Ten Baptist Churches.** 1827

Tull, James E., **A History of Southern Baptist Landmarkism in the Light of Historical Baptist Ecclesiology** (Doctoral Dissertation, Columbia University, 1960). 1980

Valentine, Foy D., **A Historical Study of Southern Baptists and Race Relations 1917-1947** (Doctoral Dissertation, Southwestern Baptist Tehological Seminary, 1949). 1980

Wayland, Francis, **Notes on the Principles and Practices of Baptist Churches.** 1857

Whitsitt, William H., **A Question in Baptist History.** 1896

Wood, Nathan E., **History of the First Baptist Church of Boston (1665-1899).** 1899